THE CONTEMPORARY POET AS ARTIST AND CRITIC

Eight Symposia

LEONIE ADAMS   W. H. AUDEN   JOHN BERRYMAN

ROBERT HORAN   DONALD JUSTICE   STANLEY KUNITZ

ROBERT LOWELL   JOSEPHINE MILES   JOHN FREDERICK NIMS

MURIEL RUKEYSER   STEPHEN SPENDER   WILLIAM STAFFORD

Eight Symposia
edited by
ANTHONY OSTROFF

ROBERT BELOOF LOUISE BOGAN PHILIP BOOTH WILLIAM DICKEY

BABETTE DEUTSCH RICHARD EBERHART GEORGE P. ELLIOTT

W. D. SNODGRASS JOHN CROWE RANSOM THEODORE ROETHKE

KARL SHAPIRO ADRIENNE RICH MAY SWENSON RICHARD WILBUR

THE CONTEMPORARY *Poet*
AS *Artist*
AND *Critic*

Boston and Toronto
LITTLE, BROWN AND COMPANY

Published simultaneously in Canada
by Little, Brown & Company (Canada) Limited

PRINTED IN THE UNITED STATES OF AMERICA

ACKNOWLEDGMENTS

The editor is grateful to the following publishers and
authors for permission to reprint the materials listed:

ATLANTIC-LITTLE, BROWN AND COMPANY for "Father and Son" by
Stanley Kunitz from *Selected Poems 1928-1958*, copyright © 1958 by
Stanley Kunitz, reprinted with the permission of Atlantic-Little, Brown
and Company and J. M. Dent & Sons (London).

W. H. AUDEN for his permission to use his poem, "A Change of Air."

RICHARD EBERHART for his permission to use his poem, "Am I My Neighbor's Keeper?" Copyright © 1963 by Richard Eberhart. From *The
Quarry*, published by Oxford University Press, Inc.

FABER AND FABER LTD. for "Skunk Hour" from *Life Studies* by Robert
Lowell, and for "Love Calls Us to the Things of This World" from
Poems, 1943-1956 by Richard Wilbur.

FARRAR, STRAUS & COMPANY, INC. for "Skunk Hour" by Robert Lowell.
Reprinted from *Life Studies* by Robert Lowell, by permission of Farrar,
Straus & Company, Inc., Copyright © 1956, 1959 by Robert Lowell.

Cover artist: Edith Allard
Cover photograph: Donald Preston

FOREWORD

THE PLAN OF THIS BOOK may be simply explained: In each of our eight symposia, three distinguished poets write independent critiques of a recent poem by an important contemporary—who then writes a commentary in response; the poem, the three critiques, and the author's comment together constitute the finished symposium. As the reader will be aware, the scheme introduces something new in literary criticism, first, in calling upon *poets* to perform the essential critical task; second, in calling upon the authors of the poems under consideration to comment directly on their work and on criticism of it. One effect is that critic and author are placed in a somewhat more intense relation of responsibility to each other than is usual, which provides a special interest of its own. But the most valuable effects are more direct. The authors' comments, informing us of original intention in the poems, giving us details of background and composition we could not otherwise know, and calling our attention to aspects of the poems which the critics may have missed, are uniquely helpful both as critical sources and as critical controls. The critiques, because they are written by poets, are exceptionally free of critical prejudice, attentive to the integrity of poem and poet alike, and sensitive to the entire range of those events and devices of imagination and language whereby experience becomes poetry.

Clearly, the central purpose of the symposia is exploration and illumination of the poems that are their subjects—and it is as handsomely accomplished as one would expect from the array of talent gathered here. The essays are remarkable in several respects, but perhaps above all for the ways in which they require that we be active in our response to them—and thus to the poems they are about. The dramatic interplay of ideas among the contributors (who contradict as well as complement each other) does not allow us to retire comfortably to a single, official view. And there is the liveliness of the essays. We are always aware of somebody there, of a particular voice, a distinct personality. This is a direct source of delight in itself; it also reflects and enforces upon us a fact which all the contributors take as a principle: that experience is individual—and that communication of experience, therefore, must always in some measure be personal, intimate, and subject to unpredictable eccentricities and limits. Thus the broad measure of tolerance and humility our critics usually supply; thus their frequent willingness to be tentative, not to press conclusions too hard, and their steady reminders that what is said is offered as reflection of personal response and experience; thus, yet again, the constant obligation upon us to think and feel and judge for ourselves.

This is not to imply that the essays give us less than a great wealth of information and insight relevant to the poems, or that the contributors do not make their judgments clear and emphatic. The symposia are finally most stimulating precisely because honesty extends as far as tact in them. The views they offer of the poems which are their whole occasion are as direct as they are various, and match the extraordinary breadth of possibility they present to us with an individual concentration and keenness that makes them important.

But so much for comment on the main event of the book—the humane and irresistible conduct the essays give us into our poems. There are other things that take place, however, which deserve mention. For one, we are granted considerable insight into the nature of poetry and the creative process itself—most richly, of course, in the authors' comments (where a good deal more than first meets the eye is revealed about the relation of the poets to their work), but also by observations on these matters by the critics, who speak with the authority of their own experience as poets. We are also enabled to see and understand a good deal about problems in the critical process. Here, indeed, is a major fascination of the book. Disagreements among the critics expose limits or flaws in critical method as often as they expose flaws in the poems being examined. The juxtapositions of essays in the symposia permit us to judge the relative efficacy of various critical approaches as well as their limits. There are, furthermore, a good many little texts in criticism— critical asides, strictures, speculations, comments on theory, and the like—which appear naturally in the course of most of the essays. These make a surprisingly consistent and useful body of principle for the reader who may be interested enough to gather them together.

As examples of practical criticism, the essays collectively (and often individually) demonstrate a marvelous, common-sense eclecticism. There is no general adherence to a single school. Rather, all the disciplines, all the techniques, all the devices of criticism seem at one time or another to be brought to bear. The rule is that what matters is what best yields results in the critical task at hand, not concern with the superiority of one method over another, or of one man over another.

A few notes on procedure in arranging for these symposia may be of interest. The participants all served at the editor's invitation. Those who were to serve as subjects were asked to submit four or five recent poems—previously unpublished, if possible—from which one might be chosen for a symposium. Instructions for the essays were minimal: length was to be roughly between two thousand and four thousand words; form and substance were entirely up to the individual, with the one stipulation that the poem serving as subject be maintained as the ultimate focus. Normally, at least two months were to be allowed for the critics to write their essays, and another two for the poet to prepare his response. Among the few exceptions to procedure, three should be noted. John Crowe Ransom was asked to submit only one poem, the one we have here, which marks his resumption of the writing of poetry after a pause of over twenty years in his distinguished career as poet. Stanley Kunitz had been working for some time on a long poem and so had no recent work suitable for submission, for which reason we relaxed the general rule of using current or nearly current poems and chose a poem from several he suggested in his *Selected Poems*. Karl Shapiro also had been working on a long poem, but its nature, we agreed, permitted considering excerpts from it. The symposium on his work, thus, constitutes a departure from the usual scheme in offering less than a whole poem for subject.

As will be evident, the poems considered in this book are of quite different levels of difficulty and quite different in the tasks they set themselves. The symposia, however, are arranged simply in the chronological order of their completion, not in terms of any sense of the relative difficulty or interest or value of the poems on which they focus. Some readers may find it to their advantage to read all eight poems first, and then read the accompanying symposia in whatever order of interest suggests itself.

So brief an introduction as this can scarcely touch on those qualities of intelligence, conscience, and passion that characterize our essays, but these, as they are finally what give substance and life to this book, are amply demonstrated in the pages which follow. I doubt that any reader will fail to appreciate them, or to feel grateful, as I do, to all of our contributors for their courage and generosity in making themselves available to us as they have done here.

Anthony Ostroff

CONTENTS

RICHARD EBERHART

ROBERT HORAN

MAY SWENSON

RICHARD WILBUR

On RICHARD WILBUR'S

"Love Calls Us to the Things of This World"

Richard Wilbur

LOVE CALLS US TO THE THINGS OF THIS WORLD

The eyes open to a cry of pulleys,
And spirited from sleep, the astounded soul
Hangs for a moment bodiless and simple
As false dawn.
                    Outside the open window
The morning air is all awash with angels.

Some are in bed-sheets, some are in blouses,
Some are in smocks: but truly there they are.
Now they are rising together in calm swells
Of halcyon feeling, filling whatever they wear
With the deep joy of their impersonal breathing;

Now they are flying in place, conveying
The terrible speed of their omnipresence, moving
And staying like white water; and now of a sudden
They swoon down into so rapt a quiet
That nobody seems to be there.
                    The soul shrinks

From all that it is about to remember,
From the punctual rape of every blessed day,
And cries,
              "Oh, let there be nothing on earth but laundry,
Nothing but rosy hands in the rising steam
And clear dances done in the sight of heaven."

    Yet, as the sun acknowledges
With a warm look the world's hunks and colors,
The soul descends once more in bitter love
To accept the waking body, saying now
In a changed voice as the man yawns and rises,

    "Bring them down from their ruddy gallows;
Let there be clean linen for the backs of thieves;
Let lovers go sweet and fresh to be undone,
And the heaviest nuns walk in a pure floating
Of dark habits,
                  keeping their difficult balance."

3

RICHARD EBERHART

The important thing about Wilbur's poem is that it celebrates the immanence of spirit in spite of the "punctual rape of every blessed day." The conflict is between a soul-state and an earth-state. The soul wins. The soul, felt as a vision of angelic laundry on awakening, must still be incorporated into the necessities and imperfections of everyday reality. Man is redeemed by the angelic vision.

"Rosy hands" in the beautiful suds recalls Homer's "rosy-fingered dawn." The poem is typical of the author in its amiability. Its "halcyon feeling" predominates over dark realistic forces which are indicated but which are not unduly stressed. It is not an angry poem but a poem of acceptance. It is a serene evocation, with a touch of the whimsical, of angelic immanence.

The slight narrative frame allows the burden of meaning to fall on images and their suggestions. There is some shock in "rape," "hunks," "terrible" and "bitter," enough as clothes-pinning to keep the poem down toward the earth, to keep it from becoming too airy or abstract. (I feel that "terrible" is uncommunicated, fails of its meaning, and to a lesser extent that "bitter" does not work, but that "rape" and "hunks" freshen the language.) The pleasant vision of angelic immanence establishes the real feeling of the poem. The poem is neither too long nor too short for what it says. It is neither too hard nor too soft, cannot be got entirely in one reading but does not need to be worried into sense.

The poem is not a willful nor a dynamic one. It is static and a psyche poem. It makes nothing happen. It states what has happened, what may or could happen. It erects a psyche state which embodies its own truth for contemplation. The soul must be put on the things of this world. The world cannot live by world alone but must hark back to the soul. This dichotomy is accepted with the value-judgment or value-suggestion in favor of spiritual reality.

When fully awake man must accept full responsibility, the heaviness of the Fall, evil, the Adversary (thieves, undone lovers, heavy nuns figure here). When half- or dream-awake in false dawn man's delight is perfect in the Platonically perfect angels and angelic vision, but it seems crucial with Wilbur that the sure-to-come knowledge does not overwhelm everyday reality with evil, pessimism, darkness or death, and that his view is optimistic. The poem is also playful. Criticism should not be too ponderous about it. The pleasure is in not taking it too heavily; his sun does not overwhelm or menace but "acknowledges / With a warm look." We can bask in the warmth.

And I ought to add that it is a man's poem. Certainly not all women would like a laundry poem which pays no heed to hard work and coarsened hands. They might say, poet, have your ruddy dream, but give us better detergents.

Note: Criticism of the above. The first paragraph states my conception of the poem. Should it not end there? Is a general statement about a poem enhanced by particulars?

Perhaps I ought to explain my strictures on "terrible" and "bitter." My Webster gives for "terrible": 1. Causing terror; fearful; frightful; dreadful. 2. Extreme; intense; severe. 3. (*Colloq.*) Very bad, unpleasant, or disagreeable. Somehow the adjective weakens the noun speed. It is not sufficiently motivated or does not motivate itself in the context according to the above definitions, at least for me. Likewise, I feel that "bitter" for love has not been motivated and that some more conclusive or more evocative word might have been better. These feelings may well come from my own critical imperfections and I do not stress them. What Wilbur is talking about, in fact, is the imperfection of life. My response may be wrong on these two words and in any event I esteem the poem and delight in it so much more than I object to what seem to me blemishes that I do not consider my strictures damaging to the piece. Incidentally, students of mine have objected to "hunks" but I applaud this word along with Wilbur's use of "rape" as original.

P.S. Instance of a self-motivating adjective: "multitudinous" in "rather / The multitudinous seas incarnadine / Making the green one red."

P.P.S. When Wilbur reads this poem my adjectival animadversions are ironed out. These words are absorbed into the general and whole meaning. A poem is greater than its parts.

ROBERT HORAN

Hearing Richard Wilbur read, recently, the title poem from his new book, "Love Calls Us to the Things of This World," I recall his making only one comment: "The title, I think, comes from somewhere in Johnson." Certainly the psychological repercussions of the title are a beautiful provocation to our concern. Perhaps a part of the poem's final persuasiveness is locked in that first emblem, however fine Mr. Wilbur's extensions and ornaments. The insight is humble and assertive: Love calls us, not only out of ourselves, from our deserts of tedium and impasse, nor toward a single "other," but toward various realities, "the things of this world."

The poem begins with a man's emergence from sleep. In this state the body and soul are separate. There is an intrusion of sounds, "a cry of pulleys." This is insistent and mundane, of a kind with the laundry and ropes of the poem, though the hanging wash is quickly enough metamorphosed to angels. The waking soul, amazed, is "spirited from sleep," as if conspiratorially, before it can stabilize or flesh itself for whatever encounter. It hangs "bodiless and simple as false dawn." Immediately, the clothes on lines outside the window are transformed by metaphor: "The morning air is all awash with angels." The intimate relationship established through an overlapping of connotations applicable to more than a single image is typical of Wilbur's sensitivity to the overtones of language, and results in an instrument both of ambiguity and of clarity. Simple examples here, such as the relation of *soul* to *spirited, hangs, bodiless,* all prepare and echo the image of the clean wash itself hanging bodiless as an angel. The dawn is *false* because it is premature, incomplete, a thinly-bodied ghost.

The second stanza further particularizes the washing. *Bed-sheets, blouses* and *smocks* are various habitations, they billow with "halcyon feeling," are swollen with an impersonal exultation of spirit and season and flight. There is motion in these lines and those which follow, as the washing is streamed out, hollowed by wind and with flapping pennants, in a fixed but rapid flutter, like waterfalls or rapids we know to be rushing in constant ribbons and eddies, yet seem as if arrested. Then there is a fainting of action in the lapsed wind, and the wash, like ghosts emptied of their ether, falls into vertical rest.

6

On Richard Wilbur's "Love Calls Us to the Things of This World"

We return to the soul, which now draws back from collision with painful memory, the multiple past and the mirroring future. The day is always "punctually raped"; it is violated and possessed by things, demands and confusions. The world is worked; the shirt sweated; the sheet stained. But the soul pleads that there be nothing but these scrubbed and bodiless vestments in cold air, nothing but the hands, rosy with water and rinsed with dawn, and these lucid and spiritual dances of goblined cloth under "the sight of heaven."*

Yet now, that other eye of heaven, the sun, "acknowledges / With a warm look the world's hunks and colors," and is benign toward the riant confusion of forms. Now the soul (like the laundry emptied of too seraphic a breath), *descends* to *accept* the *waking body,* even though it be in *bitter love.* The man "yawns and rises." The soul speaks in an altered (wakened) voice another invocation: Let the wash, hanging its folds in dawn-streaked air like cloths of crucifixion, be brought down from these *gallows.* It will serve as "clean linen for the backs of thieves." (I find numerous crossings and allusions in the *ruddy gallows, linen,* and *thieves,* the decapitated smocks, the "hanging" rope, the two thieves of the Crucifixion, etc.) Fresh-scented in innocence and morning, let the lovers go "to be undone"; this, too, is a part of the "punctual rape of every blessed day." In a more hermetic and self-conscious world of grace, even "the heaviest nuns" must "float," buoyed up and supported by their dark habits (both costume and custom?), keeping their own personal and precarious *balance.* So, however lovely the pantomime against this little horizon, the angels must be brought down from their halcyon heaven, as from a gallows; while the soul descends, the body wakes and rises to the world in all its "hunks and colors"; thieves, lovers, nuns; compassion, effort, grace; ushered here by love, all are clothed and contending with "the things of this world."

Like all paraphrase, this bleak account oversimplifies and, where it does depart from the literal, risks the idiosyncratic. Such commentary simply does not take into account the untranslatable compound of music and image, tone and

---

* This reminds me of a related concept, though with a very different image for it, in Elizabeth Bishop's "The Imaginary Iceberg," where the iceberg is an impeccable, jewelled fantasy, fleshed by our appetite for iced abstraction, and "fair and indivisible" like the soul. In this poem, the moving ship, peopled and plowing toward warm life, is the traffic of "ordinary" reality. The poem reiterates: "We'd rather have the iceberg than the ship."

structure, which makes this, like any fine poem, a total world resisting any prosaic reduction. Though bare of the poem's art and ambiguity, this is simply a skeleton of my own view of a few of its implications.

To me, what is, initially, so sharp and pervasive in the imagery is the look, the light, the promise and the peril of morning. The air "all awash," the "halcyon feeling," the reassurance that the footless ghosts are angels—"truly there they are," these chaste guardians—these details remind me strongly of a painting by the young Italian, Cremonini, of rooftops and upper windows and cornices all strung with washing (*angles* and *angels,* Cocteau reminds us, are words of a feather), an area dissected by light, blue-white sails and diapers, the sheets and blouses with merely a hint of flesh, or contour of failure.

The moving cry,

> Oh, let there be nothing on earth but laundry,
> Nothing but rosy hands in the rising steam
> And clear dances done in the sight of heaven.

is Utopian. It is the spirit's hope for an immediate and impossible eternity of the uninhabited, yet gracious, form.

It is in the concluding stanza that the soul asks that the linen be permitted to become a robe or bandage, an emblem of love or compassion. The laundry loses some of its lovely aerial fiction as it is humanized. Love calls us, whether in darkest habits or heavy and difficult grace, or thinnest veils of innocence, back into the awakened, intricate and culpable world of reality. Note that we are called to this world not by dream nor ennui nor the bodiless mask in the mirror, but by *love,* which is the instrument that defeats our solipsism.

If there is any irony in such an openly lyrical poem, it would seem to me a situational irony; though love be bitter, the poem is not an underscoring or celebration of that bitterness. It is, rather, an *acceptance* of the fact that the sweating, ruined, half-penitent world must be clothed with our compassion. The angel must become human, as heaven must become the street where we walk.

Unless I am much misled, the poem is not difficult, nor its central observation, once reflected, surprising. It is almost as if we must know at least this much, if we are to know anything better. But the statement of the poem is focused like a changing chord or prism; and it does not merely reassert, it exfoliates. It en-

8

On Richard Wilbur's "Love Calls Us to the Things of This World"

riches the poor, forgotten fact of that lovely title, which we so rarely animate in our lives. It relates different hierarchies and distances, which is one of the wonderful powers of metaphor; just as, in another poem of Wilbur's, the *grimy rainbow* thrown from the charwoman's sudsbucket as she washes down the steps of an elaborately gilded Mexican church bridges their separate worlds, so often doomed merely to genuflection. It accomplishes this bridge with a plain but exuberant symbol—the scrub-water rainbow, a secular devotion in a palace stuffed and jeweled with devotions, humanizes and harmonizes the scene.

In its metrical or formal devices, the poem I have been discussing is not altogether typical of Wilbur's techniques. The rhythm is fairly free, the syntax simple, the echoes of sound are delicate and internal rather than heavily chimed. The musical structure is both less even and less intricate than in many of Wilbur's poems.

> Some are in bed-sheets, some are in blouses,
> Some are in smocks: but truly there they are.

This is more casual in cadence than his usual practice, though still not "conversational." (I am reminded of a remark Dylan Thomas made in the course of a conversation some ten years ago. Perhaps because I have so long agreed with it, I am able to recall it quite totally, in meaning if not in color: "Whatever it ever is, poetry is *never* conversational. It's based on *un*common speech.") This is to reinforce an earlier remark in relation to Wilbur's diction and composition. His style is not arch when witty, nor academic in its irony, nor slack and prosaic, but most often lyrical. There are few enough fine lyric poets these days, but this sad fact leads some hot-rod prose-poets to the odd conclusion that the lyric is outdated, as if one were to say that flowers were less contemporaneous than plastics.

Wilbur's lyricism is often more convoluted than it is in this poem—for instance, in his "Baroque Wall Fountain in the Villa Sciara." Perhaps "Love Calls Us to the Things of This World" has at least a greater tonal relation to poems like "At Year's End," or "Beasts." Whether tighter or more relaxed, however, Wilbur's structure is never flabby nor the diction drab. His words, which move as if to shadow and reflect one another, seem to have both the unity and uniquity of leaves.

On Richard Wilbur's "Love Calls Us to the Things of This World"

Yet, though this poem remains for me a fine one through many readings, there is in it, as elsewhere in Wilbur, some fastidiousness or remoteness that dissipates power. Some of these fine distances assist clarity and perspective. At other times, however, Wilbur's hand seems gloved, muffling passion in favor of finesse. Most often, the poetry is superbly controlled, and the craft and careful observation are beautiful because they are not mere embroidery. Nevertheless, in many poems, I miss a more urgent involvement, emotive, not sermonic; some real risk or riot of the head and heart and nerve. This need not involve any efface-ment of his particular lucidity or lyricism, nor any relation to the shouting self-crucifixion that is, at the moment, so often litanized in public and enjoyed in private. But when Wilbur's poems aren't edged with wit, or other tonal complex-ity, there is frequently an amber quietude for all their music, a finish that ap-pears to polish away intensity as if it were a flaw.

The charge of *elegance* is leveled against Wilbur, in particular by a number of younger writers whose oracles, though various, are often Whitman and Wil-liams and Charlie Parker. (Here, Dylan Thomas is a strong influence as a per-sonality, but hardly at all as a poet.) This charge of fatal elegance seems to me a vague if not specious label. Coherence, control, design, and then a line gleam-ing like a bar of enamel in the light; this, and the patience of a lizard until the relationships of a scene are memorized, are powerful virtues. But they are often trained upon nature. Of course, the poetry of barns and ponds, stemming from Dickinson's Amherst, and corruscated with Molière and Italian fountains, were-wolves and love, may have an index insufficiently violent and indigenous to some, especially when the metaphysician of the academy is suspected hiding heretically in Emily's cupola.

I think the subjects and allusions in Wilbur which fail or bore such jazzy young readers are not really pedantries or orthodoxies, but clear and personal uses of a sense of history and event sometimes more remote, though no less alive, than the Charleston. Certainly in comparison with a more fashionable master like Pound, the chief genius of anagrams, Wilbur is forthright as a poster; his real puzzles are few, and his mortar is not chiefly pebbled with rage. This lack of explicit rage and rebellion may be the real complaint underlying the charge of elegance.

Though I cannot join the occasional cries of "elegance" or "preciousness," I

On Richard Wilbur's "Love Calls Us to the Things of This World"

do miss, or find muted, a certain largesse, a more dramatic gesture, a stroke at stature; a passion that grips rather than graces; an engagement that proclaims the person as well as the persona, and the ache, not just the symbol, of the event. (I am aware, and consequently wary, that just some such urgency and spontaneity would be of the greatest value to me in my own poems, and might even help to free them from a crust of oblique images and useless armours. For this reason, I hope I have not projected personal problems where I feel so much sympathy with aims and achievements.)

The concern of Wilbur's poem, with which I began these remarks, involves a reciprocity between the multiple emotion which we call *love,* and the multiple kaleidoscope, *the world.* The poem that articulates this is subtle without opacity, musical without rigidity, moving without sentimentality. It contains no Apocalypse nor explosion. Its virtues are quiet, humane, poetic.

In view of all these qualities, it may be uncharitable to demand others not vividly present in this poem, and perhaps outside the intention, rather than the range, of the poet. It is as if I reiterated: Everywhere in Wilbur's poetry there is acuity, craft and honesty; subtle, fine ribbons in the marble, deceptive simplicity of figure, or disarming fugues of light and melody . . . But then felt that I must add to this gratitude, as I do, the poem's own admonition to the bodiless laundry hung high in the false dawn: "Bring them down from their ruddy gallows." I see an intenser pavilion for these ghosts and graces, fleshed with the marvelous mundane; and fired, then, in a real blaze of love for "the things of this world."

MAY SWENSON

The modern lyric is autonomous, a separate mobile, having its own private design and performance. It may be little on the page, yet project a long and versatile dance in the mind. Its total form and gesture is not a relative, it is an absolute, an enclosed construct. Some readers, opening the volume of a lyric poet, are apt to approach the poems sequentially, comparatively, considering them as an independent row of things in the box of the book—when, in fact, each poem is a package individually wrapped. I like to see the poem first as a shut box or package to be opened, within which is an invention whose particular working I hope to discover. Something can be felt about it even before beginning to read: its profile on the page, its regular or irregular pattern of stanzas, length of lines, their symmetry, its wide or thin shape, its look of bulk or lightness. For instance, before reading, I see that Richard Wilbur's poem is a squarish vertical, built of six stanzas, five lines each, running to thirty lines. Each stanza is indented, and there are dropped-line indentations within some stanzas. The lines show a regular rhythm pattern with an occasional eccentricity. I now read the opening line of the first and last stanza, and find a four-beat line; I see that the title announces this beat. (Later I discover that five as well as four-beat iambics are used.) Glancing down the end-words of the lines, I find no outer rhymes. I suppress attention to the content, and quickly read through the poem for its sound alone. I want to determine the mainsprings of its music before releasing its images into consciousness. There are no deliberate internal rhymes either, yet the poem has evident harmonic values: there are numerous assonances, alliterations, consonant matings, recurrent *ing* endings. The meter seems not to be one obviously selected and imposed; it is consistent in the over-all, elastic in its parts; it rises, flows, expands, sinks; it has a billow or a bump now and then. It comes to a noticeable halt in the very center of the poem, at the middle of the last line of the third stanza. The movement of the top half is fluid and swift, that of the lower half slower, more dense—this is felt not only in the leap or walk of the meter, but in the vowels and consonants predominating (i, e, and l, for the most part, in the first half, and principally u and k in the latter half).

So far, the box has been opened and the mobile examined as a *still*; its top surfaces have been handled coolly. Any number of other poems could show the

On Richard Wilbur's "Love Calls Us to the Things of This World"

above superficial features but give a different performance when "turned on" in the mind. For me, it is the images and their expansion into metaphor that constitute the main motion of a poem—for these awake concrete associational responses and, while the sound must augment, in fact be inevitably welded to, the image, by itself sound is the more abstract feature, for me.

With the flow of the images into the mind, I give myself up to the magicianship of the poem, postponing analysis until later. I let myself be caught up, uncritically, and ride within the poem, to experience as intuitively as I can *its* experience, which I hope will be a fresh one. Wilbur's "Love Calls Us to the Things of This World" proves to be that. My reactions after a first reading are these: 1. I enjoyed it. 2. It was an exciting ride. 3. There was something unique about it; at the same time, it felt familiar. Up to the middle, to the conclusion "That nobody seems to be there" it felt as if I had seen and recognized the very simile he has found: clean clothes, blowing on a line, are disembodied souls or angels. This partly because the incident is so common that everyone has seen it, and partly because the analogy is so fitting in each of its details: a shirt is white, it is empty of body, but floats or flies, therefore has life (an angel). Wilbur here has brought an unconscious association of my own into light; this is a joyful shock, and it seems magical. But were this all, it would be a "little" poem, exquisite, playful, nothing more. It might be dismissed with the thought, "I could have done it; I've had the same experience." The unique, and more mysterious part of the poem is the lower half, where *he* reacts to his own metaphor, as an individual and as a representative of modern man. The philosophical content adds unexpected solidity and durability—so that my impulse is to read it again, and several times, to find out "what he is really saying." And doing so, I find that I cannot reach a point of final decision as to whether he is saying "only *this*" or "underneath this, also *that*" and perhaps "underneath *that*, etc." This is what keeps the poem from being too quickly "grounded"—to land in the box of no-longer-played-with-toys. Since it gives a somewhat different performance each time it is set going in the mind, it stays alive.

Attempting to lift the layers of meaning, I see several sets of clues, all having to do with physical sensations. There are at least six, pertaining to Sound, Relative Tension, Shape, Color, Motion, and Relative Weight. The poem begins with the "cry of pulleys" as a line of wash is hoisted into the morning air. This *Sound*

On Richard Wilbur's "Love Calls Us to the Things of This World"

(1) opens the poem (and the eyes of the sleeper). Later "The soul shrinks . . . and *cries*" and later, the soul *says* "in a *changed voice* . . ." Similarly, contrasts of *Tension* (2) may be followed throughout the poem. Consider these words and their placement: *pulleys* (with its extra association of being pulled), hangs, shrinks, gallows; and then: calm swells, impersonal breathing, yawns. There are these allusions to *Shape* (3) or its absence: bodiless, angels, bedsheets, blouses, smocks, white water, steam, dances, world's hunks and colors, waking body, man, nuns' habits. *Color* clues (4): *White* is indicated or suggested for: soul, dawn, angels, water, steam, linen, pure. *Red* is suggested in: rape, rosy, warm look, love, waking body, ruddy gallows, swoon, nobody seems to be there, shrinks, *punc*tual (with its extra association of punched holes). *Black* is suggested in: bitter love, gallows, thieves, undone (with its double meaning), heaviest, dark habits, difficult. *Motion* clues (5): *Angels:* rising, swells, breathing, flying, conveying, speed, moving and staying, swoon down, quiet, dances. *Soul:* hangs, shrinks, descends, accept. *Steam:* rising. *Man:* rises. *Nuns:* walk in a pure floating. *Relative Weight* (6): bodiless clothes / souls, heaviest nuns.

The whole poem (in its material, structure and expression) is in fact an epitome of relative weight and equipoise. As noted in regard to its rhythm, the imagistic action is also brought to a point, a pause at the very center, with the words "that nobody seems to be there." The lower half of the poem is made into a ground, a base of thought (reaction) for the emotion that is unfurled in the upper half. There is a descent, a hardening, a graveness (the result of gravity!) in the last three stanzas. But then, with the sense, the sound, the image of the final two lines, "And (let) the *heaviest* nuns walk in a pure *floating* / Of dark habits, keeping their difficult balance" the ethereal is joined to the earthy (soul to body, imagination to reality) and *balance,* the significant concluding word, is revealed as the synthesis of the whole poem, simultaneously giving the clue to its meaning *and* its form.

A single large metaphor emerges from a series of exact observations, its separate features closely corresponding to the mundane event that takes place, the hanging of the wash. The "soul *hangs*"—and one of the bodiless "persons" on the line is Richard Wilbur. By an act of possession (the obverse of being possessed, but just as useful for the seizing of poetic power) he becomes a part of his subject. He then experiences in each of its particulars the dramatic life of the row of

On Richard Wilbur's "Love Calls Us to the Things of This World"

souls in the air: he is one of the angels. He is one of the "hunks and colors" acknowledged by the sun; he "descends in bitter love to accept the waking body" of the man.

Taken at face value, the poem is direct and transparent. It seems to project a mood of primary exuberance, freedom, playfulness; air, space, clean forms, spontaneous motion are its atmosphere—a poem to free the muscles and freshen the mind—for so skilled without stiffness, so lighthearted without gaucherie, is Wilbur able to be. But it has the added weight of its somber accents. It is anchored and steadied by a guy of thought, just as is the line of flying clothes, so that it is "moving and staying" at the same time. There are ominous, painful, even violent suggestions in this fair and bouyant poem. They are not noticed at first, but they are what furnish its intricacy and constitute enough ambiguity so that its analysis cannot be exhausted. With his very first image, he warns himself (and us) with the innocent/ugly word "hangs" that is resounded later in "ruddy gallows." Hidden in the whiteness, the cleanliness of the angelic crowd, a *hanged soul*, a *false dawn*. There is at one extreme "the terrible speed of their *omnipresence*" and at the other "a swooning down into so rapt a quiet that *nobody* seems to be there." That there are thieves among the nuns, that they are heavy in their "dark habits" (with the double meanings of these two words) and the wish for only "clean dances done in the sight of heaven" may indicate other levels of meaning having to do, perhaps, with the poet's conscience, with doubt about his own equilibrium, with a questioning of his self-faith, or with criticism of a larger Faith. If I look to the title to name a single intention for the poem, I can arrive at several possible equations. Does "Love" that "calls us" equal the "angels" that cry us awake in the squeak of the pulleys? Do "The Things of This World" equal "the heaviest nuns" who in "dark habits" must keep "their difficult balance?" Are the (pure) "things of *this* world" presented here as opposed to a false, a hypocritical, even cruel "heaven"? I would as soon be content with the unparadoxical first-thought meaning that, with the insights of love, we see deepest beauties and miracles in the simplest things "of this world"—our daily lives.

Something more—much more—could and should be said about Wilbur's sonic devices which are integral to his imagery and magnify the charm of the poem. A full analysis would consume more space than I am allotted, but if I now read the piece aloud, chief emphases seem to ring out, in the first half, from words containing the vowel sounds *i*, *e*, and *a*. If my count is correct, there are, respectively, 7, 6, and 7 such words. Alliteratively, as well as within words, the *l* sound occurs 14 times. A delightful fusion of music, movement, image and emotion is seen, for instance, in the lines: "Now they are rising together in calm swells / Of halcyon feeling, filling whatever they wear / With the deep joy of their impersonal breathing." In the second half of the poem, *u* is the most emphatic vowel sound, occurring, as I count it, 12 times, and the *k* sound is the ruling consonant, beginning, or included in, 16 words. Example: "Yet as the sun acknowledges / With a warm look the world's hunks and colors." The lower part of the poem takes on a darker, harder cast for me, partly because of this, while the upper poem is higher pitched, lighter, more fluid. The response to sound in a poem is so subjective that it has not as much value for analysis as does image. For instance, the *a* tone conveys mystery for me (probably from association with the word *awe*); the *u* sound repeated suggests bluntness, heaviness mixed with fear. Curiously, in stanza three, the sequence of the words *place, conveying* and *staying*, because of the vowel sound *a*, suggests intense whiteness, even apart from the image. While confirming my other theories about Wilbur's poem, these sonic impressions I believe to be too personal to carry any but secondary importance for the interpretation of content, although they sharpen my total appreciation.

RICHARD WILBUR

Dear Mr. Ostroff:

I find just one assertion in these essays which I can confidently correct, and that is Mr. Horan's attribution of the title to Johnson. The title comes from St. Augustine. Since the error lies within a quotation from me, it's perfectly possible that I am correcting not Mr. Horan but my own lapse.

For the rest, I can only say that it is good to be so thoroughly understood. However troubled by the desire to please, poets soon come to ignore most of the criticism they receive; approval or condemnation are not interesting in the absence of understanding. It is not gratifying to be praised as perspicuous by a critic who proceeds to obscure one's work by wild misquotation. Nor is it disturbing to be damned by a critic who concludes (on the basis of Italian title, girl, and stair) that one's poem *"Piazza di Spagna"* is a rehash of *"La Figlia che Piange."* After a time, what one most desires from criticism is the assurance that someone somewhere, with or without complaisance, has stooped to seeing the point.

Miss Swenson and Messrs. Eberhart and Horan give me this assurance three times, and I thank them. Being poets, they have been willing to perform the humble, fundamental task of criticism—the interpretation of the work in the light of its apparent intention. Three critics would not have been so modest or so penetrating.

Miss Swenson's remarks on sound-patterns in the poem I found extremely interesting. Of course, most poets would not be conscious of selecting i-sounds or e-sounds in composing a particular passage; but I am sure that one's feeling of "rightness" in a developing poem most often depend on the half-conscious achievement of appropriate vowel-and-consonant color.

As for what sounds are appropriate to what ideas, it is as Miss Swenson says a relatively subjective matter. Yet I think that I'm on her side about l's and k's, and there are certainly sounds which suit one idea more than another.

Let us alone.—Tennyson, *Lotus-Eaters*

For an old bitch gone in the teeth,
For a botched civilization.—Pound, *Mauberley*

RICHARD WILBUR

On "Love Calls Us to the Things of This World"

A child-psychologist told me once of a five-year-old boy in her care, who really wanted to be a girl and was totally lacking in aggressiveness. When asked to count, he'd begin each number with L, so as to avoid the fricatives and other assertive sounds. Lun, Loo, Lee, Lour, Live. Teased, he would sometimes, in momentary anger, admit to being FFFive.

Dame Edith Sitwell has repeatedly gone too far with sound-analysis, discovering for instance "the whole sound, gathered through ages, of the sea" in Pound's lines "And doom goes with her in walking." But subjective excesses of that sort shouldn't put us off noticing and mentioning the more demonstrable sonic aspects of a poem.

Lee Anderson, so far as I know, is the only poet in America who writes *deliberately* in sound patterns; the patterns are nevertheless there, in everybody.

I feel some sympathy for Mr. Eberhart's objections to "terrible" and "bitter," and I can guess why he lets the other "shock-words"—"rape" and "hunks"—get by. The latter pair are nouns. If the surprising words of a poem are also adjectives, they seem (first-off, at least) like chromium accessories on a jalopy, or flashy costume jewelry on a woman with a bad figure. Nouns and verbs make the power and figure of a poem.

Nevertheless, the general strategy and local syntax of a poem will sometimes force one to put into an adjective what might be stronger elsewhere. Both "bitter" and "terrible" are saying something I thought needed to be said. Omnipresence is a dreadful or awful concept; one way to *feel* the concept is to approach it through the idea of speed, until the imagination faints; "terrible" should have the effect of greasing the track—of saying to the reader, "go ahead, imagine infinite speed." Doesn't Shakespeare's "multitudinous" work somewhat in this way—supplying something of the reaction, so that the hearer will venture to feel a monstrous image, and through that a monstrous guilt?

Plato, St. Theresa, and the rest of us in our degree have known that it is painful to return to the cave, to the earth, to the quotidian; Augustine says it is love that brings us back. That is why the love of line 23 has got to be bitter—for the sake of psychological truth. Again, I agree that the necessity would be plainer, at first look, if the extrusive word were not an adjective. Had I been able to afford another "speech" at that point in the poem, I might have conveyed the notion of bitter love dramatically, in the manner of the last of Elizabeth Bishop's fine poem "Sleeping on the Ceiling":

But oh, that we could sleep up there . . .

Mr. Horan's observation about "some fastidiousness or remoteness that dissipates power" and his suggestion that I could do with "an *engagement* that proclaims the person as well as the persona" interests me extremely. I've always agreed with Eliot's assertion that poetry "is not the expression of personality but an escape from personality," and I suppose that it has been temperamentally convenient for me to do so. I've thought of the poem—in Miss Swenson's phrase—as "a box to be opened," a created object, an altar-cloth, Japanese garden or ship of death. Not a message or confession. Mr. Horan's remarks, and Mr. Eberhart's opinion as to the tone of the poem, have moved me to sharpen these ideas.

We do inevitably treat any poem—in part—as the utterance of a person, and react to it as we would to a person. A poem should "bring the whole soul of man into activity," and we look in a poem as in conversation for signs of passion, intellect, judgment, and the harmony of these faculties. It is hard, in life, to read these signs, because we are obliged to take ourselves as normal, and because modes of expression vary. In poetry, it is both easier and harder to assess the signs of the soul. Easier because all is verbalized, and because literary convention and tradition are being employed, defied, or both. Harder, because poetic technique translates all signs into a new and condensed language, and because "acting a part" is not only legitimate but unavoidable.

When technically adequate poetry doesn't satisfy, it is either because the persona seems a forced version of the person (as when Yeats is writing what Graves calls his "hard, burnished rubbish"), or because the persona, though a true derivation of the person, does not seem to express a "whole soul" (as Dylan Thomas, with his lack of moral imagination, sometimes does not).

I think one generally knows when one is faking too far. But can anyone truly judge whether or not he is imparting a "whole soul" to his poetry? I doubt it, and I am reminded of a ludicrous character of Cabell's whose secret opinion it is that the force of human passion is greatly exaggerated. Descartes observes that everyone thinks himself abundantly provided with common sense, and

On "Love Calls Us to the Things of This World"

doubtless every poet feels that he has confided the proper amount of passion, intellect, judgment and harmony to his best lines.

The farther one gets from the dramatic, the harder it is for the poet or reader to judge the presence or absence of these qualities in a poem. Juliet's speeches in Act III, Scene 2 ("I am not I, if there be such an I") have often been thought absurdly tricky and frigid, but it was surely Shakespeare's intention to convey distraction and despair. He was using rhetorical rather than dramatic means. The passions are there, or meant to be there; but they are represented in a manner more remote from ordinary emotive expression than one finds—for instance—in the great speeches of the later scenes. Our reaction to Juliet's rhetorical speeches is complicated, too, by the fact that rhetorical conventions are transitory.

Until recently, I have inclined I suppose to avoid the direct, dramatic expression of feeling, and to convey it through rhetoric or through hints imbedded in apparently objective description. My best poems seem to me to account somehow for my whole experience and to engage my whole nature. When sympathetic critics find what seems to me a passionate poem merely "amiable," or are troubled by a sense of "fastidiousness or remoteness," I hardly know what I can sensibly say. I must concede the possibility, as all must, that I am not a "whole soul." I must also wonder whether my poetry may not be too indirect for its emotion to transpire. What I must not do, I am sure, is to attempt a manner which might satisfy my critics; there is nothing to do, in art, but to persevere hopefully in one's peculiarities.

"Love Calls Us" is, for me, a departure in the direction of the dramatic. I am not essaying the dramatic on principle; it's just happening. The first six drafts of the opening lines may interest some of your readers, and therefore I shall close by quoting them. What I see now in these drafts is a gradual moving-away from too much objective detail, and a liberation of the rhythm toward the abruptness of speech.

(1) My eyes came open to the squeak of pulleys
   My spirit, shocked from the brothel of itself

(2) My eyes came open to the shriek of pulleys,
   And the soul, spirited from its proper wallow,
   Hung in the air as bodiless and hollow

On "Love Calls Us to the Things of This World"

(3) My eyes came open to the pulleys' cry.
    The soul, spirited from its proper wallow,
    Hung in the air as bodiless and hollow
    As light that frothed upon the wall opposing;
    But what most caught my eyes at their unclosing
    Was two gray ropes that yanked across the sky.
    One after one into the window frame
       . . . the hosts of laundry came

(4)   The eyes open to a cry of pulleys,
    And the soul, so suddenly spirited from sleep,
      Hangs in the air as bodiless and simple
      As morning sunlight frothing on the floor,
        While just outside the window
      The air is solid with a dance of angels.

(5)   The eyes open to a cry of pulleys,
    And spirited from sleep, the astounded soul
    Hangs for a moment bodiless and simple
    As dawn light in the moment of its breaking:
        Outside the open window
    The air is crowded with a

(6)   The eyes open to a cry of pulleys,
    And spirited from sleep, the astounded soul
    Hangs for a moment bodiless and simple
    As false dawn.
        Outside the open window,
    The air is leaping with a rout of angels.
      Some are in bedsheets, some are in dresses,
        it does not seem to matter

Yours,

RICHARD WILBUR

JOHN CROWE RANSOM

BABETTE DEUTSCH

STANLEY KUNITZ

THEODORE ROETHKE

On THEODORE ROETHKE'S

"In a Dark Time"

Theodore Roethke

IN A DARK TIME

I

In a dark time, the eye begins to see:
I meet my shadow in the deepening shade;
I hear my echo in the echoing wood,
A lord of nature weeping to a tree.
I live between the heron and the wren,
Beasts of the hill and serpents of the den.

II

What's madness but nobility of soul
At odds with circumstance? The day's on fire!
I know the purity of pure despair,
My shadow pinned against a sweating wall.
That place among the rocks—is it a cave
Or winding path? The edge is what I have.

III

A steady storm of correspondences!—
A night flowing with birds, a ragged moon,
And in broad day the midnight come again!
A man goes far to find out what he is—
Death of the self in a long tearless night,
All natural shapes blazing unnatural light.

IV

Dark, dark my light, and darker my desire.
My soul, like some heat-maddened fly,
Keeps buzzing at the sill. Which I is I?
A fallen man, I climb out of my fear.
The mind enters itself, and God the mind,
And one is One, free in the tearing wind.

JOHN CROWE RANSOM

We are glad to be invited to look at Theodore Roethke's new poem; and the first look that I take seems to discover a poem about a decisive moral experience. But I can do better. The poem is later than that; it is a religious poem, about a "dark time" of inner conflict—it might be about a "dark night of the soul," except for my strong impression that this poet never lapses into established schemes of imagery—into which at last comes the serene light of a triumphant resolution. The true self or soul or mind of the highly compounded authorial "I" asserts its authority and makes its peace in the name of God. And, in the name of poetry, the critic welcomes the poet who has converted his reckoning with that blunt and homeless "categorical imperative" of the moral experience into metaphysical images. Now it becomes a reckoning with God. But in this poem it passes so quickly! It is not slowed by the sweet clang and clog of some profuse conventional rhetoric, which we may have come to expect for our greater ease when we are being persuaded to religious themes. But it is not as if there were any failure in the sharp images; they offer themselves punctually line by line to denote the pain, or the peace. Still we feel that they are too terse and spare for so great an event—if we are not quite familiar with this poet's severe economy. A poem made mostly out of pure images often taxes the mind of the reader who would make out the scheme of its argument. Very soon I confessed that I was not prepared to read this poem justly.

But I could still prepare myself. So I took many hard close looks at some of the hundred and more poems which had preceded it, as I find them in the poet's collected edition, *Words for the Wind*, of 1958. When this book first came into my hands I had postponed too long already my proper study of Roethke, and my preoccupations were such that even then I looked at it only hurriedly; a sad betrayal as I think now. To make amends I can at least advise my readers here that it is much to our advantage if we can possess ourselves of the earlier poems, in order to establish this poet's habit of mind, and the commonplace of his actual or imagined experiences, as the "situation" for the new poem to plunge into (*in medias res*) with its own special drama. No other background will do, only the actual one, which we shall never light upon within our own independent imaginations.

On Theodore Roethke's "In a Dark Time"

The poems of the first section of *Words for the Wind* are out of Roethke's first book, published in 1941; the author had been born in 1908. They are accomplished; and various, as is right when the new poet is taking stock of his powers, and the several directions his further work may take; Apollonian in their tidiness and roundedness. Then other books are drawn upon, and finally many single poems not previously in book form.

But after the opening miscellany the poet becomes much more programmatic and consecutive. It is as if he were writing in retrospect and intentionally, like Wordsworth, about the growth of a poet's mind; but hardly with Wordsworth's bland and macroscopic vision, which takes its scenes whole, and panoplied in their atmospheres of light and shade, and pays little attention to the small things, and the incessant little fantasies which compose the minutiae or substance of a poet's experience. This is a different mind. We say to ourselves that now Roethke has found the main line of his history, and is getting on with it by dramatizing in chronological order many recollected or possible experiences under new technical forms.

First comes the stage of early childhood. Like Wordsworth, this is a nature poet, and an "I" poet. But this child is prodigious in his perceptions, and the bold fancies to which he fits them instantly. He feels deprived and lonely in the family group, in that human society which lifts and keeps itself so painfully off the natural earth and its teeming life. At some tender age he begins to alienate himself; this is the sight of the metaphysical man, the artist and/or religionist who is to come. The child is the great metaphysician; he entertains one marvel after another, the evil and the good; it is not strange if we have been advised after we are old to "become as a little child" if we would believe in wonders again. So it is not enough for the child to frequent his father's greenhouse; he must go to the field and the wood, where he becomes intimate with many curious forms and stages of vegetation, and the habits and bodies of small animals. We have not had the like of that in our poetry before, so far as I know. Yet this body of experience is known to most of us; it has only lacked its literary development. Certainly we have not before had the odd emphatic rhythms by which the poet becomes a child in order to think as a child again. At this point of my study it was a beautiful coincidence to find Roethke in a recent issue of *Poetry* of Chicago talking about the rhythms of Mother Goose, and especially the joy of the freer

On Theodore Roethke's "In a Dark Time"

rhythms in the adaptable old folk medium; it was a clue to the oral quality he meant for his own child poems. But they are not exactly for the conventional nursery. Here is a passage from the poem, "Where Knock Is Open Wide":

> I know it's an owl. He's making it darker.
> Eat where you're at. I'm not a mouse.
> Some stones are still warm.
> I like soft paws.
>
> Maybe I'm lost,
> Or asleep.
>
> A worm has a mouth.
> Who keeps me last?
> Fish me out.
> Please.
>
> God, give me a near. I hear flowers.
> A ghost can't whistle.
> I know! I know!
> Hello happy hands.

The rhythmic structure here is a singular and happy invention which Roethke often uses. Each of the upper lines is the half of a full folk line, but each half has two halves of its own which are complete small sentences. In a few poems a top or major line may have three sentences! After this formal opening there is a slower and more irregular movement of focus and conclusion.

I must hurry. Next comes the stage of adolescence: the boy is racked by the furtive stirrings of a wild animal in his own person, and therefore, in the same degree, by the twitchings of another self which we call conscience.

And is that to be all of this story? Do we not need continuation, till the boy has become the full-grown man? Luckily it is still possible, working with the poet's own text if he will allow it, to push the story to its proper conclusion. Certainly the part which we have seen is broken off, and succeeded by new reflective poems in the present tense of their author. But before long appears the remarkable sequence of *Love Poems* in the past tense, and I beg to consider this as the sufficient culmination of the retrospect. A difficulty arises in the style,

On Theodore Roethke's "In a Dark Time"

which is no longer the boy's style. But now it is as if, with the arrival of the grand passion, he had come into his artistic as well as his physical maturity; from now on, we say, his characteristic voice is going to meter itself cleanly and beautifully in what we must call the syllabic or high style of this art. First love is a spiritual experience, and we should have expected that for this as for other poets it would prove the most mystical as well as the most animal engagement that has yet claimed him. And to have it the grown-up boy must return whether he will or no to the human society, though for the woman as for the man the natural setting is the right place for it. In vain I think our imaginations will turn the pages of our sophisticated modern anthology for another set of love lyrics as fresh and utterly successful as this one. It is a great triumph.

And now our history of the young poet's growth is complete. Its world is nature, and the dominant symbol is sex. It will occur to us that this little formula holds probably for many other poets' youthful histories, if only they had been written; and for example, John Donne's, and John Keats's and William Butler Yeats's; it would hardly do for that famous *Prelude* of W.W.'s.

The collected poems of course go on past the retrospective poems, and show to what powers the mind of the poet has actually come. There is much reference to Yeats, who has influenced him, but our poet is original, and quickly reasserts his own voice in paying tribute to the other poet. And now he is much occupied with a new interest, and a fearful one: the theme of death. Probably many readers have observed that John Keats, like the poets of some centuries preceding him, thought of the act of love as a sort of Little Death (in view of the anticlimactic and death-like void of the spirit which followed it); and, as his mortal malady advanced, dwelt upon the thought of the Big Death which would end everything for him. But we should not forget that a third Death has played a great role with some poets, as well as the systematic religionists. This we may call the Symbolic Death which the mind embraces by a religious conversion. The mind prevails upon itself to acquiesce in the Big Death as the right prospect as well as the sure prospect of a mortal man. Mr. Roethke's new poem is about this event. It has to take place on his own terms; he is fastidiously a modern, exuberantly an American, the man of a New World; just as Walt Whitman and Wallace Stevens were; as William Carlos Williams, happily, is. Whatever his future poetry may be, a considerable chapter will already have been written about a

On Theodore Roethke's "In a Dark Time"

long clashing of violent and original images till an authentic conversion was accomplished.

There is a strong theological strain in Roethke. Is not that an intellectualism complicating the poetry? (We are aware of the same complication in Wordsworth's early verse.) The new poem, with its predecessors which lead up to it, may belong to an order which is classical in the history of religion rather than the history of poetry. The poets typically do not make formal avowals of their conversion or of "dying unto this world" forthwith, as the saints do. Perhaps the poets grow into their new mind and do not have to fight for it. Conversion is of the mind; yet, avowals or not, its effect is a conversion of the whole scheme of the natural world, to make it wear a new look. Poets discover how much is added to life by the premonition of death. The best moments of life are the poignant and clinging ones which are most informed of the fact of death; life is being rescued by death from what would have been its pure indifference, void of history and of drama, a mode of action which would be unconscious, physiological, mechanical. Would not goodness itself be meaningless, be just nothing at all, if goodness prevailed universally and did not have to reckon with the fact of evil? Death is the curse which time brings, but if it is not valuable in itself it is the cause of whatever else is of value. Without it our good moments could never be exalted and kept in memory, nor could the poet set them up in that handsome though specious "immortality" which is said to be within the power of his magic. This is the classical wisdom of poets; typically it does not follow from a formal theology. A great piety plays over the poets' representations of this world, and might seem to indicate no mean religious habit for mere poets to possess. But if we would still insist on seeing their technical or theological credentials, the best we should ever get out of them might be some wide and windy proclamation like this: How excellently is the world made, that death should have been provided in order to achieve life: do we not faithfully testify to the best of all possible worlds?

There is nothing I can think of which is lacking in Mr. Roethke's equipment as a regular or classical poet; but there is something more, in the plus sense; and it agitates and complicates his surfaces. As we go along we may perhaps reflect upon the difficulty of his poetic strategy. A poet dedicated to pure images, as Roethke is dedicated in an extreme degree, is faced with the huge problem of finding what Mr. Eliot has called his "objective correlative," if he wants his images to do justice at the same time to the mixed emotions of the painful protagonist and the intellectual niceties of the theologian. We are apt to think it might have been easier if the poet had been simply a man of some reputable faith, let us say simply a Christian poet, and could draw upon a multitude of familiar images which might conceivably be adequate, having been employed for many centuries; or even in spite of this last qualification. But the strategy must be left, without prejudice, to the poet.

Apologies to Miss Deutsch and Mr. Kunitz my colleagues, and to Mr. Ostroff our moderator, for the time I am taking! But I have explained my disabilities, which they will not have had. And now we must take a quick look at two or three of the late poems, in the collected edition, which are about death and the Symbolic Death of conversion.

One poem is called "The Dying Man (In Memoriam: W. B. Yeats)," and I quote the part called "The Wall":

A ghost comes out of the unconscious mind
To grope my sill: It means to be reborn!
The figure at my back is not my friend;
The hand upon my shoulder turns to horn.
I found my father when I did my work,
Only to lose myself in this small dark.

Though it reject small borders of the seen,
What sensual eye can keep an image pure,
Leaning across the sill to greet the dawn?
A slow growth is a thing hard to endure.
When figures out of obscure shadow rave,
All sensual love's but dancing on a grave.

The wall has entered: I must love the wall,
A madman staring at perpetual night,
A spirit raging at the visible.
I breathe alone until my dark is bright.
Dawn's where the white is. Who would know the dawn
When there's a dazzling dark behind the sun?

On Theodore Roethke's "In a Dark Time"

This is a furious piece, and the speaker nearly wins his victory. The ghost is the speaker's father, still saying, "Just go on with your work," as he used to say. But such maxims are for children; clearly the father is no friend to the remembered boy who is again neglecting his work; really the boy is a man now and has his own mind to make up. In the second stanza the speaker is trying for a more than natural vision, but having his difficulties; the images of sensual love still beset him. Then the wall enters, and "I must love the wall." The wall is the barrier to the vision, but it is made out of the unworthy images of the natural man, and therefore he must love it. Nevertheless he keeps trying to pass beyond the visible, and is not far from succeeding; so that this passage almost anticipates the new and triumphant poem at which we (and he) are aiming.

The very last poem in the book is to our purpose; it is mostly an item out of the classical tradition of poetry, and surely it is one of Roethke's finest. The title is "Meditations of an Old Woman." A good woman who lives in nature without much benefit of theology, and without fear, will keep the child's grace and spontaneity; perhaps she makes the best kind of saint which it is advisable (for those who are qualified) to try for. When she is old, and death is coming before long, she says cheerfully, at the end of her Second Meditation, and in the rhythm of the child,

> If the wind means me,
> I'm here!
> Here.

This old woman is knowledgeable as well as innocent; her learning shows brilliantly sometimes, but in the long monologue it is never a burden to the argument. And Mr. Roethke, who wears his own learning with a poet's indifference, may here be taking on an old woman's mask in order to have his last fling with the racy idiom of folk speech; but we hope it will not be his last. Her medium is a free verse which sometimes rises into folk rhythm, and again into ambitious pentameters. I quote the ending of her Fifth Meditation on the last page of the collected poems:

> The sun! the sun! And all we can become!
> And the time ripe for running to the moon!
> In the long fields I leave my father's eye;

And shake the secrets from my deepest bones;
My spirit rises with the rising winds;
I'm thick with liberties a short life permits,—
I seek my own meekness;
I recover my tenderness by long looking.
By midnight I love everything alive.
Who took the darkness from the air?
I'm wet with another life.
Yes, I have gone and stayed.
What came to me vaguely is now clear,
As if released by a spirit,
Or agency outside me.
Unprayed-for,
And final.

She is now adjusted to the last imminence of death. She has not had to pray for this revelation, and does not bother as to where it came from, being scarcely conscious of her metaphysics.

The acceptance of death symbolically, and in advance, is harder for the usual masculine "I" of Roethke's poems. Let us take up the poem "In a Dark Time," for we are home at last. I imagine that readers who have followed my quotes and remarks are about as well prepared as I to make a few suitable observations.

The poem is a recapitulation of the old compulsion upon the poet's mind to exceed its finite bounds for one mystical moment to be forever cherished. But now its conclusion is as assured as that of the old woman, and ever more joyful. The peace is hard-won. It has been wrestled for, prayed for; the long frustration was a sort of madness; each failure intensified the fear. It is a well-structured poem, having a beginning in Stanza I, a middle in II and III, a conclusion in IV. The opening of any stanza has a fine rhetorical resonance; the images which follow and conduct the action are specific and clear, and, having met with most of them before, we know the better how to construe them.

In Stanza I there are images which gave me a little trouble. But I think the weeping of "a lord of nature . . . to a tree" signifies the extreme abasement of the man, and is explained in the two asides which follow:

On Theodore Roethke's "In a Dark Time"

> I live between the heron and the wren,
> Beasts of the hill and serpents of the den.

The weeping image represents the speaker in the role of wren. Living between heron and wren represents his vacillation between power and pride as of the heron, and weakness and meekness as of the wren. The two poles shift a little in the next line, where the vacillation is between the open and public life of the beasts of the hill, and the evil secrecy of serpents.

In II the image of pure despair occurs when the light at the speaker's back presents him only with his own shadow "pinned against a sweating wall"; we know the wall, but now it is the façade of the wood, sweating with the heat of the sun; perhaps the things of the wood are what the desires of the natural man are fixed upon, what he wishes to be delivered from. The image about the place among the rocks, whether cave or winding path, is not extended enough for my perception to grasp. Here, frankly and with regret, I choose to go outside the poem and identify it with an old and familiar image. It becomes a cave or pit to stay in, or else an uphill path going out; this is according to the *Purgatorio* of Dante.

In III comes the question of what the true "I" of a man is. But it is not the natural self; that self wants to die, symbolically. Already the unnatural light is blazing.

In IV that blaze once more is dark for the speaker, darkened by his natural desires. But the soul buzzes at the sill of consciousness, more insistent than ever. At once the fallen "I" begins to climb out of his fear. Is he ascending the mount that leads to God? Not exactly. For here comes a radical shift in the imagery, where the new images leave the physical ground and are all but disbodied, being metaphysical and factitious only as physical entities invented in order to clear up the mysterious structure of the mind.

> The mind enters itself, and God the mind,
> And one is One, free in the tearing wind.

If we wish to be hard and close critics we have a little boggle over this procedure. Do we understand the fact which is being represented in these crucial lines? I think we do if we are willing again to leave the poem and refer the lines this time to a famous text out of the Wisdom of the East, offered by Krishna himself as he counsels the troubled King Arjuna in the *Bhagavad Gita:*

> Let each man raise
> The Self by Soul, not trample down his Self,
> Since Soul that is Self's friend may grow Self's foe.
> Soul is Self's friend when Self doth rule o'er Self
> But self turns enemy if Soul's own self
> Hates Self as not itself.

That is the Arnold translation, and we like to think that the text of Krishna was more perspicuous than this; Roethke's text is more perspicuous, but our difficulty is in its brevity. And in justice to Krishna, he is a beautiful poet after laying down this rule of life when he elaborates upon its glories. Roethke and Krishna are the same in the fundamental sense they give to the rule, whose acceptance denotes the religious conversion. In the proper mind the divine soul is sovereign, the natural self obeys it gladly, and even the human mind becomes a fragment or station of God's own mind.

I am sure that Roethke knows the *Bhagavad Gita,* which has elevated so many Western minds; perhaps Roethke smiles (as Mr. Eliot must have done a lot of smiling) while he wonders if we know what we are reading here. Do we mind this invasion from the ancient East? No, it doesn't matter. This is a tremendous poem, but a religious or philosophical poem, and ordinary images are not sufficient for it. And this is so good a poet that we will take him either way, in the style of the natural images or in the high philosophic style to which the earthbound have to climb.

It is true that we are startled, thinking that our poet has gone out of character. Let us take comfort from the final phrase: *free in the tearing wind.* It is as if the suffering hero had been set free, and a storm from heaven had come to signalize the happy event, with a tearing but cleansing wind to sweep all the foolishness of the mind away. Is not that a lovely conclusion?

35

BABETTE DEUTSCH

Contemporary poems so often seem anonymous that one which readily allows us to identify the author makes a special claim upon us. In the stanzas of "In a Dark Time" Theodore Roethke's voice is clear. It is recognizable in the cadences, which make grave lyricism of normal iambic pentameter, in imagery taken from the natural world to signify the climates of the soul—movement and metaphor together exploring the more obscure regions of consciousness and, with equal boldness, pointing to the emergence of an exalted awareness. The poem declares a misery that appalls, a rescue that demands spiritual athleticism in the teeth of continued threat.

The paradoxical truth stated in the opening line, "In a dark time, the eye begins to see," announces the theme. It is one touched upon in a lyric by Goethe, that most hale of poets:

> *Wer nie die kummervollen Nächte*
> *Auf seinem Bette weinend sass,*
> *Der kennt euch nicht, ihr himmlischen Mächte!*

When, however, Roethke follows his initial affirmation with the words: "I meet my shadow in the deepening shade," the reader may find matter for wonder. But only if he reads hastily. "Shade" is a dusk all the gloomier for being amorphous. A shadow is usually well defined and is cast by a definite object; it may nonetheless be terrifying. This one is cast by the speaker. As he advances into "the deepening shade," suggestive both of the encroachment of physical death and of the mind's beclouding, he may well be afraid to meet his own shadow. If it does not take on the aspect of a ghost, it is yet mutely eloquent of unreality. Certainly it is a darker self. The sense of a hovering Double is immediately adumbrated again: "I hear my echo in the echoing wood"—where "echo" and "echoing" carry a weird resonance. Nor can we escape here the further "echo" of the poet who, soon to venture into Hell, found himself

> *per una selva oscura,*
> *che la diritta via era smarrita.*

The connotation of "the echoing wood" is, of course, not the sunless brambles of political life in thirteenth-century Florence, but a more general Wood of

Error, where there is no trace of the right path. And the reader may also remember the cry in an earlier poem of Roethke's, "The Lost Son":

Tell me:
Which is the way I take? . . .

Here the lost man is not so bewildered as to be unable to comment ironically on his situation: "A lord of nature weeping to a tree." Yet his self-mockery leaves him no less sadly alone, with the trees, the birds of the air, the "beasts of the hill and serpents of the den."

The birds that he names, "the heron and the wren," are creatures of nature, yet they have fabulous kindred. The first, present only as the invisible thunder of the Great Herne, symbolized Deity for Yeats in *The Herne's Egg.* What he called his "strangest and wildest" play was too wild to be staged. It deals with man's war upon God. The image of the heron, a recurrent one in Yeats's poems, has its nobler prototype in the avatar of Zeus in "Leda and the Swan." The heron is also notably prominent in *Calvary,* where, however differently, it again seems linked to the theme of man's opposition to God. In a note to that play Yeats spoke of the bird, along with the hawk, the eagle, and the swan, as "a natural symbol for subjectivity" and so, by implication, of the poet himself. Is it a like symbol here? And what of the wren? It used to be known as the king of the birds, and was annually hunted, killed, carried in triumph from one house to another, and ceremoniously buried, in villages in the British Isles, in many countries of Europe, in southern France as recently as the first half of the nineteenth century. Roethke may have had no thought of these matters when he wrote: "I live between the heron and the wren." Yet Yeats is one of his masters, and he is familiar with folklore; in any event, the reader is aware, however vaguely, of the beating of supernatural wings.

The second stanza opens with abstractions infused with vigorous life. The question so forcibly posed seems italicized for us here and now.

What's madness but nobility of soul
At odds with circumstance?

Roethke is clearly not referring to Socrates' observation, à propos of the inspired poet: "The same man is nowhere at all when he enters into rivalry with the madman." Nor is he recalling the passage in *A Midsummer Night's Dream* in which the poet, being "of imagination all compact," is equated with the lover and the lunatic. This is a more radical madness, not to be confused, either, with the insanity of powerful criminals. True, it has seized upon men who never made a verse, but when Roethke names it he summons up for us those poets who have been forced to take asylum from a world they never made. Not all of them have shown the "nobility of soul" of a Christopher Smart or a Friedrich Hölderlin, but the noble among them continue to bear witness to the outrage that the world perpetrates upon the sensitive mind. The stanza does more than imply that by the cultivation of callousness men save themselves from madness. The power of the lines lies largely in the presentation:

> The day's on fire!
> I know the purity of pure despair,
> My shadow pinned against a sweating wall.

What response is there but the cry of recognition: "Why, this is hell . . . ?"

Yet as long as a question can be asked, the purity of despair may be impugned. And a question *is* asked:

> That place among the rocks—is it a cave
> Or winding path?

A "place among the rocks" is almost inevitably associated for us with the parched landscape of the Waste Land, the more so here because it recalls "Rocks and no water and the sandy road / The road winding above among the mountains / Which are mountains of rock . . ." For all the bleakness of this scene, Roethke's mention of a "cave," with its promise of shelter, offers hope; provided, of course, that the place is not inhabited by the "serpents of the den" or, if it is, that they can be overcome. Even the "winding path," in spite of its intimation of arduous climbing ahead, seems to point toward freedom. "On a huge hill, / Cragged and steep," we remember, "Truth stands, and hee that will / Reach her, about must, and about must goe." He who achieves truth, the assurance goes, will be set free. But there is another and more pressing association here; indeed, in "Byzantium" we find the very phrase that Roethke uses:

On Theodore Roethke's "In a Dark Time"

. . . Hades' bobbin bound in mummy-cloth
May unwind the winding path. . . .

The reference, as every reader of Yeats knows, is to the idea that the dead, living in their memories, unwind the thread of past experience. The "winding path" is the serpentine course that it is natural for men to take, as distinct from the straight path followed by saint or sage. If Roethke is harking back to Yeats here, as seems not unlikely, then "That place among the rocks" may be supposed to set him again on the tortuous road of real life, with its miseries that have no origin in fantasy, and that allow no escape, except madness. At this point one thing seems clear: "The edge is what I have."

It is a risky having. As we discover again when the third stanza opens with "A steady storm of correspondences!—" For one who has nothing but an edge to cling to, a "steady storm" is an unwelcome phenomenon. Not less so when the "correspondences" fling wildly out of the echoing forest of symbols familiar to another haunted poet. Terror mounts in "A night flowing with birds"—one imagines neither heron nor wren, but darker shapes against "a ragged moon." Then the thunderclap: "And in broad day the midnight come again!" Yet on the heels of horror there is another glimmer of hope. The assumption is that he will find out what he is, though the discovery must come during the dark night of the soul:

Death of the self in a long tearless night,
All natural shapes blazing unnatural light.

The strangeness of the light becomes more frightening in the final stanza, as darkness thickens:

Dark, dark my light, and darker my desire.
My soul, like some heat-maddened fly
Keeps buzzing at the sill.

The epithet "heat-maddened," since the fly is a simile for the soul, is a reminder of the earlier horror, when the day is on fire and the desperate man sees his shadow "pinned against a sweating wall." The homely image of the insect "buzzing at the sill" calls up as well, for me, the deathbed scene, indelibly drawn by

BABETTE DEUTSCH
On Theodore Roethke's "In a Dark Time"

Emily Dickinson, when a fly "With blue, uncertain, stumbling buzz" inter-posed between one dying and the light, till at the last he "could not see to see." Thus, after another fashion, in "broad day" was "midnight come again." Possibly the Dickinson poem came to mind not only because of the buzzing fly, but also because the death wish looms in the opening line of Roethke's last stanza.

The fight for identity is sharpened as the poem proceeds. In this last stanza it takes shape in the shrilling cry: "Which I is *I?*" But relief comes at the close:

A fallen man, I climb out of my fear.
The mind enters itself, and God the mind,
And one is One, free in the tearing wind.

There is something subdued in the tone of this affirmation. It seems to speak of the stunned aftermath of a confrontation not wholly unlike the struggle between Jacob and the Angel, at least in its terror and in the hardly wrung blessing of its conclusion. But the release is less fully realized than the conflict and the dread that haunts it, and so haunts the major part of the poem. The change from ap-palled uncertainty to what one might call "the comfort of the resurrection" (with a lower-case "r") is too sudden to be quite convincing, especially since it comes directly after that piercing cry. Another reader might not be disturbed as I am by the abruptness of this reversal. The last three lines, taken by themselves, I find wholly acceptable, and the phrase, "free in the tearing wind" is a fine and moving conclusion, and one way of defining the human condition.

Not the least notable feature of the poem is that, dealing with madness in so intimately revealing a fashion, it exhibits such extraordinary control. The simplicity of the language—most of the words are monosyllables and the fewest have more than two syllables, the quiet tone in which the drama is set forth, help to make it impressive. The pattern of the rhymes, and the use of consonance and internal rhyme, delight the ear, as the tendency to repetition in the placing of the caesura gives the phrasing the quality of insistent speech. The poem is the story of a purgation. One of its virtues is that it purges the reader, alike by what it says and by what it intimates.

STANLEY KUNITZ

The Taste of Self

"Searching nature," noted Gerard Manley Hopkins in 1880, "I taste *self* but at one tankard, that of my own being." Comparably, Theodore Roethke searches for a language, a lyric process, in and through a world of multiple appearances, to convey the sensation of the torment of identity. Logic told Hopkins that he was doomed to fail in his effort to distill "this taste of myself, of *I* and *me* above and in all things, which is more distinctive than the taste of ale or alum, more distinctive than the smell of walnut leaf or camphor, and is incommunicable by any means to another man (as when I was a child I used to ask myself: What must it be to be someone else?)." But logic did not prevent him from writing "in blood" the sonnet beginning "I wake and feel the fell of dark, not day," with its harrowing lines from the far side of anguish, "I am gall, I am heartburn. God's most deep decree / Bitter would have me taste: my taste was me." In Roethke the self is divided, and the hostile parts are seen as voraciously cannibalistic: "My meat eats me."

Like much of Roethke's recent work, "In a Dark Time" is marked by a style of oracular abstraction. The vocabulary is plain, predominantly monosyllabic; the pentameters are strictly measured and often balanced; the stanzaic units, with their formalized combination of true and off-rhyme, adhere to a tight pattern. If these fiercely won controls were to break down at any point, the whole poem would collapse in a cry, a tremendous outpouring of wordless agitation.

With lesser poets we are inclined to stay in the poem itself, as in a closed society that satisfies our public needs. Roethke belongs to that superior order of poets who will not let us rest in any one of their poems, who keep driving us back through the whole body of their work to that live cluster of images, ideas, memories, and obsessions that constitutes the individuating source of the creative personality, the nib of art, the very selfhood of the imagination. In my reading of "In a Dark Time" I shall try to indicate, selectively, how its configurations are illuminated by the totality of the poet's vision and intuition. Page references are to *Words for the Wind* (Doubleday, 1958), Roethke's most comprehensive collection.

STANLEY KUNITZ
On Theodore Roethke's "In a Dark Time"

Stanza I

The poem begins with a paradox, the first of a series of seeming contradictions to establish the dialectic of the structure. The "dark time," like Hopkins' "fell of dark," bespeaks the night of spiritual desolation, that *noche oscura del alma,* in which, according to the testimony of the mystics, the soul is tortured by the thought "that God has abandoned it . . . that He cast it away into darkness as an abominable thing," in the classic description by St. John of the Cross. "The shadow of death and the pains and torments of hell are most acutely felt, that is, the sense of being without God. . . . All this and even more the soul feels now, for a fearful apprehension has come upon it that thus it will be with it for ever." Such desolation is not an obsolescent state, nor one reserved only for the religious. Modern philosophy and psychiatry have been much concerned with the condition of anxiety, defined by Dr. Rollo May as "the subjective state of the individual's becoming aware that his existence can become destroyed, that he can lose himself and his world, that he can become nothing." In simpler terms, "anxiety is the experience of the threat of imminent non-being."

Roethke's first words inform us that the speaker has already entered into his land of desolation. If a poem is to be made, which is tantamount to saying if a spirit is to be saved, it will only be by a turning to the light, by a slow recognition of the beloved diurnal forms. As is true of Roethke's major sequence, *Praise to the End!* (pp. 63-110), the archetypal journey of the poem is from darkness into light, from blindness into vision, from death into life. The emergent landscape is already familiar to us: "Eternity howls in the last crags, / The field is no longer simple: / It's a soul's crossing time" (p. 101). We have listened before to this poet's invocation of the creatures of earth that arose out of the original deep and that alone can show him the way back to the baptismal source: "Wherefore, O birds and small fish, surround me. / Lave me, ultimate waters" (p. 100).

His first encounters, as he struggles to recover his identity, are not with things in themselves or even with himself as object, but with shadow and echo, the evidences at one remove of his existence. "Once I could touch my shadow, and be happy" (p. 205). In his need for self-esteem he describes himself as a lord, though only "a lord of nature weeping to a tree": he is not ready for the world of human sympathy. His place is in the lower order of creation, in the kingdom where he is most at home. One of Roethke's earliest poems celebrated the heron (p. 24), not as the philosopher bird, in the manner of Yeats, but as the antic lord of his observed amphibian environment. The leg on which the heron balances in the marsh is his visible connection with the primordial element. As for wrens, they are forever flitting through Roethke's poems. They belong to his world of "lovely diminutives" (page 91), the most blessed and light-hearted of God's creatures, free as they almost are of the gross burden of corporeality. "The small" are associated with beginnings; they invariably excite the poet's tenderness (p. 37) or his joy, not always unalloyed with dread (p. 178). The implicit question in this passage is spelt out in another poem (p. 203):

Where was I going? Where?
What was I running from?
To these I cried my life—
The loved fox, and the wren.

Roethke's quadrupeds, except for those who live in holes, such as the bear and the fox, are not usually "loved"; most of the time they appear as rabid and predatory, "dogs of the groin" (p. 81), the running pack of sex. Reptiles are either overtly phallic (p. 136) or emblematic of "pure, sensuous form" (p. 181).

Stanza II

As if in reply to an accusing voice, the poet launches into an impassioned self-justification. The world may call him mad, but it is only because he refuses to compromise with the world that he suffers this sacred disorder. Madness knows an ecstasy, a burning revelation, that is denied to reason. "Reason? That dreary shed, that hutch for grubby schoolboys!" (p. 104). In his ordeal of despair and terror he has faced the absolute. "Who else sweats light from a stone?" (p. 207). "Tell me, body without skin, does a fish sweat?" (p. 101). The momentary clarity of vision, born of the authenticity of suffering, fades. "That place among the rocks" would seem to be suggested by the "sweating wall" in the previous line. In one sense it is Golgotha, the place of suffering; in another, it is a place beyond, but dimly apprehended, as through a clouded window—a habitation fit for one who identifies himself with the "beasts of the hill." Is it a promise of rest, of hiding, of Being? Or of departure, journeying, Becoming? Caves and nests, in Roethke, are womb images, representing the sub-world of intuition and the unconscious. Conversely, the "winding path" signifies the world of one's unfolding fate, realizable only in terms of action. The "edge" that the poet lays claim to, in an abrupt return of certainty, is expounded in several other contexts:

> I was always one for being alone,
> Seeking in my own way, eternal purpose;
> At the edge of the field waiting for the pure moment . . . (p. 205)

> I have gone into the waste lonely places
> Behind the eye; the lost acres at the edge of smoky cities . . . (p. 195)

> The edges of the summit still appall
> When we brook on the dead or the beloved . . . (p. 190).

> On love's worst ugly day
> The weeds hiss at the edge of the field . . .
> The bleak wind eats at the weak plateau,
> And the sun brings joy to some.
> But the rind, often, hates the life within (p. 193).

As evidence of the presence of a creative syndrome, it should be noted that in writing "The Shape of the Fire" more than a decade before "In a Dark Time," Roethke introduced the figure of "the edge" in recognizably the same fixed constellation of images:

> The wasp waits.
>   The edge cannot eat the center.
> The grape glistens.
>   The path tells little to the serpent.
> An eye comes out of the wave.
>   The journey from flesh is longest.
> A rose sways least.
>   The redeemer comes a dark way (p. 95).

If I read Roethke aright, he is differentiating between the spiritual life, which is achievable through discipline, prayer, and revelation, and "the life within," which is the soul locked inside the cabinet of flesh, the cave, and not locked in alone but with the central devouring worm. Hell is the trap where one is forever tasting oneself. To be saved one must undertake in the dark the long journey from flesh, that is, from the country of one's birth and bondage, that bloody incestuous ground, to the other side of the field, or to the appalling height, the jumping-off place, where the clean light falls on everything one has learned to love. Is this a parable for art? Blake tells us that "the road of excess leads to the palace of wisdom," and again, that "improvement makes straight roads; but the roads without improvement are roads of Genius." There is a kind of poetry that, in its creative excess, insists on pushing itself to the edge of the absurd, as to the edge of a cliff, at which point only two eventualities remain conceivable: disaster or miracle. The real and beautiful absurdity, as every artist knows, is that the miracle sometimes occurs.

Stanza III

The voice is one of growing assurance, as the things of this world emerge more and more sharply, not only in their bold lineaments but in their metaphorical radiations as well. No contemporary poet can use the word "correspondences" without harking back to Baudelaire and his Symbolist heirs. For Roethke, nature is the wayward source of joys and illuminations, the great mother of secrets, from whom they must be wooed or pried, out of urgent necessity, and at any cost.

> Sing, sing, you symbols! All simple creatures,
> All small shapes, willow-shy,
> In the obscure haze, sing! (p. 102).

> The moon, a pure Islamic shape, looked down.
> The light air slowed: It was not night or day.
> All natural shapes became symbolical (p. 203).

At the visionary climax of the poem, under the transformations of the cloud-torn moon, the air becomes electric with the agitated flight of birds. Everything is in motion, plunged beyond the syntax of time, to the brink of incoherence, where there are no divisions between night and day, reason and unreason, ecstasy and despair. The steadying thought is that "a man goes far to find out what he is"; in other words, that the life justifies the journey to the "edge." Elsewhere, in a variant of this maxim, Roethke has written, "I learn by going where I have to go" (p. 124). The last two lines of the stanza are a triumphant collocation of the spiritual and phenomenal levels of this total experience: the self dying, the world revealed. Past pity for himself and past tears, our "lord of nature weeping to a tree" hardens to a man arrived "in a long tearless night." The light that he sees blazing from "all natural shapes" is termed "unnatural," largely in the sense of "supernatural," transcending nature, but certainly also with the force of an epithet transferred from witness to object. Roethke has answered for himself the question that he posed in an earlier poem:

> Before the moon draws back,
> Dare I blaze like a tree? (p. 209).

The answer may well be: Yes, by becoming like a tree.

Stanza IV

As the transcendent moment fades, the poet returns to the prison-house of his senses. The slow rhythm, the massed percussive effects suggest the heaviness of his tread, the weight of his body. He can scarcely untrack himself from the word "dark." Where once he wrote, "The dark has its own light" (p. 108), he now asserts the counter-truth. In the blindness of desire is the deepest dark. Even the soul is seen as contemptible, an insect frenzied with heat (desire) that keeps batting itself at the window of perception, trying to get out.

> In the slow coming-out of sleep,
> On the sill of the eyes, something flutters,
> A thing we feel at evening, and by doors,
> Or when we stand at the edge of a thicket . . . (p. 199).

The true ancestor of this ominous apparition can be found in "The Lost Son":

> Sat in an empty house
> Watching shadows crawl,
> Scratching.
> There was one fly (p. 79).

As Yeats asked, "How can we know the dancer from the dance?" and as Hopkins when a child puzzled, "What must it be to be someone else?" Roethke inquires, pressing the same question of identity, "How can I find myself in the confusion of my separate and divided selves?" What desolates him is the thought that he has no true identity, and what makes him whole again is the recognition and confession that he is "a fallen man," whose quintessential taste is that of being lost. To embrace this knowledge is to overcome the dread of non-being, is to be redeemed or, so to speak, reborn. In the final couplet the separation between mind and God is dissolved in the mystery of interpenetration. Having found the divinity in himself, man is free—free to fly, like the birds of the preceding stanza —in the chancy wind that will leave him "torn and most whole."

"In a Dark Time" recalls the lamentation that more than a century ago John Clare wrote in madness, beginning "I am: yet what I am none cares or knows." The parallelism extends to the sestet structure as well as to the theme, whose history of explicit formulation runs back through Descartes and Iago to the eternal Yahwe's "I am that I am." Roethke's poem seems to me more solid, more profound, more terrible than Clare's, altogether finer, but I must grant that it is curiously less affecting, perhaps for the simple reason that it is less naïve, more ambitious. Amid so much nobility and injured pride one longs for the artless human touch. At his infrequent best when Clare writes, "I am the self-consumer of my woes"; when he speaks of living "like vapours tost / Into the nothingness of scorn and noise"; when he deplores "the vast shipwreck of my life's esteems," we cannot doubt that he is eating dust without an inch over his head; his long sigh overrides the beat and surges through to the final word. Roethke's admirable restraints on his cold rage have not permitted him the liberty of sustained action. Each self-enclosed stanza is conceived as a separate stage for which new scenery must be set up for a repetition of the drama of rebirth. Only an extraordinary creative energy, such as is manifestly present here, could set the stages rolling, like a procession of pageants in a medieval mystery. Roethke succeeds, for me, in effecting this illusion through three complete stanzas of mounting intensity and almost halfway through the fourth, where I stumble on his rhetorical question. The fussy grammar of "Which I is I?" is only part of the trouble; I am more concerned with the clinically analytic tone, which jars on the ear that has been listening to a stranger music. Furthermore, I am not wholly persuaded by the final couplet, superbly turned as it is. It may be my own deficiency that leads me to resist whatever seems to smack of conventional piety, but I cannot agree that anything in the poem prepares me for so pat a resolution. The "natural" climax remains, marvelous though unresolved, in Stanza III.

Despite the foregoing, "In a Dark Time" is one of a handful of contemporary poems to which I am most attached. What it says and the grandeur of the saying are important to me, as much after thirty or forty readings as after the first. If it required an epigraph, I should be happy to supply one in the form of a sentence by Paul Tillich: "The self-affirmation of a being is the stronger the more non-being it can take into itself."

THEODORE ROETHKE

It is given to few writers in their own lifetime to receive such close, acute, and, dare I say, devoted reading as these three essays reveal. One does not expect exactitude and detachment, intensity and love from contemporaries. I quail before these mentors who have pursued me so closely, even down to some of the reading I was doing at the time of the writing of the poem. Any words of mine, then, are unnecessary and bound to be graceless.

Another reason makes any comment of mine unseemly: the nature of the poem itself. It is the first of a sequence, part of a hunt, a drive toward God: an effort to break through the barrier of rational experience; an intention not unmixed with pride, as Mr. Kunitz has pointed out, accompanied by a sense of exhilaration, and only occasional seizures of humility (in the usual sense of the word). This was a dictated poem, something given, scarcely mine at all. For about three days before its writing I felt disembodied, out of time; then the poem virtually wrote itself, on a day in summer, 1958.

Presumably, in the poem, the self dies, for a time at least. I was granted an insight beyond the usual, let us say. To speak of it further is a betrayal of the experience. One forces the self, with all its trappings of vanity and guilt, its "taste," as Mr. Kunitz would have it, upon what seems to me the essential otherworldliness of the poem: one defiles whatever purity has been achieved.

I take the central experience to be fairly common: to break from the bondage of the self, from the barriers of the "real" world, to come as close to God as possible. If the clumsy paraphrase or running comment which follows reveals even one incidental insight about spiritual experience, it will have served its purpose. I write, then, not to enhance the poem, or to quarrel with other interpretations, but to find out further what really happens when one attempts to go beyond "reality."

Stanza I

In a dark time, the eye begins to see:

The reader may ask, how does one get to the "dark time"? Is it a willed experience? There are those who believe the true artist is impelled by forces

49

outside himself. It is possible that he who risks this dark, the dark night of the soul, is doubly driven. But the conscious will can be a factor, I have found, in either a rise or a fall of a cyclic phase. The danger to the human condition lies in excessive acceleration, either way. The way up and the way down may be the same, but the pace often varies, sometimes disastrously.

It is important to remember that the eye only *begins* to see: this is only a stage in a long process.

I meet my shadow in the deepening shade;

I find Miss Deutsch very pertinent here. And Mr. Kunitz; he has not missed the importance of *meets*—but what one meets, the other self, is already "in" part of the "deepening shade," the self-created dark of the echoing wood. I meet my shadow, my double, my Other, usually tied to me, my reminder that I am going to die, in the "deepening shade"—and surely "shade" suggests Hades, if not hell. I hear my echo, that verbal shadow, in the wood that is likewise ringing—with my own name? No. I am not Tennyson, muttering Alfred, Alfred, over and over. But there *is* a sound, a ringing, and this, I am certain, is psychologically exact, for all consciousness of sound is enormously increased in this heightened or sometimes exalted state.

This "lord of nature"—self-mockery, a partial irony is intended—is "weeping to a tree." I must quibble with Mr. Ransom, who takes the gesture as "abasement," and Mr. Kunitz who feels that the protagonist is "not ready for the world of human sympathy." I believe the tears fall, not from self-pity or self-denigration, but out of an awareness of the human condition that has not, as yet, been transcended. The speaker is weeping to a *tree*, a growing thing, which, as a primitive man, he can touch and feel and understand.

I live between the heron and the wren,
Beasts of the hill and serpents of the den.

The heron and the wren are both literal and fabulous—the heron for me a beautiful, a solitary bird that nested in the corner of my father's preserve (we often drove out seven miles of an evening to watch it and listen to the whippoorwills), a symbol of purity, wisdom, toughness—tough on the nest, particularly. I live between this heron (mine, not Yeats's) and the wren or "wran" of folklore, a happy, courageous, lecherous little bird that always nested in our back yard. (By no means meek, Mr. Ransom—it would go after a kingbird.)

"Beasts of the hill," etc. I would gather the beasts, I would call upon their powers in my spiritual ascent or assault. "I live between": I partake of them all —heron and wren, beast and serpent. They surround me; they protect me; they are my nearest and dearest neighbors. True, sometimes I may be one, sometimes another: to this extent I vacillate between identities.

Stanza II

It is possible that with the rhetorical question ("What's madness but nobility of soul / At odds with circumstance?") I am calling to my aid, in addition to the animal world, a literary ancestor: Yeats. Behind the possibly highfalutin rhetoric lies a simple truth. "Madness" is a sociological term, a good deal of the time: what is madness in the Northwest is normal conduct in Italy, and a hero's privilege in western Ireland.

"The day's on fire!" means, I suppose, the mind is on fire: this is the ultimate burning of revelation. In that condition the purity of despair is realized in all its finality, but in the place of suffering, it is the other, the shadow which is "pinned against a sweating wall." The true self still maintains its choice, its mobility.

As for the question in the final couplet,

That place among the rocks—is it a cave
Or winding path? The edge is what I have.

I must disagree with Miss Deutsch, who would have me more aware of my elders than I really am. As a child, I was always a passionate cave—and path—watcher, curious as to where things led. The cave and the winding path are older than history. And the edge—the terrible abyss—equally old.

Stanza III

In this state, a stream of correspondences—that term out of mystical literature —of analogies, keeps breaking in upon the protagonist: there is a steady stream, a veritable storm of signs, reminders of the invisible, the divine world. Birds, the symbols of song, still flow in the dark night, the moon is ragged, night and day reversed. The time sense is lost; the natural self dies in the blaze of the supernatural.

Stanza IV

And perhaps *should* die, say the next lines:

Dark, dark my light, and darker my desire.

The paradox again, but this time with at least a modicum of humility: my desires are "dark," unfathomable, sense-ridden. My soul itself is "like" a disease-laden, heat-maddened fly—to me a more intolerable thing than a rat.

And this is where the turn comes. It seems to me that Mr. Kunitz ignores the intensity of the identification with the fly: Am I this many-eyed, mad, filthy thing, or am I human? "Which I is *I?*" The cry comes shrilly, says Miss Deutsch. I am with her in this. If this is not understood, the poem does indeed falter.

The moment before Nothingness, before near-annihilation, the moment of supreme disgust is the worst: when change comes it is either total loss of consciousness—symbolical or literal death—*or* a quick break into another state, not necessarily serene, but frequently a bright blaze of consciousness that translates itself into action.

"A fallen man" (literally and symbolically), I return to the human task of climbing out of the pits of fear—and this is not an ambiguous word: fear, unlike anxiety, has a definite object; I am afraid of God until—and here the transition is very swift—"The mind enters itself." The mind has been outside itself, beyond itself, and now returns home to the domain of love.

The conclusion puts a heavy burden on language, most certainly. One could wish that the divided opinion at this point indicates a real, a genuinely rich dramatic ambiguity. Naturally I rejoice that Mr. Ransom can take things "either way, in the style of the natural images or in the high philosophic style." That Mr. Kunitz finds the concluding couplet smacking of conventional piety, bewilders me. The lines say, "The mind enters itself": this suggests (visually at least) an androgynous act, a hole disappearing into itself, "crawling into your hole and pulling your hole after you," the folk saying has it. An unpleasant image. It is stock myself, and maybe stock mystical doctrine. And perhaps the next part of the line, by itself—"and God the mind"—is right out of the hymn books, though it is usually the heart He enters, if we believe the hot-gospelers.

But the next line? "And one is One." This seems a genuine double, at the least. In the Platonic sense, the one becomes the many, in this moment. But also —and this is what terrified me—the one not merely makes his peace with God (Mr. Ransom's phrase) he—if we read One as the Godhead theologically placed above God—transcends God: he becomes the Godhead itself, not only the veritable creator of the universe but the creator of the revealed God. This is no jump for the timid, no flick from the occult, no moment in the rose garden. Instead it is a cry from the mire, and may be the devil's own.

But we are not done with the line. The protagonist *one* and/or the Godhead are "free" in the "tearing wind"—free to be buffeted by their own creation. God Himself, in his most supreme manifestation, risks being maimed, if not destroyed.

I feel there is a hope in the ambiguity of "tearing"—that the ambient air itself, that powers man once deemed merely "natural," or is unaware of, are capable of pity; that some other form or aspect of God will endure with man again, will save him from himself.

53

JOSEPHINE MILES

ROBERT BELOOF

ROBERT LOWELL

STANLEY KUNITZ

On STANLEY KUNITZ'S

"*Father and Son*"

Stanley Kunitz

FATHER AND SON

Now in the suburbs and the falling light
I followed him, and now down sandy road
Whiter than bone-dust, through the sweet
Curdle of fields, where the plums
Dropped with their load of ripeness, one by one.
Mile after mile I followed, with skimming feet,
After the secret master of my blood,
Him, steeped in the odor of ponds, whose indomitable love
Kept me in chains. Strode years; stretched into bird;
Raced through the sleeping country where I was young,
The silence unrolling before me as I came,
The night nailed like an orange to my brow.

How should I tell him my fable and the fears,
How bridge the chasm in a casual tone,
Saying, "The house, the stucco one you built,
We lost. Sister married and went from home,
And nothing comes back, it's strange, from where she goes.

I lived on a hill that had too many rooms:
Light we could make, but not enough of warmth,
And when the light failed, I climbed under the hill.
The papers are delivered every day;
I am alone and never shed a tear."

At the water's edge, where the smothering ferns lifted
Their arms, "Father!" I cried, "Return! You know
The way. I'll wipe the mudstains from your clothes;
No trace, I promise, will remain. Instruct
Your son, whirling between two wars,
In the Gemara of your gentleness,
For I would be a child to those who mourn
And brother to the foundlings of the field
And friend of innocence and all bright eyes.
O teach me how to work and keep me kind."

Among the turtles and the lilies he turned to me
The white ignorant hollow of his face.

JOSEPHINE MILES

This poem sets one tone against another, surrendering the major active to the minor passive tone at the end, so that the minor becomes dominant.

First it gives us the quality of simple narrative: *Now I followed him . . . Mile after mile I followed . . . strode . . . stretched . . . raced.* Then it continues by asking *How bridge the chasm in a casual tone?* and carries out the middle and final stanzas in that casual active tone, the speaker pleading, *O teach me how to work and keep me kind.* But then it comes up square against that other tone, begun early in "falling light," "curdle of fields," "smothering ferns," when it comes to the final passive "white ignorant hollow of his face."

The *and* in the title "Father and Son" is an irony, then. *Son to Father* is what it means; not a partnership, not a co-ordinate, but a pursuit of a powerfully sad past by a firmly courageous present looking for sustenance and finding oblivion. Like the structure of the title, the structure of the poem purports to be active in its narrative, its first stanza of vivid following, its second of telling, its third of promising and petitioning by the son, but in every stanza the father's heavy substance outweighs the action, *steeped in the odor of ponds.* The son has been held at home after his father's drowning—*whose indomitable love kept me in chains.* He seeks some strong word about work and love from that father, and gets, from the water's edge, from among the turtles (doves?) and lilies (which do not spin?) a white and hollow look, more powerful in its ignorance of meaning than all his effort for understanding has been.

How beautifully Mr. Kunitz makes the sound sustain this sense! Ostensibly, like the title and the argument, the sound-pattern is firm and direct and regular: twelve-, ten-, and twelve-line stanzas of iambic pentameter, strongly assonanted. Within this smooth regularity there are two or three meaningful breaks, at crucial places. First, the many assertive inverted stresses in the beginnings of lines slacken toward the end of the poem, as if the vigor of action were slacking. Compare, for example, *Kept me in chains. Strode years; stretched into bird;* with the easier later *For I would be a child to those who mourn.* Second, early in the first and third stanzas, where the father's influence is strongest, the pentameter breaks to tetrameter, as heavy quality takes over from action, *Curdle of fields, where the plums,* and *Your son, whirling between two wars.* The sheer weight of quality and pause in these places seems to take the place of an extra stress.

And at the end the variation from the norm, in both number of syllables and placing of stress, is particularly sharp:

"O teach me how to work and keep me kind."

Among the turtles and the lilies he turned to me
The white ignorant hollow of his face.

Son has hit his stride in his pleading; he is running on all five iambic cylinders. But then the father's lines turn metrically sticky: *Among the turtles and . . . he turned to me* would be regular; why three extra syllables and a stress? Because father's passive objects are taking over from the meter and the action. They present finally, in full passivity, *The white ignorant hollow of his face*—a juxtaposition of heavy accents prepared for by two earlier significant lines: *The night nailed like an orange to my brow,* and *We lost. Sister married and went from home.*

All three of these reversals of the second stress, bringing it up beside the first, not only jar the expectations established by the speaker's iambics but also create a solidity of assertion, a sort of *this is it* emphasis which is not to be denied, because it is not really a statement, just a presence; an emphasis not *innocent,* but *ignorant.*

When I first read "Father and Son" I disliked yet admired it, and I still do. I hate the father's victory, the persistence and eventual dominance of the *sweet curdle of fields* and *smothering ferns.* "Poor son!" I feel like saying of the son in this particular poem. But not "poor poem!" It seems to me a very good and successful poem in doing what I gather it intended to do: bitterly to betray the *and* in the title, the sureness of meter, the busy consequence of action and structure; to belie the Fisher King.

Many poems of Mr. Kunitz's *Selected Poems* are of this kind—a lively narrative search ending in a blank sorrow and static symbol. The reader may feel sad, even misled, because he cannot always understand what lies behind the loss; he may feel a sudden sense of loss beyond what he has been literally prepared for, so that mind and heart, like son and father, end in conflict—of admiration for the poem against regret for the self that is the human self. This is part of the critical problem referred to I think in Mr. Kunitz's poem, "A Choice of Weapons."

Many others of his poems avoid this danger of conflict by using but a single tone, winning the reader directly and rationally, as in the intellectual arguments by which I first came to admire his work in *Intellectual Things*. But I think these are somewhat easier to achieve, and thus possibly less fully characteristic of his work, than a third kind, which takes some of the white ignorance to itself and makes it not only dramatic but also lyric. A good example, and one I'd like to quote in full because it seems to me so right is "Goose Pond":

> Goose Pond's imaginable snows,
> The fall of twenty years at once,
> Like subtler moons reflect the rose
> Decompositions of the sun.
>
> A feather tumbling from a cloud
> Scrolls thunders of the natural law;
> The cattails rattle; cinnamon fern
> Raises rag banners towards the thaw,
>
> And early footed ghost flowers scour
> Through willow-dapplings to a cave
> Where secrecy grows fur. Self burns
> At the pulpits where Jack-preachers rave!
>
> Now a sulky weather dogs the heart,
> There is no bottom to the day,
> The water lily's Chinese stalk
> Drags heavy, as the white-lipped boy
>
> Climbs from the detritus of his birth,
> The rusted hoop, the broken wheels,
> The sunken boat of little worth,
> Past balconies of limber eels
>
> Until, along that marshy brink,
> The springy trails devoid of plan,

On Stanley Kunitz's "Father and Son"

He meets his childhood beating back
To find what furies made him man.

This poem belongs beside "Father and Son," and for me belongs ahead of it, not because it is more skillful—indeed perhaps in some small phrases it is less so—but because it has got further into that marsh and come out alive. It wins the cinnamon fern away from symbol to situation. Its turtles would be clearly not doves, its lilies not literary. It is sulky but angry, and I am glad it is not going to let the scenery take over the action.

So a critical evaluation of a poem represents the critic as well as the poem. The statement of *I like this* represents the *I* as well as the *this*. And as I like Mr. Kunitz's poems, I like especially some of their happy endings.

ROBERT BELOOF

In speaking of "Father and Son" I find myself called to place it, briefly, in the larger context of the poet's work. It is not always that an individual poem is best studied in this way, and indeed there are some of Mr. Kunitz's own poems in relation to which I would have taken little notice of what came before and after. "Father and Son," however, occupies ground crossed by some of Mr. Kunitz's most important directions and it is only because I feel that a brief summary of some of these will offer, in the end, the most succinct opening into certain textual matters, that I beg patience through what might appear an indirect approach.

Mr. Kunitz is about as far from the imagist as it is possible to be in this time and place, and this arises directly out of the fact that all his landscapes are internal, his wars are internal, his characters are internal. He has been, so far as I can tell, from the beginning true to those themes which are his, rather than to those which are merely fashionable. The flagrant prosperity of the 'twenties, depression, war, his life has spanned them all, and, excepting a few poems here and there, his central theme has been a persistent search for a unity of self. He seeks upward to the nourishment of a divine air, downward to a firm and nourishing human community. Occasionally in the religious poems ("He," for instance), one feels a firm faith, an acceptance of the traditional meaning of the Passion, and a sense of the meaning of suffering in human society. Yet more characteristically it is the decay of the body which haunts him,

> Here at the monumental door,
> Carved with the curious legend of my youth,
> I brandish the great bone of my death,
> Beat once therewith and beat no more.
> ("Open the Gates")

and the loss of a sense of the wholeness which ended somewhere with his youth.

> Concentrical, the universe and I
> Rotated on God's crystal axletree,
>
> So perfectly adjusted in suspense
> I could not mark our split circumference,

On Stanley Kunitz's "Father and Son"

. . . .
Now cubical upon a fractured pole
It creaks, scraping the circle of my soul.
        ("Geometry of Moods")

Another way he has imaged this conflict is in a rather eighteenth-century sense of discontinuity between the mind and the body; between that which the mind perceives and that which the body can do, between the mind's cry of the need for union with others and the body's monadic isolation, between the vegetable-animal reality of the body and the "crystal brain." Of course, this modern poet is saved from the complete bifurcation of the eighteenth-century poet. Kunitz knows too well the limitation of the mind, of reason, to resign his total being to reason's tyranny. Yet more than most he feels the power of the mind, and we note the title of his first book (1930), *Intellectual Things*.

His sense of the disparity of being is realized in yet a third way, through familial images, and this is most relevant to the specific poem under consideration. It is not accidental, I think, that some of his very best poems evoke family figures in a symbolic way—mother, father, son, daughter, wife—capitalizing on certain of these figures' rich connections with the world of flesh as well as with the world of abstractions, with the society of the living as well as of the dead.

   . . . Tolet gave sixty reasons
Why souls survive. And what are they to you?
And father, what to me, who cannot blur
The crystal brain with fantasies of Er . . .
        ("For The Word Is Flesh")

In the year of my mother's blood, when I was born,
She buried my innocent head in a field because the earth
Was sleepy with the winter. . . .
        ("Poem")

I suppose I might generalize about these images from a broadly social viewpoint by saying that Mr. Kunitz shares the profound sense of dissociation which was such a mark of certain writers of that self-designated "lost" generation—Pound, Eliot, Hemingway, Fitzgerald—which came of artistic age in the 'twenties. Their differences were no doubt at least as significant as their similarities, and certainly Mr. Kunitz is a decided variant. He differs primarily, it seems to me, in certain qualities frequent in those who follow hard upon a great event. For he is not really of that generation. Twenty years old in 1925, his sensibility could scarcely have missed the after-clap of World War I; and yet he could scarcely have known profoundly the shape of the world before the war, nor the reality of the event itself. It might be said he was of those who walked directly into the literary scene of dissociation and despair before time could much alleviate or ameliorate it, without having suffered the larger social shock himself. Therefore his might be expected to be a more private dislocation, the death that haunts the interstices of his poetry's dissociation might understandably be of a more strictly personal nature. Again and again his poetry is an attempt to stay a shadowy advance which always turns out to be an eternally feeding presence.

Kunitz, in the power of his idealistic mind, hates the "good-enough" that spoils society, yet while he admires the mind's constructs he also distrusts them as sterile, an ambivalence he once succinctly expressed in this phrase, "Brain, be ice, / A frozen bowl of thought." It is not surprising that he should turn to dreams as a frequent device for exploring the no-man's land between the abstract and the real, between eternity and the flesh, between thought and action, between that family wanted and the family-that-is. There is an early poem, using female rather than, as in "Father and Son," male images, which may in a sense be seen as the latter poem's companion piece. I have already quoted briefly from it, with the image of the mother burying the speaker's innocent head. As the poem moves on in its fantasy the child dies and is then reborn into the world of sex, "I pulled life's long root, slow inch / By inch, from its loamy trap." Then,

> . . . Womanly, a shadow combed
>
> Her dark tremendous hair beyond the violet border
> Of my sleep. Strong passionate hands I had, but could not find
>
> The red position of her heart, nor the subtle order
> Of her lips and breasts, nor the breathing cities of her mind.
>
> Lovingly, lovingly, I wept for her absent eyes,
> Large pity of her thought; I broke the spine of my pride

On Stanley Kunitz's "Father and Son"

Upon a stone, seeing she did not recognize
My tears, because our sorrows did not coincide.

Softly grieving, ironic with a smile forlorn,
I took my baffled heart and buried it under the corn.

O Heart: this is a dream I had, or not a dream.

("Poem")

This is admirable as a summary indication of the obsessive theme, the dissocia-
tions social and personal, and above all the inevitable triumph of death in view of
the complete failure to close the gap.

But equally interesting, in this poem we see the deliberate exploitation of the
ambiguous area of the dream. The early poet's withholding of himself from the
inevitable form of his material is showing in his insistence on "This is a dream I
had, or not a dream," both at the beginning and at the end of the poem. By the
time we come to "Father and Son" the poet can cast himself fully into surrealism
—the questioner's equivalent of allegory. What is gained is much of the gain of
allegory over fantasy—a clearer moral structure, greater power in the denotative
core, greater literalness of visual delineation permissible in the images (for if
allegory is symbolic, it is much more closely related to the peculiar physical simili-
tude of the emblem than is most symbolic writing).

The surrealistic style of "Father and Son" leads directly to some of its major
successes as well as its few problems. The apocalyptic nature of the statement is
served very well, on the whole, by the technique. The particular is translated into
the archetypal with great ease—in fact a whole wealth of ambiguity reaching in
many directions is at once created, and I should say that the great question is
whether these are sufficiently delimited for imaginative communication to take
place.

The basic ambiguities, of course, cluster around the nature of the father and
of the son. On the simplest level, the poem is related by a man whose isolation
and sense of futility is complete, and who seeks, as the bridge back to life, memories of his childhood and his parentage, particularly of the father whose drowning in a pond has left a substantial though undefined lesion in the man's life. But
it also seems to be, on another level, the search after God.

ROBERT BELOOF

On Stanley Kunitz's "Father and Son"

The ambiguities of literary reference urge us in this direction. The initial hint of Thompson's poem, "The Hound of Heaven" (here ironically reversed, with the man pursuing the elusive Godhead), the allegorical quality of the narrated story in the middle stanza, the Talmudic reference, all serve so to deepen in significance the son's spiritual search for his father, that one is left ambiguously poised between the reality of the father whose blank unanswering face the boy really saw in the pond, and the God for which he searches in that element which is so often, in religious traditions, used symbolically as the source of life. His final plea for help is, certainly, less the plea of the modern Freudian, "I am sick, make me well," and more the ancient plea of the religious, "How, in this world, may I be merciful and righteous."

The seeking goes out of the urban center to the country, where life and death, ripeness and decay, mingle and interconnect without a visible seam, and the journey is accomplished with the speed of dreams, effortlessly. It is autumn. The fruit has fallen, the fields are "curdled"—broken into clods with the fall turning. The country is "sleeping," thus, not only in the primary sense. The poem starts in dusk, and quickly moves into night. The fictive collapsing of time here is convincing. "Strode years; stretched into bird." And this collapsing has three dimensions. There is the one evening and night of the surrealistic flight. There is the sense of a season having passed in the countryside—the ripening and fall of the fruit. There is the sense of the passing of a human life, the plunging back into the country "where I was young." The ambiguities of the reality of the countryside and of its imaginative, symbolic import are beautifully maintained. In this first stanza there is a certain amount of rhetorical repetition: "Now in the—," "and now down—"; "one by one"; "mile after mile"; "I followed—," "I followed." One notices that all these relate to time and serve their valid purpose in aiding the reader's acceptance of the temporal hallucination. They are quite properly unobtrusive, unoriginal (it is of the essence of the hypnotic phrase that it is repetitive, undisturbing, unprovoking). Yet carefully the poet has kept these rhetorically important but linguistically dull elements to the absolute necessary minimum for the achievement of his emotional purpose. The author's purpose here is not to mesmerize the *reader* (an aim which has only limited if legitimate artistic purposes), but rather the more difficult feat of conveying a conviction to our relatively objective minds that the *speaker* was mesmerized and, further, to make us feel something of the reality of that condition of the speaker. We are meant to accept—almost to the point of participation—that the mind of the speaker is "kept in chains."

Everything is muted. The ear seldom is consciously aroused; alliterations are rare, assonantal and consonantal effects are seldom heavy. Yet always they are there, and the texture is never conversational, never bare, always singing with an unobtrusive sound. Thus, while the action of the speaker is seemingly violent ("with skimming feet," "raced"), yet the countryside is silent, motionless, the music subdued. The speaker is thus not only the psychological but also the pictorial center of the picture. Nothing offers competition to the vision of his headlong pursuit, all offers vivid contrast and heightened meaning to it. This is, in fact, both a pursuit and a flight. Ambivalently, the son "follows" the father, yet he remembers the "chains" of his "master." The focus lies in the word "indomitable"—this is a key to the seeking and fleeing—for it is the unconquerable ability to love which the speaker pursues. It is in this very lack, so exposed, that we see why the speaker is forced at the same time to acknowledge his need for the father's power to love, yet to recall that same power in unpleasant images.

I have mentioned the visual, pictorial directness of figures usually found in allegory and surrealism, and we see that, with a single exception, all the images surrounding the flight are visual. When the father (the at-this-point vaguely characterized goal of the pursuit) is first evoked, it is not through the visual sense. At this point the poet, while hinting of *the* fateful pond, is careful to evoke it only as an odor. Suspense begins to build toward the father's appearance; and yet our focus on the son is not allowed to wander. Not only are the images of his progress visual, but they are evoked in a natural and logical way. If one starts from the city one goes through the suburbs to the country, with its "sandy road." The falling light, the road, the curdle of fields, the remembered plums, all the images have a naturalistic base, and get their surrealistic quality rather from the speed with which they are evoked, the constant stream of them, and from the subdued insistence on their symbolic overtones. It is the combination of these qualities of the landscape—naturalistic, surrealistic, symbolic—that gives dramatic dimension to the central figure. These qualities are sustained and generalized in the line "The silence unrolling before me as I came," where even the silence, which somehow dramatizes the length of his journey, becomes a visual quality and emphasizes the speaker's continued isolation in the landscape. The very last line of the stanza is another matter, however; we shall return to it later.

Developments in the middle stanza reinforce the ambiguity of the father's character—his strange place, poised between reality and apotheosis. One senses the defeating separation between the father and the speaker. As a child finds no adult words to express his world, finds his fears real, but feels his life, somehow, to be apart, and, in some sense, fabulous, so the chasm for the speaker is not merely one of speaking across the Styx, but of speaking from a limited to a very much greater vision. The double level is sustained through the loss of the father's house, and the subsequent breakup of the family. Certainly the sister's leaving home and "nothing" coming back can be taken as a parable of the breaking of the chain of religious instruction and belief, parent to child. The man himself left home and "lived on a hill that had too many rooms." Our feeling that this refers to the life of the intellect, with its limited vision of reality and its multiple and disparate ideas of knowledge, is reinforced by the next line, with its pointing out that knowledge can make light (increase mastery of the physical), but cannot create warmth (human love and affection). When the light fails—that is, when the intellect ceases to be enough, then the speaker climbs "under the hill." I am not sure of the exact symbolic meaning here, but the overtones of a retreat into an inner life, a withdrawal into self from a world whose rewards have failed, seem to me clear. This withdrawal is dramatized in a fine line of understatement. The papers come; the speaker's connection with the world is regular but at second hand, and he is unmoved by its daily tragedies and melodramas. More, it seems clear he feels himself *unable* any longer to make an emotional connection outside his private self.

The second stanza adds a new twist to the distortion of time. We suddenly have what is, in effect, a frame story. The first stanza begins in time present with developmental material concerning the father relating to a distant past, introduced discreetly. In the second stanza, however, by means of the speaker's imagining what he will say when he finds his father, the middle ground of the story is filled in—the salient elements of the speaker's life between his early memory of his father and the present. Essentially, this stanza completes the presentation of developmental material, at the end of which the crisis takes place in a return to present time, in the arrival at "the water's edge," and the confrontation of the father.

Breaking the normal temporal sequence in so constricted a space serves its function in helping to create the fabulous quality, but perhaps even more importantly permits compression and narrative speed. For instance, while it gives us vital information of the speaker's spiritual history, it at the same time permits us to make a contrast between what he *thinks* he may say and what in fact he *does* say when the confrontation occurs. And we note that in that hopeful speech we all-too-frequently prepare in our minds before a vital interview, his emphasis is on his failures since his father's death, on his retreat from the father's house and his ultimate withdrawal from life. But the speech he actually makes is a plea for the father's return, and an idealistic statement of what he hopes to achieve with the father's help. The ironic insight into the speaker is reinforced by not the least meaningful ambiguity of the poem, namely, the fact that though the father is dead, he is in the water, the very source of life, while the speaker, alive, must remain at its edge, and the ferns that arise from it appear to him "smothering." The next to last line confirms these implications.

But before going on to one of the best lines of the poem I would like to contrast its successful development of the basic visual imagery with the poem's weakest moment. I refer to the last line of the first stanza, which seems to me to partake, alone of the surrealistic images of the poem, of the peculiar kind of melodramatic inaccuracy to which surrealism is addicted. The failure, of course, may very well lie in me rather than in the line, but I cannot see why the night is an orange, or why it is nailed to the protagonist's forehead. Further, even if the symbolism of the orange could be explained to my ignorance, there is a bizarre and garish quality to the image which I think I would still feel and which would still throw it out of context. It is a fact that it suddenly violates the naturalistic visual base of the vision. It is dreamlike all right, but it seems to come from another dream. I wonder whether the author did not subconsciously feel some of this, and whether this feeling might not be attested by the presence here of the only simile of the poem.

By contrast, the turtles and the lilies seem to me unobtrusively brilliant in their ability to perform a variety of functions. They are, of course, literal and real as they relate to a literal, real pond. Yet they come here with the clarity and the richness of emblems, serving as ambiguous contrast to each other as well as creating the framework for the face of the father—demonstrating in a literal way the place and fate of physical man in the physical world as one in a row of physical things, and in a symbolic way the dualities in man's own spiritual nature.

We notice in how many ways the father's appearance is prepared for, notably how the passivity of the reply contrasts with the frantic activity of the son. And it is here that the whole dream quality of the poem is invoked to save us from a disastrous sense of anticlimax. The surrealistic technique, the handling of time, have permitted a gradual revelation of the kind in which the ultimate moment is neither exactly a repetition of information nor exactly a surprise. In the same way, in light of all we know of the speaker's psyche by now, we must feel the father's silence to be inevitable. Yet that very inevitability has its surprises, its extensions and reinforcements into the poems' final ambiguities.

The functional phrase is "white ignorant hollow," and without the previous insistence on the surrealistic ambiguity of the images one would be left merely confirmed in the suspicion that the dead are unable to speak. But while on the simplest pictorial level we see a skull, yet "white" is a color which means purity and innocence as well as death, and nothing in the poem indicates that they might not perfectly well apply to the father. Likewise "ignorant" seems strangely difficult. Is this ignorance a good or bad or neutral thing? Is the "light" of the "hill" preferable? "Hollow" seems terrible enough, yet is the father dead any more hollow to the son than he was alive? Alive, was he able to communicate to the son the source of his power to love? Apparently not. And whose fault was that? The poem does not tell, unless in the information that the father was a veritable learned commentary of "gentleness." All of which leads us back ambiguously to the search for God, and the eternal question as to whether the fault is that God does not speak, or we do not hear. The mystic has his certainties as does the materialist. In any case, one is aware of the son's total failure, and one would be hard pressed to say whose face—white, ignorant, hollow—the son sees there, his father, his Father, or his own, and what success or failure it signals.

ROBERT LOWELL

I suppose the fashion of looking very, very closely at poems began with *The Waste Land*. This poem was widely attacked as immoral non-sense. Many who liked it found it complex yet unintelligible. The author's footnotes had a breezy, pedantic dash to them that was in itself a warning. They assumed more knowledge than most readers had, yet everywhere in their inadequacy pointed to more work to be done: myths to be pondered, symbols to be harmonized, books to be read. Soon there was a crackling controversy among the admirers of *The Waste Land,* as to whether it was religious, anti-religious or without beliefs. Long analytical essays began to appear; soon this kind of writing spread, and everything, ancient and modern, was being explained.

Eliot seemed to gaze on this new industry from the background, a friendly god, silent and brooding. But when he broke silence, his remarks were far from helpful. The footnotes, faithfully reprinted according to the author's wishes in each new anthologizing of *The Waste Land,* turned out to be a publisher's afterthought, a trick to make a book out of a poem that was too short to be one. Far from being a devotee of analysis, it seemed that Eliot read it, if at all, with weary, incredulous amazement. Commenting on a book of close critical studies of "the poem," he had many doubts and ended by saying that such writings certainly didn't make for very interesting reading.

Analysis doesn't make for interesting reading. Few of us, I imagine, spend much time pouring over *The Explicator,* that solid, dull little publication, where poems are processed into monthly exegesis. Analysis is necessary for teaching poems, and for student papers. Still, somehow, nothing very fresh or to the point is said. One knows ahead of time how the machine will grind. Conventionality has overtaken the industry; nothing new is set up, nothing bad is destroyed. There is even a kind of modern poem, now produced in bulk, that seems written to be explained. Training and labor are required for such efforts, but this can't be the way good poems are written. Inspiration, passion, originality and even technical assurance must be something that can't be produced in bulk, or merely by training and labor. Nor can good criticism be produced by training and labor and conventionality.

Dullness and the sad, universal air of the graduate schools have descended on close literary criticism. Once it was far otherwise. I can remember when the early essays on *The Waste Land*, the first editions of the Brooks and Warren *Understanding Poetry*, and Blackmur's pieces on Stevens and Marianne Moore came as a revelation. The world was being made anew. Nothing, it seemed, had ever really been read. Old writings, once either neglected or simplified and bowdlerized into triteness, were now for the first time seen as they were. New writing that met the new challenges was everywhere painfully wrestling itself into being. Poetry was still unpopular, but it seemed as though Arnold's "immense future" for literature and particularly poetry was being realized. Here, for a few, was religion and reality.

Perhaps all this was only my adolescent fever. A glow seems to be gone, but perhaps this was just my illusion. Perhaps there never was a glow; more likely, it is still there and yearly seizes new writers and new critics. For me, anyway, the fever is a chronic malaria. I will never quite disbelieve that the world is being remade by the new ways of writing and careful reading. With this admission, I feel in the right mood of warmth and naïveness to start looking closely at Stanley Kunitz's poem, "Father and Son." However, I really doubt the possibilities of the method, and even more my own talents for it.

"Father and Son" is a modern poem, one that has obviously been through the new mill and the new training. Yet when read, say twice, there seems to be an embarrassing lack of difficulty. The theme, a son looking for his dead father, must have existed in the time of Cain. The fact of the experience seems so closely joined and identical with its unavoidable symbolic reverberations that it would be banal and schoolteacherish to point them out. The pathos and dignity of expression are as open and apparent as such things are in ordinary conversation. The meter is a tolerably regular blank verse.

My first questions are cheating personal ones that mean much to me, but which are no doubt uncritical and unanswerable by careful reading. I want to know if Kunitz and his own father are the father and son. Is the countryside, the country around Worcester, Massachusetts, where Kunitz grew up and I went to boarding school? What happened to the sister? What's the point of the pond? Did the father drown himself, or was his favorite sport fishing or wading for water bugs? *Gemara* seems to be some Torah appendage to the Bible. Some sort of lonely pilgrimage? An experience of bitter purging? But I really don't know, and have no books or knowledgeable people to consult. The word *Gemara* and the poem's tone seem to say it is personal. So, I say yes to most of my questions except the suicide. The pond must somehow touch on the remembered father, and is a puff of blue smoke from everyone's childhood, when ponds, waterlilies and nature were closer and more demandingly mysterious. The sister is nowhere, an intentional question mark.

A few hard expressions stand out. "A sweet curdle of fields!" Fields don't curdle, curdle is somehow the opposite of sweet. Here is the journey in a phrase. The pathos is in its hard sterility, it's a curdle because no such journey can really be made. Finding the dead father is a pipe dream. Nothing could be more natural or idly futile. The only sand on such a road must be like "bone-dust." "The secret master of my blood" is a stern expression of filial piety. This too is hard, unconfessable, tyrannical, and in the terrible nature of things. And this particular father in life loved with a kind of love that was indomitable for him but "chains" for his son. Then several natural and impossible things happen: one strides down years, the fields are fields of childhood, the silence unrolls. Then comes an odd, violent phrase, the night nailed like an orange to the son's brow. Perhaps this is Baudelaire's "old orange squeezed dry," but oranges can be squeezed, they are not nailed. I think of the kind of contradiction I am now familiar with, a mush of obscurity and impossibility nailed to one by necessity, the inescapably absent and unshakable father. Is the orange a sop for a headache savagely nailed to the brow it is supposed to sooth? A grim, jocular reference to the Crucifixion, the torture that saves for believers, and here made low and foolish?

In the next section, three things stop me: the life that has become so unreal and meaningful that it is a *fable*, the hill so figuratively easy and literally impossible to climb *under* (Is it for warmth? Is it to get totally away from the light that is now gone, a kind of death for the son and one that has long been hinted at?) and the somehow reproachful, Stoical hysteria of "I'm alone and never shed a tear."

In the last section, the son "whirling between two wars" reminds me of a remark made by Mary McCarthy in an essay. She says that in our nuclear age it is impossible to write as Jane Austen and Tolstoy did about what we know. A house is no longer simply a house, a man is no longer simply a man in a town. The in-

73

On Stanley Kunitz's "Father and Son"

human, unreal, smashing universal is always at our elbow. All must signify and ache with the unnatural and necessary nightmare. The "white ignorant hollow of his face" is the skull, the always known unattainableness of the search and a kind of answer and reassurance. The search must be tried, though one knows that nothing solid can be touched.

Many of the things I like about this poem are simple things hardly worth remarking on but genuine and precious. They are the suburbs, the stucco house, the sister who marries as a matter of course and is not heard of as a matter of course. There's a curious distance, vagueness and dignity about the house on the hill with light but not enough warmth, and whose light fails—marriage in our wandering world perhaps and no doubt. This is our world, none of it can be put away or expunged any more than boyhood, the need to yearn, and the fact that we are all sons of someone, who is as he was. There's a boyish coziness, innocence and hopelessness to the turtles and water-lilies. The lines after *Gemara* have the vulnerable openness of a prayer. The poem is as much a struggle to recover child-hood, or the prayer once held in childhood, as it is about the father.

The other things that make this poem are of a kind that take great art and passion to accomplish. They are matters of rhythm and syntax, all that is the life blood of a poem when we read it to ourselves. These are what Paul Valéry meant when he said a poem was some huge weight carried to some height or the top of a skyscraper and dropped on the reader. The reader feels the simple brute impact, but is ignorant of the sweat and science that carried the weight into position. In the working-out of a poem, I look for two things: a commanding, deadly effective-ness in the arrangement, and something that breathes and pauses and grunts and is rough and unpredictable to assure me that the journey is honest. In the first sentence, I like plums that actually do drop one by one in their ripeness, the way they round off the sentence, and their good-natured illusory reference to the fa-ther's dropping off. There's a fine careless loosening-up of the rhythm in the "odor of ponds" line. The three verbs, "strode," "stretched," and "raced" are strong in their position, movement and pauses. The two participial lines at the end of the first section are authoritatively placed.

So is the last line of section two. So is the whole artful, broken simplicity of the speech in this section. Also the very different speech and prayer in section three. Just right is the confused rhythm describing the ferns, turtles and lilies.

On Stanley Kunitz's "Father and Son"

Are there flaws and limitations? I am not sure. I blink a little at a certain over-resolute, petrified firmness here and there, in the "master of my blood," the nailed orange, the "never shed a tear," and the "white ignorant hollow of his face." Perhaps these are just characteristics of the experience, and the binding that makes the poem a poem and not an improvisation. Certainly there's authority and honesty, a noble hallucination.

I have written under disadvantages, far from books, and in a rush to make a deadline. I haven't Kunitz's *Selected Poems* at hand to refer to. He has never published an unfelt and unfinished poem. Each line shows his fine touch and noble carefulness.

STANLEY KUNITZ

Once a poem has been distributed, it is no longer the property of the poet. By the time it is published he has become somebody else, and part of the change in him must be attributed to his knowledge that he is free from the necessity of making that poem again. Even if he could! He can try, of course, to remember who he was and how he felt during the event, but his memory is not wholly to be trusted, since it is stained with afterthought and prone to rationalize everything he has done, particularly when he has done something as unreasonable as writing poetry. The poet's professional identity is elusive even to himself: it is not a fixity to be recaptured, but rather an accumulation of quite special, often compulsive energies that disappear by flowing into the poem. After the event poet as well as reader is left with nothing but an arrangement of words on a page to testify that something more or less unusual or valuable has happened. Of "Father and Son" I can say that it is a fairly representative poem of mine—representative at least of one dominant strain in my work—and that the comments made by Miss Miles, Mr. Beloof and Mr. Lowell, even when they disagree with one another or with me, include so many brilliant perceptions as to obviate the necessity for an elaborate guided tour through the "inside" of my poem.

Mr. Lowell is right: the poem is not a difficult one at all. It is only other people's poems that have ever seemed to me obscure. The manifold tissue of experience, in Whitehead's phrase, with which one is concerned presents itself with a bewildering density, an overlay of episodes and images, both public and private. What makes art possible is that one is also, at the same time, a bundle of simplicities. But modern criticism is frightened of these simplicities. The hard and inescapable phenomenon to be faced is that we are living and dying at once. My commitment is to report the dialogue.

"Father and Son" was born of a dream and much of the dream-work has passed into the poem. I wrote it on the eve of World War II, so that there is a touch of prophecy in the phrase "whirling between two wars." Most of the landscape goes back to my boyhood in Worcester, where we lived (in a stucco house) at the edge of the city, but "the sweet curdle of fields" must have originated in the milky, sometimes clotted night-mists of the Delaware Valley, where I was resident at the time. I do not propose to launch into a full-scale autobiography here, but I am ready to say that all the essential details of the poem are true, as true as dreams are, with characteristic fusions, substitutions, and dislocations. The sister who died and the big house on the hill were not invented for the occasion; they belong to that part of my life which I keep trying to rework into legend. The line, "I lived on a hill that had too many rooms," is a distant echo of the Gospel pronouncement, "In my Father's house are many mansions," no doubt triggered by the possessive adjective. Mr. Beloof, who understands a great deal about the poem, offers an interpretation of this whole passage, in terms of the intellect, that is more abstract than my original intention but that is perfectly consistent with it. One of the oddities of poetry is the symbolic extensibility of plain facts. A literalist might say, of the nineteenth line, that I was referring, on the one hand, to the mechanics of generating electricity with a Kohler engine ("light we could make") and, on the other, to the lack of central heating in the country house ("but not enough of warmth"). In a sense I was! To seize on what is literal in a poem, what relates to ordinary human experience, is the first task of criticism. "And when the light failed, I climbed under the hill"—is a gloss required? If so, I should direct the reader to Blake's tremendous lines, from which I must have made an unconscious borrowing:

Tho' thou art worshipped by the Names Divine
Of Jesus and Jehovah, thou art still
The Son of Morn in weary Night's decline,
The lost Traveller's Dream under the hill.

How clever of Miss Miles to identify the pond of "Father and Son" with the "Goose Pond" of another poem!—the link, though obvious now, had somehow escaped me. It was a small, reputedly bottomless water-hole that I frequented in Quinnapoxet, outside Worcester, and my memory of it is alive with snakes and pickerel and snapping turtles and pond lilies (no, not turtledoves and definitely not literary lilies). A boy had drowned in it, and the legend went that his body had never been recovered. My companion, who could shoot down squirrels from the trees and birds on the wing and split a water snake in two at a hundred yards, grew up to kill his wife and her lover, perhaps with the same gun. But that, I suppose, is another story. Somewhere fact ends and myth begins, but I could not begin to determine the boundary line. As far as I am concerned, the pond in

77

Quinnapoxet, Poe's "dank tarn of Auber," and the mere in which Beowulf fights for his life with Grendel and the water-hag are one and the same. It is the pond where I am never surprised to find demons, murderers, parents, poets. Did my father really die there? No, he never even saw it; and I was the one who came closest to drowning.

Nobody, alas, seems to like my line, "The night nailed like an orange to my brow," but I have lived with it too long to think of changing a word. What is so outlandish about it? Throughout the poem the moon, though never named, is fiercely burning . . . shining in the bone-dust and the mist, reflected at the last in "the white ignorant hollow" of the father's face. Most of us must have known breathless nights, so heavy and close that the moon has walked with us. To suffer this night of the moon so intensely is to be impaled by it. To one who says flatly, "Oranges are not nailed," my flat answer is, "In this poem they are." The reader cannot be expected to know that when I was six years old, running barefoot, I stepped on a nail that protruded—God knows how—through a rotten peach and hobbled home with that impossible fruit hammered to my flesh. When I was fourteen or fifteen, I discovered Tennyson and I can still recall how enchanted I was with the sensuous mystery of the opening lines of "Mariana":

> With blackest moss the flower-pots
>   Were thickly crusted, one and all:
> The rusted nails fell from the knots
>   That held the peach to the garden-wall.

Though Tennyson was thinking of a peach *tree*, no doubt espaliered, it was years before I stumbled on that realization. Nail and fruit, then, have a long history of association in my mind, and the image that eventually sealed their connection has nothing to do with ornament or fancy, but is an emanation of my felt truth. Such moments in a poem, evident only by the pressure building behind them, can never fully explain themselves, but the poet must take his risk with them as an article of faith. In the end, for whatever it may be worth, they constitute his signature.

"Father and Son" was conceived as a dramatic lyric, with some kinship to the dramatic monologue. The divisions of the poem are not to be construed as stanzas, but as narrative blocks or paragraphs, each with its distinctive rhythm of action, and the indicated pauses are meaningful in the reading and the interpretation. The fourth and final division consists of the last two lines, which should be set off from the rest of the poem by a space. Unfortunately, in the layout of my *Selected Poems,* these lines are transposed to the overleaf, so that the break is obscured. Perhaps I magnify the importance of this small detail, but I feel quite certain now, as I examine the comments, that a clearly spaced version is essential for a firm grasp of the structure.

The way that a poem develops is largely out of one's control, since the end is willed by the means, but I sense that my impulse toward a form generally tends to move along the lines of certain ineluctable archetypes, particularly those of death and rebirth, the quest, and the night-journey (or descent into the underworld). In all three patterns—which may be consubstantial—the progress is from a kind of darkness into a kind of light. If Miss Miles is correct in asserting that passivity and ignorance win out at the end of "Father and Son," I am most egregiously at fault. As I understand the main level of the action, the son in his quest is not looking for pity or pardon. It is to be noted that he makes no confession of sins. The losses that he reviews are those peculiar to the human condition and of special interest to the father, since they involve property and family. "Instruct me how to live" is the substance of his prayer, but in the irony of circumstance it is addressed to one who is dead and who, furthermore, has destroyed himself. Presumably the son who wants to be saved is unaware of the self-destructive elements in his nature that impel him toward the father; unaware till the very instant when his begetter enters the water and becomes one with it—both source and death-trap. The last two lines, constituting a simultaneous *peripeteia* and *anagnorisis,* reversal and discovery, announce for me the shock of recognition that moves beyond despair. Now that for the first time the father shows his terrible face, the son is delivered from his bondage, from his trance of love and yearning, from his seductive loyalties. His triumph is in what he *sees.* I read the ending on a note of tragic exaltation.

Let me admit that I have written this piece with a measure of reluctance, conscious of promises but fearful of surrendering to the temptation of saying more than I should. With an intimate poem so much of the power is stored in the silences—those spacings between words and lines and thoughts—where the secret battle is being fought. The temptation to fill the spaces with verbalization is real, for the poet who returns to his own work under stress, as when he reads it in public, is engaged in a secondary act of creation, which he is liable to confuse with the first. To reply to criticism at all is to risk sounding more defensive than one has hoped to be. If the poet were a saint, he would remain indifferent to responses, resting in his knowledge that the words of the poem stand forever separate from the words about it, and that he has already had his chance.

RICHARD WILBUR

JOHN FREDERICK NIMS

JOHN BERRYMAN

ROBERT LOWELL

On ROBERT LOWELL'S

"*Skunk Hour*"

Robert Lowell

SKUNK HOUR

For Elizabeth Bishop

Nautilus Island's hermit
heiress still lives through winter in her Spartan cottage;
her sheep still graze above the sea.
Her son's a bishop. Her farmer
is first selectman in our village;
she's in her dotage.

Thirsting for
the hierarchic privacy
of Queen Victoria's century,
she buys up all
the eyesores facing her shore,
and lets them fall.

The season's ill—
we've lost our summer millionaire,
who seemed to leap from an L. L. Bean
catalogue. His nine-knot yawl
was auctioned off to lobstermen.
A red fox stain covers Blue Hill.

And now our fairy
decorator brightens his shop for fall;
his fishnet's filled with orange cork,
orange, his cobbler's bench and awl;
there is no money in his work,
he'd rather marry.

One dark night,
my Tudor Ford climbed the hill's skull;
I watched for love-cars. Lights turned down,
they lay together, hull to hull,
where the graveyard shelves on the town. . . .
My mind's not right.

A car radio bleats,
"Love, O careless Love. . . ." I hear
my ill-spirit sob in each blood cell,
as if my hand were at its throat. . . .
I myself am hell;
nobody's here—

only skunks, that search
in the moonlight for a bite to eat.
They march on their soles up Main Street:
white stripes, moonstruck eyes' red fire
under the chalk-dry and spar spire
of the Trinitarian Church.

I stand on top
of our back steps and breathe the rich air—
a mother skunk with her column of kittens swills the garbage pail.
She jabs her wedge-head in a cup
of sour cream, drops her ostrich tail,
and will not scare.

RICHARD WILBUR

When I think of *Lord Weary's Castle,* I think of a prophetic poetry directed against what Yeats called "order and outer fixity." In the name of a revolutionary Christ, the poems attack—as Randall Jarrell once added it up—"everything that is closed, turned inward, incestuous, that blinds or binds: the Old Law, imperialism, militarism, capitalism, Calvinism, Authority, the Father, the 'Proper Bostonians,' the rich who will 'do everything for the poor except get off their backs.'" The focus of the book is on this century's New England, on the times and places which the poet has best known; but for what he feels Lowell finds historical cases and precedents as far back as imperial Rome, and analogies in many reaches of literature. The crammed, hopped-up lines make continual dazzling transitions between some particular scene or occasion and the whole field of Lowell's historical, religious, and literary awareness—transitions which seem free-associational because the logic is so compressed, and which might seem virtuoso if the prophetic urgency were not so strong.

Many of the poems build toward straight prophecy—"the world shall come to Walsingham," "The Lord survives the rainbow of His will"—and there are many others in which, though the poet or someone else may figure as a character, individual sensibility is less important and less examined than the world which the poem sees and denounces. Still, the direction which Lowell's poetry was to take may be found in such a modest, relaxed, and steadily viewed reminiscence as "Buttercups," or in the brilliant monologues of "Between the Porch and the Altar." The direction, of course, is from the prophetic to the dramatic, from the world to the individual who suffers it.

The dramatic verse of *The Mills of the Kavanaughs* retains, generally speaking, the crammed and racing character of the first book; but now the quick jumps, the surprising collocations, the wrenched rhythms, the sixteen-line sentences full of avalanching particulars, are justified not by prophetic fervor but by the states of mind which Lowell allots to his characters. Dwellers in the world which *Lord Weary's Castle* described, they speak out of rumination, or revery or dream, or even from the edge of death by oven-gas; they are authorized to think with an often vertiginous subjectivity.

"Skunk Hour" is another sort of dramatic poem altogether. It is one of a

On Robert Lowell's "Skunk Hour"

series, largely reminiscent, in which the poet sheds all his personae (including the prophetic) and speaks of and for himself. Paradoxically, this permits him to sound impersonal:

> Nautilus Island's hermit
> heiress still lives through winter in her Spartan cottage;
> her sheep still graze above the sea.
> Her son's a bishop. Her farmer
> is first selectman in our village;
> she's in her dotage.

The lines are short, the rhymes off-hand, the language specific and conversational, the tone level. We are given a certain amount of verifiable gossip in simple declarative sentences, and it seems, so far, as if the poet were speaking directly and objectively to the reader. Not until halfway through the poem will we know for sure that this is selected information, evidence for something, and that we are eavesdropping on the thoughts of a troubled man alone in his house at night. Hence we make little, initially, of the bishop and selectman, and if we derive any suspicion of attitude it is from two quiet ironies. The first, emphasized by a halting *enjambement*, is "hermit / heiress"; we expect a hermit to be masculine and poor, and so the conjunction is amusing, whether as derogation or mere flippancy we don't yet know. The second irony lies in the line "she's in her dotage," which repeats the grammatical structure of the previous declarations but affects us as an abrupt let-down. The heiress and her sheep are "still" there as always, she "still" has a finger in church and state, but the vital persistence of her regime is, after all, illusory.

The form of action which her dotage takes, as described in stanza II, is wonderfully extravagant, and the neutrality of the language inclines us to see her as deliciously eccentric, an Unforgettable Character. Perhaps one also reflects that her behavior is anti-social, selfish, regressive, and life-denying, but the poem does not as yet encourage such judgments, and they seem illicitly overserious.

The humor grows more emphatic in stanza III, at the expense of a deceased conspicuous-consumer who looked, when alive, like a sporting-goods dummy, and whose death is a blow to the summer resort's economy and distinction. At the same time, we are half aware in this stanza of accumulating ideas of death and

On Robert Lowell's "Skunk Hour"

decay: to the addled heiress and the collapsing eyesores we must add the dead millionaire, the passing of summer, and the decline of a fishing port into a vacation town.

This last idea carries over into the next stanza, where fishnet, bench and awl are disnatured and trivialized by a homosexual decorator, who represents the town's new economy. (The motifs of death and decline will continue in the likening of cars to boats, in "hill's skull," "graveyard," "shelves," and the "chalk-dry and spar spire" of the church.) The last two lines of the stanza are mimicry: there's no money in his work, the decorator complains; marriage would be work, too, but at least one might be supported.

At this point the poem suddenly reveals itself as dramatic monologue, and its first half becomes in retrospect a morose private meditation on a selfish, loveless, and diseased environment. The thought of the decorator's sexual inversion makes the poet remember the prurient yearning with which, "one dark night," he spied on love-cars from his Tudor (two-door) Ford. This recollection, which argues against his mental balance, upsets him, and a car radio, passing his house in the night, moves him by a fragment of "Careless Love" to a paroxysm of balked desire. One thinks of a line from "After the Surprising Conversions"—"a thirst / For loving shook him like a snake."

"I myself am hell" (the one literary echo in the poem) is what Milton's Satan says "in prospect of Eden," and Lowell surely means us to think not only of Satan's imprisonment in self but also of his envious spying in the scenes of Book IV which immediately follow. Does the quotation aim to suggest that the poet's emotional imbalance makes him see the world falsely, that like Satan he "sees undelighted all delight?" I think not; the first four stanzas have seemed not a prophetic vision but a dour review of certain facts, and if these facts imply a diseased society—precisely the one summarized by Jarrell—their interpretation seems as much ours as the poet's. The diseased world is really there; the point is that the poet shares in a measure its addlement, "illness," deadness and aloneness, and cannot shuck off the self which the world has thrust upon him.

"Skunk Hour" has a pattern roughly similar to that of "In the Attic," the first section of Lowell's early poem "The First Sunday in Lent." "In the Attic" moves from a glimpse of the present world to a recollection which establishes the poet's complicity in that world, and finally to a prayer for man's regeneration.

On Robert Lowell's "Skunk Hour"

What replaces the prayer, in the structure of the later poem, is the poet's contemplation of a mother skunk and her kittens. What do the skunks stand for? Are they the equivalent of a prayer? They ramble appetitively at night, like the poet of "Skunk Hour" or like the husband of " 'To Speak of Woe That Is in Marriage,' " who "hits the streets to cruise for prostitutes." Their "moonstruck eyes' red fire" is wild and passionate. Yet their passionate lives are simple, as the "column of kittens" suggests; their eyes are not "homicidal," like those of the husband in "Man and Wife"; their wildness is natural and sane, and need not be "tamed by *Miltown*." To the poet, as he "breathes the rich air" on the back stoop, they stand for stubborn, unabashed livingness, and for his own refusal (in the teeth of society and of his own jangled nature) to cease desiring a world of vitality, freedom, and love.

Some have said that the poems of *Life Studies* are dilute and artless by comparison to Lowell's earlier work. They look so only if one has been so conditioned by the latter as to be irresponsive to new techniques from the same poet. "Skunk Hour" does not afford the reader a kinetic jag, does not dazzle him with its transitions, does not disarm his unbelief by a passionate violence. It cannot be read passively. As with the poems of Elizabeth Bishop (to whom "Skunk Hour" is dedicated), one must participate in the lines, discovering their implicit emotional value and generalizing from their relatively dead-pan specificities. It is up to the reader to connect "my ill-spirit" with "The season's ill," and to construe the relationship of "dotage" and "moonstruck" to "My mind's not right." There is art enough, and density enough, in "Skunk Hour"; it is a more flexible poetry than Lowell has ever written; it admits a greater range of feeling, and in particular it liberates the author's excellent sense of humor. With no disrespect to *Lord Weary's Castle*, I should argue that the later poetry, with its objectivity and its demand for collaborative reading, renders Lowell's vision of the world more probable and more readily shared. In any case, "Skunk Hour" is an extremely fine poem.

JOHN FREDERICK NIMS

A word about form: a regular basis of rhythm and rhyme gives us not something to conform to, but something to rebel against when rebellion is meaningful. In "free verse" the revolt is over before the poem begins—hence the sameness of so much of it. "Skunk Hour" has a solid framework, though the poet is continually quarreling with it, wrenching it out of shape for purposes of his own. His 6-line stanza has two pulsations of the meter in lines 1 and 6, four elsewhere. The rhythm is often "sprung"; the poet counts only his strongest syllables, sometimes disregarding conventional stresses. The syntactical unit may substitute for the foot, as in the long line of VIII, in which the four units are subject, prepositional phrase, verb, and object. Or the quaternion we soon come to feel in lines 2-4 may make us stress syllables rhetorically important ("shé búys úp áll" of II). In the norm-stanza, on which the poet rings many changes, lines 1 and 6 rhyme— this happens half the time. When it happens, the other rhymes form, typically, an internal quatrain, as in IV, V, and possibly III. (This A-BCBC-A opened many of the longer stanzas in *Lord Weary's Castle*.) Rhymes and off-rhymes run from stanza to stanza: "all"—"fall"—"yawl"—"skull"—"cell"—"pail," etc. One might well begin his reading with the cadence of IV, V, or VII in his head; this is the metrical norm varied in other stanzas. Since Mr. Lowell does not label his images, but sets them forth for us to interpret (not arbitrarily; the clues are definite), his poem will probably require many readings. The first four stanzas present three characters taken as typical of a time and place; two stanzas describe the emotional crisis to which the protagonist is brought by this and other evidence; two more stanzas resolve the crisis with the little drama of the skunks.

Stanza I

Our first character: an old lady of wealth who chooses to live alone, not without hardship. Both her son and her tenant are filling conventionally success-ful roles. Our "heiress" lives in the past; her sheep suggest the agricultural econ-omy of days long gone by. Diction is plain, almost without adjectives. The heavy genitive place-name before its noun is rugged; conventional English calls for something like "the lonely heiress of Nautilus Island." The words "hermit heir-ess" go together only with strain. Not quite oxymoron—but " 'words that surprise each other' on finding themselves together." Looking as if they began with the same sound, whereas they do not, the words are something of a tongue-twister. In the lack of parallelism in the last two sentences, the same kind of ungainliness: it would seem that the period after "bishop" and the semicolon after "village" should change places. But, as things are, the blunt last line comes out more strongly. There is little exploitation of sound either as structural or as expressive, although five thin *i*'s in line 2 dramatize persistence. With "cottage," two straggling off-rhymes; "her farmer" has sounds in common with "hermit," a grotesque rhyme; "sea" dangles unrhymed until the following stanza. With its uncertainties, this is the least tightly organized of the stanzas, as if the poem had not yet found its focus.

Stanza II

Two stanzas for this portrait, whereas the wry little thumbnail sketches that follow are done in one apiece. A few loose screws, something ramshackle—not out of place in this description of dotage. Though her cottage is Spartan, the lady "thirsts": her wasteful and self-indulgent mania squanders half the stanza on the participle and its object. Much of the emphasis comes out in the play on form: the rhyme "privacy"—"century" is jingling and false: this kind of privacy does not go with this century. Or try reading "most of" instead of "all"—far more than a rhyme is lost. The 4-beat "she buys up all" insists grimly on her fanaticism, while the 2-beat last line, apparently paced the same, yet metrically twice as fast, has a runaway speed in comparison ("shé búys úp áll . . . and léts them fáll").

The aptness of observation here is confirmed by the matriarch's resembling a synthesis of three characters in Sarah Orne Jewett's Maine classic of 1896, *The Country of the Pointed Firs.* (1) Joanna Todd: "a sort of nun or hermit person lived out there for years all alone on Shellheap Island . . . she was a well-off woman . . . there was something mediaeval in [her] behavior. . . . I called her a great fool . . . some other minister would have been a great help to her— one that preached self-forgetfulness and doin' for others to cure our own ills. . . . 'Tis like bad eyesight, the mind of such a person: if your eyes don't see right there may be a remedy, but there's no kind of glasses to remedy the mind. . . ." (2) Esther, the Dunnet shepherdess, who had given up school-teaching years before to take care of sheep. "Esther had always been laughed at for her belief in sheepraising when one by one their neighbors were giving up their flocks. . . ." (3) Abby Martin, the "Queen's Twin," who built her life around coincidental resemblances to Queen Victoria. "If you want to hear about Queen Victoria, why Mis' Abby Martin'll tell you everything."

Stanza III

The virtues of the old independent are positive ones. The summer millionaire, however, is all façade. She belonged to and endured in the difficult country; he is a fair-weather friend of vacationland, an outsider in native costume, too new, too picturesque. L. L. Bean, Inc., the Maine mail-order house, specializes in camping equipment, clothes for sportsmen, etc. The millionaire would be flaunting items like their Men's Sueded Country Jacket, "made of imported Holland Suede . . . buffed to a rich nap similar to sueded leather . . . Two slash pockets concealed in front pleats . . ." or their Moccasin Chukka, "hand burnished to a deep ivory glow." The three accented long *e*'s of the third line project him before us in all of his compulsive athleticism—a failure both as man and millionaire. Financial straits are implied by the auctioning off of his fast yawl—though the way "nine-knot yawl" wallows in its sluggish sounds suggests that the "millionaire" only claimed it could make nine knots an hour. Line 6 sprawls over the two accents we have come to expect: "a red fox staín covers Blue Híll." A wild stain, fox-red, or like the stains that "fox" old paper, or like the rash of illness—though probably just the autumn coloring on a hill whose name evokes more tranquil tones. (Blue Hill is also a town in Maine.) Sarah Orne Jewett had dwelt on the early autumn color: in September "the frost-bitten grass grew close about [the house] like brown fur. . . ." The stain is symbolic, another symptom that shows "The season's ill'—a statement not unlike Hamlet's "The time is out of joint." "Ill"—a languishing half-rhyme with "fall" above it—means more than "sick": a certain archaic strangeness shifts it from the physical to the psychical, the moral. Again Hamlet: "Thou wouldst not think how ill all's here about my heart." And the fox: what more appropriate totem for a figure of fraudulence? The rhyme: is "yawl" a far-off rhyme with the middle of "millionaire"? Or with "fall" in other stanzas? "Millionaire" then is an off-rhyme with "shore" above or "fairy" below.

On Robert Lowell's "Skunk Hour"

Stanza IV

Mounting evidence that the season is ill. In I and II, a real, if limited and withered, excellence; in III, pretense of excellence; now in IV, a corruption of human nature itself. A false man who falsifies what he deals in; who turns the gear of honest labor into objets d'art. The fisherman's corks, garish with paint, hang in their fishnet; the cobbler's bench, complete with useless awl and given an unnaturally high finish, will serve as coffee table or "conversation-piece" for some collector. In III, the pleasure craft had been degraded by being put into service. Here the reverse: the workman's tools have became gewgaws. But the decorator's work is unfruitful in another sense too: it doesn't pay. Having falsified objects, he is willing to falsify his nature by selling himself into a marriage he can scarcely have the heart for.

This stanza, with its ironic feminine rhyme in lines 1 and 6, is the most regular yet. Rhythm, at first uncertain, moves here with assurance, with even a derisive sing-song in its regularity. A sense too of excessive neatness, emphasized by the rhetorical word-order of line 4. After this line the tone falls back into plainness, in the last line particularly, with its flat *a*'s after the richer *or*'s and *aw*'s that preceded. Again the stanza is mispunctuated: lines 3 and 5 should close with semicolons. But expressiveness overrides convention: the running together of 3 and 4 dramatizes the orange jumble, the silly muchness; the comma after 5 lets the last line come blurted out.

The poet has given us a threefold classification of twisted souls: the self-centered isolation of the old woman, destructive rather than charitable; the hollowness or fraud of the millionaire; and now, and in V and VI, disordered love. Fanciers of literary parallels will recall that the most famous cataloguer of transgressions has also given us threefold divisions in his *Inferno* and *Purgatorio*. Since "Skunk Hour" is, among other things, a study of the Puritan syndrome, we may wonder if the modern poet has not deliberately inverted Dante's hierarchy of evil—assuming there is, as there should be, an order of climax here. Would not Dante have found the perverted love of the homosexual (cf. Brunetto Latini) and the excessive love of the carnal (cf. Paolo and Francesca) less censurable than selfishness, hollowness, and fraud? It is Puritanical to find the sins of the body more heinous than those of the spirit—hence the careless lovers,

On Robert Lowell's "Skunk Hour"

whose plight in hell moved Dante to a very distraction of pity and sympathy (*"pietà mi giunse, e fui quasi smarrito"*), moves the present beholder to his murderous and suicidal range (in VI).

Stanza V

In V and VI, an emotional crisis of the protagonist, prepared by the data of I–IV and now precipitated by his recognition that the illness is not only in others or in the season, but in himself. Up to now, he has been merely the observer, fairly dispassionate, through whose eyes and whose voice we have been shown the world of the poem. Abruptly, he becomes not only perceiver but participant; he implicates himself as deeply as he does the millionaire or the decorator. It would be wrong to think of this "I" as the poet speaking; what speaks is as much a character as the others. Or even more, for this is the character the poem is really about; its action is the drama within the soul of a Puritan Everyman who is combined censor and voyeur, the God and Satan of his world.

The action moves briefly into a past tense, but its urgency soon swings it back to the vivid present. The time reference, which prepares us for a greater immediacy of experience, is also a curious echo. One of the great poems of western culture begins *"en una noche oscura . . . ,"* "One dark night . . ." How consciously the American poet echoes the *Noche oscura* of St. John of the Cross we cannot be sure; but we do know that the Muse of the Unconscious—perhaps the only Muse—caught the echo and permitted it. St. John's poem, also in the first person, describes how a girl (*el alma*) steals forth one dark night for an ecstatic meeting with her Lover:

> I gave all I own,
> gave all, in air from the cedars softly blown.
>
> All, in wind from the wall
> as my hand in his hair moved lovingly at play.
> He let soft fingers fall
> and I swooned dead away
> wounded: all senses in oblivion lay.
>
> Quite out of self suspended—
> my forehead on the lover's own reclined.

On Robert Lowell's "Skunk Hour"

> And that way the world ended
>   with all my cares untwined
> among the lilies falling and out of mind.*

Such sweetness of passionate self-surrender is what the Puritan on his island psyche can never manage; his own dark night is a ghastly burlesque of the Spanish adventure, though he too finds release and reconciliation, among the skunks if not among the lilies.

The protagonist, with his morbid curiosity, goes forth. Fascinated by a carefree indulgence he despises, he rages at it and at himself. The manufacturer's name for his "two-door" model identifies the driver ironically with the pageantries of the past. His car goes up the "hill's skull"—again the misplaced genitive is a deliberate ugliness. Hill . . . Skull . . . as the words rub together we realize that the most famous hill in our tradition was named for a skull: Calvary, from the Latin *calvaria*. The experience, then, is some kind of emotional crucifixion for the speaker? He goes as voyeur, but his ambivalence refuses to let him contemplate, even in imagination, the lovers. His attention instead is displaced to the "love-cars" which "lay together." Love is debased to the mechanical, as in the seduction scene of *The Waste Land*. Headlights are dimmed, in token of light rejected. The cars are seen as ships—the ship image is already, through the yawl, a something bought and sold. "Hull to hull" sustains the ship imagery, contrasts "skull" and "hull" (car or flesh), and also suggests "hull" as husk, a container that contains only hollowness. Our lovers' lane is near a cemetery, another place of skulls. Moralists are fond of mingling images of the body alive and pleasure-loving, with the body dead and decayed, as in Hamlet's words to the skull: "Now get you to my lady's chamber, and tell her, let her paint an inch thick, to this favor she must come." The last line of the stanza again goes off on an abrupt tangent. The mind, attracted by what it condemns, seeing the careless lovers in terms of coupling mechanisms, is no less corrupt than what it contemplates. Yet it is still sound enough to perceive and agonize over a dilemma from which the only escapes are madness and suicide. "My mind's not right." For most of us, the line will carry Shakespearean reminiscences, perhaps of Lear's "I fear I am not in my perfect mind." But more particularly echoes of Hamlet, whose derange-

---

* From *The Poems of St. John of the Cross* (Grove Press, 1959).

ment also had its origin in sexual shock: he saw his very home "a couch for luxury and damnèd incest." The madness of young Ophelia and old Lear was sex-obsessed.

Technically, two things are interesting. The most unsettling experiences of the poem are expressed in mellifluous liquids. As if the attraction, forbidden disclosure in the imagery, had come out caressingly in the sound. And nowhere before has there been such recourse to metaphor. Indeed, there has been almost none. Successful metaphor, like an elctrical discharge, comes from emotions at high enough tension to leap considerable distances—as they do in this stanza.

Stanza VI

"Careless Love," which the goatlike metal voice is bleating, is about seduction, pregnancy, desertion, violence:

When I wore my apron low . . .
You'd follow me through rain and snow.

Now my apron strings won't pin . . .
You pass my door and won't come in.

Now you see what careless love will do . . .
Make you kill yourself and your sweetheart too.

A theme-song and dirge, then, for the careless lovers in their cars. (The capital L of "Love," if deliberate, would seem to imply a deity heedless if not evil— deeper reasons for dismay.) Upon hearing the song, the protagonist's mind projects a schizophrenic monster of its own: an ill-spirit in the flesh itself. The hyphen hypostatizes the illness, makes it a morbid presence to be exorcised, by killing if necessary. This waking nightmare has brought the protagonist to the verge of murderous violence—his awareness of this, his endurance in that awareness, is his hell. The phantom sobbing in the blood is not mere ghost-lore; it has a basis if we remember that "spirit" means breath and that the red blood-cells carry breath. It is this breath, this life, which the sufferer, in his self-hatred, imagines himself strangling. "I myself am hell"—these words are spoken by Lucifer in Book IV of *Paradise Lost* as he makes his way toward the Garden of Eden for his "dire attempt" on Adam and Eve:

"Mee miserable! which way shall I flie
Infinite wrauth, and infinite despaire?
Which way I flie is Hell; my self am Hell;
And in the lowest deep a lower deep
Still threatening to devour me op'ns wide,
To which the Hell I suffer seems a Heav'n."

"In the lowest deep a lower deep"—the escape which Hamlet pondered in his torment. "Nobody's here" is the wish-fulfillment of the self-loathing, self-destructive soul—but here too we may have the Muse of the Unconscious at work. If V opens with an echo of the *Noche oscura*, VI may close with another echo. The fourth stanza of St. John's poem ends: *"en parte donde nadie parecía*—"where nobody appeared." Not only the idea but its positioning hint a relationship. In the *Noche oscura* the emptiness is only apparent:

where there waited one
I knew—how well I knew!—
in a place where no one was in view.

In "Skunk Hour" there is a saving presence also, not so much the little animals who now appear as a spirit of resolution in the suffering soul itself.

Broken syntax expresses the distraction. The 2-beat norm hurries the first line: "a car rádio bleáts"—the words come with a silly insistence after the grave line preceding them. They come also with a dissonant half-rhyme—followed by a further raucous dissonance in "throat." The emptiness of the last line gapes in the vacuous "hear"—"here." The only rhyme that rings out in this turbulence is "hell" in the strongly accented fifth line, a rhyme clinging also to the *el* of "myself."

Stanza VII

The only stanza run on from the preceding one without a sentence break is paradoxically the only one that opens with a sense of time elapsed. The observer has moved onward, progressed in place and state of mind. There must have been a tormented struggle between the distraction of V and VI and the health and quiet breathing of VII and VIII. We are not shown this conflict, but we know where the victory lies: the destructive urges have been resisted; the victor, calm of mind as clear of eye, is looking outward at the mother skunk and her column of kittens. Actual skunks, and yet also a little string of metaphors moving down Main Street in the moonlight, which for more than one poet has meant the enchantment of the imagination. The crisis of the poem was on a dark night; the love cars had refused illumination; Blue Hill had been obscured. But the skunks appear in the softest and dreamiest of natural light—light with its many connotations of hope and truthfulness. Unlike the avid heiress, the millionaire living his lie, the decorator perverting what he touches, and the lewd pursuing the lewd, the skunks are engaged in a natural quest: the search for "a bite to eat." Most of the human types have been somehow furtive; the skunks go about their business openly, "determination's totem" and "noble little warriors," as Marianne Moore described them in "The Wood-Weasel." Their vigor stiffens the verse: this is the only stanza with internal couplets, aligned as smartly as the marching columns. They march on their "soles"—at least one classic dream-interpretation has "sole" for "soul"; poets, like dreamers and writers of hiero-glyphs, respect the pun. A trochee in the iambic movement brings the weight down heavily on "soles." The next line is a series of solemn spondees with four long *i*'s, our most vibrant vowel sound, brightening the white stripes and lighting the eyes with fire, as if they were inspired by the mystical moon. In contrast with this natural vitality, the church has only its "chalk-dry and spar spire," chalky as death, or the dusty controversies that divided Trinitarian from Unitarian. The thinness of the spire and of the doctrine it stands for is mocked by the harsh jingle of "spar spire."

Stanza VIII

The image of the mother skunk and her young contrasts with the sterile human types seen earlier. Nonchalant but earnest, oblivious of all but her mission and her young—so she appears in the longest line of the poem, itself indifferent to the obligations of meter. The young skunks move in a "column," with almost institutional stability. But a real stability, unlike that of the "spar spire." Obstinate virtue, indomitable confidence—these come out of the final image; the skunk, disdainful of attack, drops her menacing tail, airily beautiful as ostrich plumes. Her solidity bulks in the muscular non-Latin vocabulary: jab, wedge, sour, scare. Some interpreters might relate the wedge and cup of these lines to the Lance and Cup of Grail legends—images that Miss Weston says are "sex symbols . . . originally 'Fertility' emblems . . . employed in a ritual designed to promote, or restore, the activity of the reproductive energies of Nature." We cannot insist this is "meant," but we are not bumbling in wrong directions if it occurs to us, for the "wood-pussy," sturdy head in the garbage, is certainly a rank, rich, fertile, unashamed physical essence, and, as such, enjoys the benediction of the moon. Meanwhile, the protagonist stands on top of his steps, breathing the rich air. The struggle he has been through, which may well have taken longer than one symbolic night, had brought him to some verge of turbulence. But, in the drama we did not see, he has mastered the vertigo, and (again using a dream-technique) sees himself standing "on top of" something arduous. In VI, his spirit was threatened with strangulation; now it is breathing easily an air rich with the musk of an animality not lewd and furtive, like that which so unsettled him, but frank and confident. Release is felt even in structure: after the strain and constriction of earlier stanzas, the last two move fluently to the close.

But what, basically, is the poem saying? Surely nothing so banal as that people are corrupt but skunks are noble. The greater the poet—one might hazard —the less interested in animals: the great poets, after all, are out for bigger game. No, the poem is not about skunks; it is a human drama, a sort of *Hamlet* or *Lear* in miniature. Shakespeare's heroes were shaken by a disillusionment that plunged them into a nausea of world-weariness, world-abhorrence. Each agonized to a kind of serenity, a kind of reconciliation, if only at the moment of death. "Skunk Hour" is about a similar ordeal. The protagonist, already disillusioned with humanity, finds himself, one dark night, involved in deepest horror. Somehow— and how could we be shown the process in so short a poem?—he struggles through. A strange sort of reconciliation, this amid the skunks—but a restoration of balance none the less. In the struggle he seems to have discovered that if pretense and meanness exist, so do candor and courage; he comes down from his hill's skull prepared to admit these qualities, looking for an image for them, as we do in dreams. And if, by a ruse of displacement, he acknowledges them in animals rather than in man, it may be because the earlier aloofness, the earlier suspicion, have not had time to wear away. One does not have to look far to find a man as brave as skunks are, a mother as maternal as they. It is certain qualities (they are human qualities) he has come to respect and is looking for; otherwise no number of wood creatures could have dragged him from his slough of despond. Whatever is received, say the Schoolmen, is received according to the manner of the receiver. More than that: we see what we seek to see. Without his change of mood, the protagonist might have seen the skunks quite differently:

> Flat-footed skunks that prowl
> In the lewd moon to stuff their gut;
> Up Main Street, stinking-proud, they strut,
> Little eyes reddened, jailbird stripes . . .

Just as, with more compassion, he might have seen a pathetic courage in the failing millionaire (as E. A. Robinson did in that type) or in the decorator with his desperate problem. But the skunks have served their purpose in triggering the release he was ready for.

The little animals have close relatives in modern poetry: the *"dos lindas comadrejas"* (two pretty weasels) in one of the greatest poems of the century, Antonio Machado's *"A orillas del Duero."* Largely in terms of an allegorized landscape, Machado had been deploring the degeneracy and inertia of his homeland, when suddenly the two weasels (which in my translation turn to mink) appear —lively, interested, and committed children of the earth. Church bells (from a spar spire) are heard and

> Now gather for their rosary-beads the grannies all in black—.
> Suddenly two lissom mink glitter from the rock,
> Look at me with jewel eyes, flash away, and come
> Back at once, so interested!*

Machado's poem ends less reassuringly than ours, because his eye turns sadly back to a darkening country and an empty road, whereas the final image in "Skunk Hour" is one of sturdy triumph.

* From *Knowledge of the Evening* (Rutgers University Press, 1960).

JOHN BERRYMAN

Despondency and Madness

A title opaque and violent. Since it throws, at once, little or no light on the poem, we inquire whether the poem throws any light on it, and are under way. Our occasion is the approach of a crisis of mental disorder for the "I" of the poem—presumably one leading to the hospitalization, or hospitalizations, spoken of else-where in the volume, *Life Studies*, where it stands last. Mr. Lowell's recent poems, many of them, are as personal, autobiographical, as his earlier poems were hieratic; and it is certain that we are not dealing here purely with invention and symbol. One thing critics not themselves writers of poetry occasionally forget is that poetry is composed by actual human beings, and tracts of it are very closely about them. When Shakespeare wrote "Two loves I have," reader, he was *not kidding.*

Back to the title then. The Hour of the Skunk, I suppose, would be one of the most unprepossessing times of the day, far less livable than the Hour of the Bear, say, or the (Chinese) Month of the Dog. Noon is held a luckless time for Sikhs. Up and down India, when anything goes wrong for a Sikh near midday, all nearby Hindus and Moslems have a ball. Skunk hour: the poet's Sikh noon. The skunk is a small, attractive black-and-white creature, affectionate and loyal when tamed I believe, but it suffers (or rather it does *not* suffer, being an ani-mal) from a bad reputation, owing to its capacity for stinking. (The poet, in the identification, knows; and suffers.) Cornered, it makes the cornerer wish he hadn't. Painful, in symbolization, is the fact that its sting, so to speak, can be drawn, its power of defending itself removed—as the poet can be made helpless by what is part of his strength: his strangeness, mental and emotional; the help-lessness of a man afraid of going mad is the analogue. The skunk is an outcast; this is the basis of the metaphor, and how a mental patient feels. I hate to call the associations complex, but they are, and with a poet so daring or offhand that he once arranged a masterly elegy around his literal translation of the gambling expression *"Rien ne va plus,"* we must take it. The skunk, its little weakness or weapon apart, is charming; cheer-up. But nobody likes; paranoia. It is not what it seems: the reality belies the benign appearance—as with the statesman For-restal who supervises American industry's brawl-for-contracts with scrupulous

99

On Robert Lowell's "Skunk Hour"

honor and kills himself, or the poet, brilliant, famous, appearing, who goes off his rocker. We like, in mature professional life, to know who we are; which may be on the point of becoming out of the question for the "I" of the poem.

If the topic seems to anyone theatrical, may I mention suicides: two of the three or four most important early Soviet poets, Essenin and Mayakovsky; while Hart Crane and Vachel Lindsay (and for that matter Sara Teasdale—writing really well toward the end) who destroyed themselves here were not our worst poets. Poets in odd ages have killed themselves or gone mad, Poe and Dylan Thomas as clearly as Swift, Chatterton, Smart, Beddoes, and many have written about it from inside and outside, from Cowper's posthumous "The Castaway" to Miss Bishop's wonderful "Visits to St. Elizabeth's" and Rilke's *"Das Lied des Idioten."* It is better not to feel so strongly:

> We poets in our youth begin in gladness,
> But thereof comes in the end despondency and madness.

Wordsworth once said that if he had written what he most deeply felt no reader could have borne it, Coleridge that he gave up original poetical composition (but the fine, bleak "Work Without Hope" is late) because he was unable to bear it. One poem does not edge into the terror but starts there and stays there: Jon Silkin's "Death of a Son." This you will find in the Hall-Simpson paperback anthology of recent verse, and it is as brave, and harrowing, as one might think a piece could be. But Lowell's subject is different from all these others'.

His target is the dreadful aura—in epileptic analogy—the coming-on, handled by Hölderlin in *"Hälfte des Lebens,"* which may be the deepest European poem on this unusual theme. You feel you're going too fast, spinning out of control; or too slow; there appears a rift, which will widen. You feel *too* good, or too bad. Difficult subject. Perhaps there is a quarter-inch of mordant humor, by the way, very like this author, in the title: dogs have their day, even the skunk has an hour, characteristic. An inverted celebration. Take the poet's arrangements in three parts, and one critical problem will be to determine how they culminate in the hallucinatory intensity of the seventh stanza. We have the opening stanzas (*praeparatio*), then statement—understatement ("My mind's not right"), then the skunks. One of the poem's desperate points is their *cyclical* approach, each night; as episodes of mental illness are feared to recur. The skunks too, can we wonder, replace him (they will survive as he goes or is taken off) as well as figure him. But we're getting too far ahead.

Very good poem, incidentally, and gets better, explored. Perhaps one of his absolutely best; early to say. Maybe the Faustus allusion is overdrawn. Who cares to hand grades to a writer who could first *make* the Ovid stanza in "Beyond the Alps" (I believe it appeared in the *Kenyon* version) and then delete it? The reader may not have come on this, so I put it in evidence.

I thought of Ovid, for in Caesar's eyes,
That Tomcat had the number of the Beast.
Where the young Turks are facing the red east
And the twice-stormed Crimean spit, he cries:
"Rome asked for poets. At her beck and call,
Came Lucan, Tacitus and Juvenal,
The black republicans who tore the teats
And bowels of the mother wolf to bits.
Beneath a psychopath's divining rod,
Deserts interred the Caesar-salvaged bog.
Imperial Tiber, O my yellow Dog,
Black earth by the Black Roman Sea, I lie
With the boy-crazy daughter of the God,
Il duce Augusto. I shall never die."

Mr. Lowell once told the present writer that the stanza took him a hundred hours; it is worth every second of the time, and may be read, despite its author, for as long as things not formular are read.

I hear the first four stanzas of "Skunk Hour" as a unit. Grandiose figures—the senile aristocrat, the summer millionaire—from the past, outworn, gone, or not gone: the theme of the first stanza is Survival—but survival how?—doting; anti-gainfully employed (second stanza, and the "eyesores" "let fall" are the first prefigurings of the paranoid aspect of the skunk-symbol), living in the past. Relevance?—for re-reading (all poems are built of course for re-reading, but this more than most): the poet is afraid of outliving himself, going away, like Hölderlin, Swift, Maupassant. Destructive second stanza, but queerly abstract and arbitrary, anachronistic; as for "privacy," in the modern world (so the underground thought goes) unattainable, hospital life is unspeakably public—one is available without will to doctors, nurses, even (usually) other patients. The sheep have things easy, so to speak, and the radio "bleats" to the untense satisfied lovers in stanza VI; no human responsibilities, any more than the skunks are to have. The poem makes use of the animal-morality tradition without quite belonging to it. "Spartan" I reserve. "Hermit" and "winter" make nearly standard associations with madness.

Note that we have first a true aristocrat, irresponsible ("heiress"—mental illness can be inherited), then a pure money-figure; an ominous declension. (L. L. Bean: I haven't seen a catalogue for years, some boys at my school in Connecticut had them; they were beyond Sears Roebuck and even Alex Taylor for fascination—compare Abercrombie & Fitch, if they put out a catalogue.) Somebody rooted, but off; somebody rootless, gone. Blue Hill I take to be Blue Hill, Maine, where I never saw foxes but don't doubt that they flourish. This is the poem's hard line. "A red fox stain covers Blue Hill." Even the syntax is ambiguous—the stain may be red, or it may merely be that red foxes stain with their numbers (a plague to farmers) Blue Hill. Is the sportsman accused of having shot foxes?—but this seems sentimental and improbable; or is the fox population said to have increased since he quit shooting foxes?—but this seems even more implausible. I can't feel the implied narrative is clear. Perhaps there is no implied narrative (but shouldn't there be, tied to the millionaire as the line is?) and we have a straight dream item: for the meaning is certainly to be found in the association backward to "Spartan." This is the boy who stole a fox which, hugged to him in public, ate his vitals, the stain spreading, until stoical he fell dead; clearly a figure for the poet, still unheard of, with his growing hidden wound. At this point "Blue Hill" becomes extra-geographical and macabre: the dying Spartan boy turning blue, the tall poet sad, "blue" (the use of a popular song presently makes this likely).

Now in a succinct modulation from blood (and courage) to pale "orange," appropriate to the "fairy," comes the decorator, to fix things up inside (as psychiatrists will try to do for the poet); miserable, though, things not going well. "Marry" is callous and fraudulent, a last resort. The three figures, on their descending scale, are fruitless. The useful put just to decoration (fishnet), deprived of function, looks on to the poet's fear. One will get, in the poem, no sense of his *doing* anything, only waiting, driving about, skunk-watching, sleepless. (In the opposite conversion, just before, the sporting being put to work, the yawl, I hear as the dominant affect: longing.) This is a late-summer poem, idle, apprehensive.

It's half over. Outworn, gone, queer; analogous figures, tangential all—the first *having been* central, the second having mattered to local revenue. The four stanzas are unemphatic, muted. But their quiet, insistent mustering of the *facts* of an extant world opens toward the danger of its being swept away, into delirium. I have seldom seen stanzas (and by this poet, composer of the Ovid stanza) so un-self-evident. He's holding his fire, let's say. Down-rhyme, casual, unlike earlier Lowell, suggests Miss Bishop's practice; to whom the poem is dedicated; though the heavy, fierce rhyming of "The Quaker Graveyard" will be admitted in the final stanzas. Money-wellness, however misused (compare Eliot's ruined millionaire, Adam, in the *Quartets*—the auctioning off of the boat does not suggest that this one is doing very well), seems important all through the three figures and winds up in a "rich" air, freedom, the poet's to lose. The "fairy," poor, is already sick with perversion.

Since, on the entrance of "I" in stanza V, he climbs a sort of Golgotha (Place of the Skull), I will observe that there is more Christian detail in the poem than might have been expected. There's the bishop (I see no assimilation here to Chekhov's overwhelming story, which however I haven't read for years), the Marlovian hell of stanza VI ("where we are in hell," as Mephistophilis says at line 554 of Tucker Brooke's criminal edition, and compare other texts in that corrupt play, which even Greg was unsatisfactory with), the Trinitarian Church, and even the interior decorator goes in for suspicious properties: a fishnet (Peter, but Peter was married), cobbling (but Christ is said—on the Synoptic evidence, see Guignebert's *Jesus*, p. 106—to have been a carpenter). The detail is not, I think, systematic, and serves the purpose of a kind of hopeless casting about for aid;—unavailable, as in Hemingway's "A Clean, Well-lighted Place," in *The Trial*, in *Waiting for Godot*, you name it. I should say that Lowell works rather in parable-form than in forms of allegory. There is no point-to-point correspondence, the details are free. The (hoped for?) rescue-figures are simply sinister and pathetic, the senile old lady who lets houses decay, the unhappy homosexual who would like to fix up their interiors. Who knows where the bishop is?

On Robert Lowell's "Skunk Hour"

In stanza V there is much more than: furtive love, furtive madness. But both come out loud and open in stanza VI, and the loss of the person, in its last line, leads to the oneiric vision of the skunks.

Their ceremonial line, for (their kind of) nourishment, may belong with the religious traces. They have taken over the world; the poet has a final instant of freedom at the start of the last stanza. "Moonstruck" and "ostrich" (I am lunatic, hidden—hidden?) then take over. We began with one mother (of a bishop) and wind up with another (of a column of little skunks) in a sort of greedy parody of the Eucharist; the ultimate help. Some of Lowell's early poems were savagely Marian. I would not call this poem at all friendly to Christianity, which appears to have failed the shelving (and to be shelved) man. We feed instead on garbage. The "cream" is sour. The last line equals: "I will, I *do* 'scare.'" It is man's right, foreseeing, to be frightened. But the stubbornness of the mother skunk, like that (merely in association) of the Spartan boy, make up a small counterpoise to the poem's terror.

We attend, so, to a sense of having been failed by the biological and mental and emotional (and religious) probabilities: not all, or most, have to feel this way; many can believe. There is a staving-off, with dramatization, of self-pity; an implied (at the end) confession of fear. I have a feeling that the poem may look better fifty years from now, even better. Snatching at war-terms irritates one, as of writers; Baudelaire hated "avant-garde"; but it takes moral courage, at least, to write in this poem's direction.

I must pause, briefly, to admire its administration of Time. In general for it Time narrows: a vista of decades, "The season's ill," *one* night, and so down to the skunk hour. But I notice two substantial exceptions to the method. The second stanza opens a longer vista still than the first, with "century." And the "Hour" is *nightly*, expanding again into a dreaded recurrence. Most real poets work in this way, but Lowell decidedly rather more than most. I will now admit that I cannot like "my ill-spirit sob in each blood cell"; the expression is just what it should not be, rhetorical, exterior, especially with "hear."

For convenience in exposition, with a poem so personal, I have been pretending that "I" is the poet, but of course the speaker can never be the actual writer, who is a person with an address, a Social Security number, debts, tastes, memories, expectations. Shakespeare says "Two loves I have": he does not say *only* two loves, and indeed he must have loved also his children, various friends, presumably his wife, his parents. The necessity for the artist of selection opens inevitably an abyss between his person and his persona. I only said that much poetry is "very closely about" the person. The persona looks across at the person and then sets about its own work. Lowell's careful avoidance, in "Skunk Hour," of the grand style he was still wielding in the Ovid stanza, for instance, makes the distinction material here. This mysterious "I" that poets deploy can certainly never be defined, but a good recent stab at characterization was Mr. Ransom's in an earlier one of these symposia, about Roethke: "The true self or soul or mind of the highly compounded authorial 'I' . . ." I would call it virtually certain that Lowell had in mind and at heart during this poem not only his own difficulties whatever they may be or have been but the personal disorders to which other poets of his age and place have been furiously subject.

Another question raised with acuteness by the poem is how far it is fair to take associations. A characteristic vice of modern criticism is taking them too far. One of Randall Jarrell's remarks sticks in my head: "as people ought to know, very complicated organizations are excessively rare in poetry." I am in ringing agreement. Hurrah. But whether the dictum applies to Lowell's poems, or to an onslaught against the Old Testament and the New Testament like Thomas's "A Refusal to Mourn . . . ," seems to me very doubtful; as I think Jarrell concedes in his handsome, better than handsome, studies of Lowell. No rules will help, naturally, but can we seek guideposts? Suppose we try two: (1) When there is something imperfectly narrative, imperfectly dramatic, which obstinately *needs accounting for,* we allow ourselves, as readers, more liberty of interpreting than otherwise; (2) Where accident and coincidence seem implausible, we stick by the textual and psychological (even depth-psychological) probabilities. Both signs point to a connection of "Spartan" and "fox stain," though fifteen lines separate them. I have several times gone too far here, deliberately, in order to repudiate my (non-) findings. But I think we must allow, with some poets, for broad and complex areas of suggestion; and I would propose a third guidepost: (3) Whatever relates, however uncertainly, to the *ruling theme* of the poem deserves the reader's intimate attention. Thus, in the fifth stanza, the fact of its being a *dark* night may suggest in our tradition spiritual despair (St. John of the Cross), and the desolate "hull to hull" may look back to the "Nautilus," adventurous, submerged; or they may not. I have made no attempt to exhaust the poem. If we were a little longer civilized here, the poet would plainly be declared, in Japanese fashion, a National Cultural Asset, and exempted from coarse analyses of his subtle, strong, terrible poems.

ROBERT LOWELL

I. The Meaning

The author of a poem is not necessarily the ideal person to explain its meaning. He is as liable as anyone else to muddle, dishonesty and reticence. Nor is it his purpose to provide a peg for a prose essay. Meaning varies in importance from poem to poem, and from style to style, but always it is only a strand and an element in the brute flow of composition. Other elements are pictures that please or thrill for themselves, phrases that ring for their music or carry some buried suggestion. For all this the author is an opportunist, throwing whatever comes to hand into his feeling for start, continuity, contrast, climax, and completion. It is imbecile for him not to know his intentions, and unsophisticated for him to know too explicitly and fully.

Three papers by three poets on another's poem! Perhaps they should be considered as short stories and variants on my original. I shall comment on them later; here, I only want to say that I learned much from them. Very little of what I had in mind is untouched on; much that never occurred to me has been granted me. What I didn't intend often seems now at least as valid as what I did. My complaint is not that I am misunderstood, but that I am overunderstood. I am seen through.

I am not sure whether I can distinguish between intention and interpretation. I think this is what I more or less intended. The first four stanzas are meant to give a dawdling more or less amiable picture of a declining Maine sea town. I move from the ocean inland. Sterility howls through the scenery, but I try to give a tone of tolerance, humor, and randomness to the sad prospect. The composition drifts, its direction sinks out of sight into the casual, chancy arrangements of nature and decay. Then all comes alive in stanzas V and VI. This is the dark night. I hoped my readers would remember John of the Cross's poem. My night is not gracious, but secular, puritan, and agnostical. An Existentialist night. Somewhere in my mind was a passage from Sartre or Camus about reaching some point of final darkness where the one free act is suicide. Out of this comes the march and affirmation, an ambiguous one, of my skunks in the last two stanzas. The skunks are both quixotic and barbarously absurd, hence the tone of amusement and defiance. "Skunk Hour" is not entirely independent, but the anchor poem in its sequence.

II. How the Poem Was Written

What I can describe and what no one else can describe are the circumstances of my poem's composition. I shan't reveal private secrets. John Berryman's pathological chart comes frighteningly close to the actual event. When I first read his paper, I kept saying to myself, "Why he is naming the very things I wanted to keep out of my poem." In the end, I had to admit that Berryman had hit a bull's-eye, and often illuminated matters more searchingly and boldly than I could have wished. Is his account true? I cannot decide, the truth here depends on what psychologists and philosophers one accepts. Berryman comes too close for comfort.

"Skunk Hour" was begun in mid-August, 1957, and finished about a month later. In March of the same year, I had been giving readings on the West Coast, often reading six days a week and sometimes twice on a single day. I was in San Francisco, the era and setting of Allen Ginsberg, and all about very modest poets were waking up prophets. I became sorely aware of how few poems I had written, and that these few had been finished at the latest three or four years earlier. Their style seemed distant, symbol-ridden and willfully difficult. I began to paraphrase my Latin quotations, and to add extra syllables to a line to make it clearer and more colloquial. I felt my old poems hid what they were really about, and many times offered a stiff, humorless and even impenetrable surface. I am no convert to the "beats." I know well too that the best poems are not necessarily poems that read aloud. Many of the greatest poems can only be read to one's self, for inspiration is no substitute for humor, shock, narrative and a hypnotic voice, the four musts for oral performance. Still, my own poems seemed like prehistoric monsters dragged down into the bog and death by their ponderous armor. I was reciting what I no longer felt. What influenced me more than San Francisco and reading aloud was that for some time I had been writing prose. I felt that the best style for poetry was none of the many poetic styles in English, but something like the prose of Chekhov or Flaubert.

When I returned to my home, I began writing lines in a new style. No poem, however, got finished and soon I left off and tried to forget the whole headache. Suddenly, in August, I was struck by the sadness of writing nothing, and having nothing to write, of having, at least, no language. When I began writing "Skunk Hour," I felt that most of what I knew about writing was a hindrance.

The dedication is to Elizabeth Bishop, because re-reading her suggested a way of breaking through the shell of my old manner. Her rhythms, idiom, images, and stanza structure seemed to belong to a later century. "Skunk Hour" is modeled on Miss Bishop's "The Armadillo," a much better poem and one I had heard her read and had later carried around with me. Both "Skunk Hour" and "The Armadillo" use short line stanzas, start with drifting description and end with a single animal.

This was the main source. My others were Hölderlin's *"Brod und Wein,"* particularly the moon lines:

> *Sieh! und das Schattenbild unserer Erde, der Mond,*
> *kommet geheim nun auch; die Schwärmerische, die Nacht kommt*
> *vohl mit Sternen und wohl wenig bekummert um uns,*

and so forth. I put this in long straggling lines and then added touches of Maine scenery, till I saw I was getting nowhere. Another source, probably undetectable now, was Annette von Droste-Hülshoff's *"Am letzten Tage des Jahres."* She too uses a six-line stanza with short lines. Her second stanza is as follows:

> *'s ist tiefe Nacht!*
> *Ob wohl ein Auge offen noch?*
> *In diesen Mauern ruttelt dein*
> *Verrinnen, Zeit! Mir schaudert; doch*
> *Es will die letzte Stunde sein*
> *Einsam durchwacht.*
>
> *Geschehen all*

Here and elsewhere, my poem and the German poem have the same shudders and situation.

"Skunk Hour" was written backwards, first the last two stanzas, I think, and then the next to last two. Anyway, there was a time when I had the last four stanzas much as they now are and nothing before them. I found the bleak personal violence repellent. All was too close, though watching the lovers was not mine, but from an anecdote about Walt Whitman in his old age. I began to feel that real poetry came, not from fierce confessions, but from something almost meaningless but imagined. I was haunted by an image of a blue china doorknob. I never used the doorknob, or knew what it meant, yet somehow it started the current of images in my opening stanzas. They were written in reverse order, and at last gave my poem an earth to stand on, and space to breathe.

III. The Critics

I don't think I intended either the Spartan boy holding the fox or Satan's feeling of sexual deprivation, while he watched Adam and Eve in the Garden. I may have, but I don't remember. The red fox stain was merely meant to describe the rusty reddish color of autumn on Blue Hill, a Maine mountain near where we were living. I had seen foxes playing on the road one night, and I think the words have sinister and askew suggestions.

I can't imagine anything more thorough than Nims's stanza-by-stanza exposition. Almost all of it is to the point. I get a feeling of going on a familiar journey, but with another author and another sensibility. This feeling is still stronger when I read Wilbur's essay. Sometimes he and I are named as belonging to the same school, what *Time* Magazine calls "the couth poets." Sometimes we are set in battle against one another. I have no idea which, if either, is true. Certainly, we both in different ways owe much to the teaching and practice of John Crowe Ransom. Certainly, his essay embodies and enhances my poem. With Berryman too, I go on a strange journey! Thank God, we both come out clinging to spars, enough floating matter to save us, though faithless.

W. D. SNODGRASS

LEONIE ADAMS

MURIEL RUKEYSER

JOHN CROWE RANSOM

On JOHN CROWE RANSOM'S

"*Master's in the Garden Again*"

John Crowe Ransom

MASTER'S IN THE GARDEN AGAIN

To the memory of Thomas Hardy

i

Evening comes early, and soon discovers
Exchange between these conjugate lovers.

"Conrad! dear man, surprise! aren't you bold
To be sitting so late in your sodden garden?"

"Woman! intrusion! does this promise well?
I'm nursing my knees, they are not very cold.
Have you known the fall of a year when it fell?
Indeed it's a garden, but if you will pardon,
The health of a garden is reason's burden."

"Conrad! your feet are dripping in muck,
The neuralgia will settle in your own neck,
And whose health is it that catches an asthma?
Come in from foul weather for pity's sake!"

"No," says the thinker. "Concede. I am here,
Keeping guard of my garden and minding miasma.
You're lonely, my loony? Your house is up there.
Go and wait. If you won't, I'll go jump in the lake."

ii

And the master's back has not uncurved
Nor the autumn's blow for an instant swerved.

Autumn days in our section
Are the most used-up thing on earth
(Or in the waters under the earth)
Having no more color nor predilection
Than cornstalks too wet for the fire
And black leaves pitched onto the byre.

The show is of death. There is no defection.

iii

He will play out his mood before he takes food.

By the bob of the Power the dark skies lower,
By the bite of Its frost the children were lost,
Who harmed no one where they shone in the sun,
But the valiant heart knows a better part
Than to do with an "O did It lay them low,
But we're a poor sinner just going to dinner."

See the tell-tale art of the champion heart.

Here's temple and brow, which frown like the law.
If the arm lies low, yet the rage looks high.
The accusing eye? that's a fierce round O.
The offense was raw, says the fix in the jaw.
We'll raise a rare row! we'll heave a brave blow!

A pantomime blow, if it damns him to do,
A yell mumming too. But it's gay garden now,
Play sweeter than pray, that the darkened be gay.

W. D. SNODGRASS

Master's in the Verse Patch Again

Our poets have a way of blooming late, often after a long sterile period. We have exciting enough early works, splendid last works, but little work of maturity—precisely that period when we might have expected the greatest work. In their middle years our poets often cannot write at all, or as a substitute for some wisdom we cannot find, will flee to theorizing, philosophy and literary dogmatism. Ofter, only the approach of death can shock us from the trance of our life; we come to terms with *it* more courageously. The artistic problems stem from the problem with love and passion.

The problem is a problem: only a fool would think he knew an answer. How could one be a first-rate artist without offending, deeply, those he most loves? First, by the mere offense of being first-rate. That, with the envy it arouses, quite commonly costs one those dearest to him. All differences, inequalities, seem unjust and odious. We have been encouraged to be feminine or childish, while our women have been encouraged to compete and to dominate. But like most executives, they dominate not through ability, but through will—a quality often rising from envy at what one takes for a *lack* of ability in one's self. Every sign of ability in others will be a very real injury. And that injury is likely to be all the greater coming from an artist, since his life involves keeping open the passions, which may be neither humane nor loyal. Meantime, the violence and faithlessness of our passions are only likely to be increased by our desire to be dominated and diminished, our childishness, which resents any loved one and will use its own faithlessness as a subtle and civilized weapon.

Not that many of us would care to reinstate the *droit de seigneur,* or to go back to an age when the male was valued for a brute physical force which we abhor. Yet it certainly seems that we have carried horrid democracy a bit far. Since the great revolutions of the nineteenth century—the Industrial Revolution and the artistic and intellectual revolutions which accompanied it—there has been no masculine, ordering force worth fighting against. In the arts, as in society, we see aimless revolt followed by aimless revolt. After the women went, then the children; the dogs appear to have their revolt fairly well under way; the vegetables are likely next. Nothing is really produced, since these rebellions are directed against powers which do not exist, and carried out by those who are lacking in either ability or purpose. We have half-men, half-women, half-adults, half-children, and nothing first rate anywhere. It is not to be expected that the poets, any more than the rest of us, could escape the problem.

Cruel as this sounds, Hardy was probably the luckiest—his wife died while he had many years to lament, to record the fierce subtleties of their marital techniques, to learn how much she *had* meant, but marry his secretary and go on with his poems. Tactless and proud as she was, his first wife had perhaps found a way to sacrifice herself into those poems so far greater (as she must really have known) than any she could herself write—a way to escape from, yet aid, a work too great to live with. This suggests both a nobility and a despair quite beyond anything Hardy credited her with, and quite beyond any reasonable demand.

Frost outlived his wife, yet for all his brilliance, was never able to make the reappraisal. Perhaps the struggle had gone too far, left too much wreckage and guilt. His earlier poems are the glory of our period—yet he never fulfilled their promise. If Cummings' feelings had reached their fullest at 25, Frost's had reached theirs at 40. When he said "How awful, yet I must . . ." he was a poet; when he says "I must, since it's right . . ." he is only a danger.

Williams truly loved his wife, yet spent years trying to injure her. Then, however, he could come back to her. Few have had his magnanimity which could forgive even someone he had so deeply wounded. After years of sterile literary dogmatism, it is to his wife that he comes back in his last great poem, "Of Asphodel"—the flower that tells of his enduring love.

To Stevens, love must have been only another expensive ornament, like philosophy or aesthetic theory, to decorate an essentially meaningless world, another wreathe for the abyss. In his old age, after *his* years of literary philosophizing, he comes back to no particular woman, but only to a "heavenly desired . . . sleek among the tintinnabula" who alone could offset the grayness of age and the shadow of trees like wrecked umbrellas. He returns to no garden, but to a greenhouse—now battered and in need of paint.

Thomas was perhaps the unluckiest, or the weakest. He had no middle age, much less whatever wisdom it might offer. He died recording the loveless lusts we associate with adolescence, the pure-sex-in-the-pants which appeals so to those with pure-sex-in-the-head. He does not lament his own age and loss, but his father's; he leaves his wife as ruined victor, to write what she can.

In Ransom we see something different from any of these—a man who has made a deep commitment and firmly stood by it, at whatever price. Whether we can be glad is beside the point. We must hold our peace before great dedication and the great loss that always may mean. There are gains, too—we have, now, a new poem just when we had given up hope for it. And it is a thoroughly remarkable poem—one that not only records this problem of love and creativity but, in that very act, partially transcends it.

Hermann Broch (in his Introduction to Rachel Bespaloff's book *On the Iliad*) defines the style of old age as an *abstractism* which impoverishes its vocabulary in order to enrich its syntactical relationships. It no longer collects the brilliant atoms of "world-content," but rather expresses its relationships, its structure. Thus, though it tends to share the scientist's concern for abstract universal structure, its productions come closer to the abstractism of myth.

This seems apt, and a proper distinction between this and Ransom's earlier poems. This is a poem of relationships; it, as a result, invites commentary as the earlier poems never did. Those first poems quite defeat criticism—one can only point to them, with perhaps a few sentences of explication, and say, "See? He's done it again!"

Even this poem's initial technical problem is one of relationships—how to use a passage from the earlier "Conrad in Twilight," now that that poem's situation has come to have more meaning with the passage of time:

Autumn days in our section
Are the most used-up thing on earth
(Or in the waters under the earth)
Having no more color nor predilection
Than cornstalks too wet for the fire,
A ribbon rotting on the byre,
A man's face as weathered as straw
By the summer's flare and winter's flaw.

This, the ending of the original poem, was never quite satisfactory. In itself it is remarkable—few poets could have handled dactyls (or anapests) so fluently, placing extra accents so skillfully to avoid the deadly dactylic bounce. But coming at the end of "Conrad in Twilight," a light and breezy poem, and sinking it into a kind of depression and flat despair, the passage was shocking and never quite right.

Ransom's answer now is not to lessen the contrasts, but rather to make them more extreme. He surrounds his original death-dull passage with two passages of the gayest and brightest sights and sounds. He even marks the sections off with numbers so that we cannot miss the contrast. It is a little like the classical sonata form: the first section is a light and high-comical scolding match between husband and wife; the second, the more serious passage already quoted, which raises the spectre of death impinging on Conrad; the last section, tonally like the first, but with an underlying grimness, a dramatization of that "show" which "is of death." The last section is a little like one of those Mahler scherzi where everything is so splendidly gay but for that *memento mori,* that one sour clarinet; or like children in their Hallowe'en costumes—gay and death-haunted, sacrificial.

Not that there is no attention to vocabulary and detail in the poem. Who else could have written that third line? After two regular dactylic lines to set the scene and tone, enter the wife:

"Conrad! dear man, surprise! aren't you bold . . ."

So metrically canny, yet so humanly alive! There is so much wife in that line, one can hardly stand it. It is as if a whole flock of bright birds had burst into the room, quarreling for territories. Fluttering and fluting, affectionate and affected, maddeningly charming, the pitches rise, fall, slide, state incredible themes.

And once begun, this jocular brilliance never leaves the poem. Again, the husband's half-joking gruffness:

"Woman! intrusion! does this promise well?"

Or the continual play of echoes and sound effects: "sodden . . . garden . . . pardon . . . burden . . . guard of my garden." Or the constant hovering on the brink of absurd and delicious puns: "asthma . . . miasma."

Yet these local pleasures are not like the brilliance of vocabulary in Ransom's earlier poems. They are not meant to define this atom of experience, but to conflict with it. They must provide a gaiety to balance the tragic grimness of the

On John Crowe Ransom's "Master's in the Garden Again"

poem's situation and theme, yet must never become too attractive in themselves.

The only thing in the poem much reminiscent of the earlier vocabulary is in the Latinism of "conjugate lovers," and I'm not sure but what that is a mistake. For me, at least, "'eldering lovers'" which one of the intermediate versions had in that place, is better. Most of Ransom's other revisions have tended to cut down the brilliance of the individual line so that the archetypical structure of the whole poem could more fully be realized. Consider these lines with their counterparts in the printed poem:

> Woman! intrusion! is this done well?
> . . . .
> Conrad, your feet are dipping in muck,
> . . . .
> Come in to your ever and loving pipe
> . . . .
> So, my loony and only, my wanton and wife,
> You may take yourself off, a while, my dear.

It must not have been easy to give those up. Yet, here again, the gains are clear.

Consider the title: "Master's in the Garden Again." Master? What does not that mean? Of course, it's something a servant might say about the head of the household as she runs to report to her real master—that is, her mistress. Therein, one of the ironies. The master himself recognizes that he is scarcely master of the house:

> You're lonely, my loony? Your house is up there.

Again, by a fine ambiguity, "Master" is just the term we might apply to a child in the family. "The Master, Conrad" is someone very different from "Master Conrad." In his rage, the old man is less like Oedipus or Lear than like a wilful child intent on his play, refusing his mother's demands that he wear rubbers, that he keep warm and dry, that he eat his meals. Just as a child may feel that the only way to preserve its identity against a devouring mother is to refuse to eat. "No!—that proves I'm alive! I'll finish my game." And typically, in his helplessness, his only weapon against the woman is to damage himself: to stay out in the cold longer, or finally to throw himself in the lake.

On John Crowe Ransom's "Master's in the Garden Again"

Then, she'll be sorry. No question but that she would; or that *he* would be sorry if she didn't come down and ask him to come in. For she must be like the constantly importunate, constantly rejected mother—which is both a cause and an effect of his helpless rage. True, in one sense, Conrad is like an Old Testament prophet, a Lear, an Oedipus, raging against those forces which he has come to resemble and which will destroy him. In this sense, too, he is the Master. But we must first see him as an old man who plays the role of a child, who, in turn, plays the role of Lear or Oedipus.

The game in which he plays that role, of course, is Art. For he must also be seen as the master artist, the Maestro. If his "show is of death" yet the management of that show is "reason's burden." Conrad is "the thinker" on guard against "miasma" and his own "loony." And it is precisely in this area that his lady attacks him—suggesting that he hasn't sense enough to come in out of the damp.

Yet, for all its concern with reason, the poem is very much more about passion. In the first version of the poem, the garden was described as "the ghost of a Forest of Arden." Good enough: not only the place of nature and exile from human unkindliness,

> Here feel we but the penalty of Adam,
> The season's difference; as, the icy fang
> And churlish chiding of the winter's wind

but also the place where the young lovers meet and miss and make love. In the new poem, however, such predilections have been transformed almost entirely into something less threatening—rage. For the poem could scarcely have been written until that transformation was possible. Rage is more easily turned back against the self, or turned against those one sees as all-powerful or impregnable. Neither could the poem be written until the two antagonistic forces, death and woman, could be identified. One of these forces is introduced in each of the first two sections; in the last section, Conrad moves to action, but only because he can identify these two forces. This is clearest in

> By the bob of the Power the dark skies lower,
> By the bite of Its frost the children were lost.

As a Limiting Power upon Life, woman and death are one. Just as it bobs, so she bobs down from her house, lowering, and calling her children home. Naughty, they will play out their games—fierce and grotesque games—the games of Art and Prophecy—games which demonstrate the blankness of the world which has formed and controlled them. "The accusing eye? that's a fierce round O." And that eye, that rage, looks high—to her house or to the skies, to the Power which dwells there and has defeated the old man, laid his arm low, and now scolding affectionately, calls him home to a final surrender. This is only an inversion of our common tendency to see death as a mother, the grave as a womb.

Just as Oedipus' ultimate identity with his Fate is never seen in any surrender on his part, but rather in an implacable rage which shows him to be essentially like that implacable Fate and basically part of it, so here Conrad's refusal to enter the house, his insistence on acting out his self-directed rage and accusation, proclaim his essential oneness with the Powers. His temple and brow frown like the law; it is clear that his laws are woman and death. In that sense, there is no defection, all appearances to the contrary. If he, momentarily, refuses to come in, he will eventually go and be glad enough for the messenger's visit. It shows a constant, almost divine, concern for his well-being. And his rage shows, finally, his lack of freedom from her.

Stanley Kunitz recently reminded us of Goethe's dictum that all Art lies in Limit, reminding us himself, however, that the artist must always try those limits to the utmost. No doubt most of us accept too readily limits which comfort us emotionally, a world conformable to a childish demand for a universe much concerned with our welfare. Still, who would accept a world of open rage, of unlimited passion? If we are too childish to be Oedipus, we are also too compassionate. Though this dilemma has itself limited the size and scope of this poem, yet the poem has defined, at the same time, that dilemma—the gain and loss, the passion and compassion, those stools between which life occurs. This seems to me a triumph.

So, in the Garden of his Art, the Master plays out a late performance; one equally composed of protest and reconciliation. For if House and Garden are separated, both still stand. If Master and Woman will never be closer, they will never be farther. If the Gardens have been long shut, we villagers must know there have been sufficient reasons. Today, Master's in his verse patch again and his formal gardens are open to the public; who can be less than grateful?

LEONIE ADAMS

Conrad as Master

The poem with its broken spacings has not quite the look of a Ransom work. The opening couplet is his unmistakably, in its every inflection. Then, for me, with the abrupt third line the impression of divergence deepened (despite gathering echoes and the recognition of the splendid autumnal passage in Section II) and has survived a thorough reading and comparison of the poem with its prototype, "Conrad Sits in Twilight." From that earlier lyric, which remained unchanged from *Chills and Fever* to the 1948 Selection,* the present poem borrows its hero's proper name, details and certain phrases relating the sodden (there "mouldy") garden to his person and ailing years, most of Section II, and the theme of age confronting a show of death. Common to both is the first repercussion of the theme and tactic of the poems: to appear to treat Conrad's lingering in this confrontation as an exasperating folly.

Nevertheless one must end by considering "Master's in the Garden Again" not as a revision or enlarged version, but as another poem. Theme and hero have been simultaneously particularized and extended in figure, the garden has taken on a stronger metaphoric 'dimension. And nevertheless, "Conrad Sits in Twilight," even if the author chooses to discard it, will for a time haunt many readers' response to the new poem. At this reading I judge the latter to be the more interesting and elaborate of the two, and the more baffling. Ears tuned to them may miss in it the continuing felicities of tone in favorite Ransom poems, and it is to the relative disappearance of the centering voice (for the voice here is more variously and directly mimetic) that I attribute the new poem's peculiar open-endedness among so many which have been notable for controlling equivocations discreetly.

A voice speaks "Conrad Sits in Twilight" throughout and is one variant on the author's uses of such a controlling voice. For it would be a mistake to assume because we recognize this voice as "his" in its combination of personal rhythm, metric habits, and verbal sensibility, that it is identically employed in different poems. Mr. Ransom has said that he considers the dramatic monologue the *central* poetic form, and this is one of his critical dicta rather subtly related to his

* In Mr. Ransom's *Selected Poems* of 1948, the poem's title becomes simply "Conrad in Twilight." [Ed. note]

On John Crowe Ransom's "Master's in the Garden Again"

practice. He has not made the dramatic monologue in the usual sense his characteristic form. But the voice which speaks his poems is always crucial to their effects, and is only deviously the poet's own. Like the fictional point of view it is maneuvered, in its more contracted space, to lead us through a series of perspectives to the essential apprehension. These perspectives may suggest roles, attitudes of participants, may be only the inflections of the unsaid. Sometimes, as with the fictional device, the point of view becomes the real protagonist.

What we have in "Conrad Sits in Twilight" is someone ruminating the elderly Conrad's ruminatings (and situation) and enforcing their savor upon the reader. "Conrad, Conrad, aren't you old" it begins, "To be sitting so late in your mouldy garden?" and goes on with an odd suggestion of mimicking the accents of a proper and prudent scolding the old gentleman in; and then again of those same accents mingled with his own promptings (or temptations) to flee his misery where

> Chips on Conrad's hearth are blazing
> Slippers and pipe and tea are served,
> Butter and Toast, Conrad, are pleasing.

Or is all this the voice of rage and outrage at the flimsy intrusions of solace? The reader has not many clues to Conrad. He will suppose him to have been given to gallantry, though perhaps not much more than is common since the knees he "nurses" are here

> . . . too rheumy and cold
> To warm the wraith of a Forest of Arden

and there is a ribbon (rather incongruously) rotting on the byre of the last passage. The most direct statement of his situation follows on the opening quoted above, and is a telling one:

> And I think Conrad knows it well

says the voice, with an eery sardonic note. The voice that speaks this first portion (three stanzas) of the poem, though so versed in the matter, is an elusive one. The innocent reader may begin to read in a tone of tender chiding, and find he cannot keep it up; he is receding to a maximum distance of empathy. The strains of feeling meet in the last word of the third stanza:

On John Crowe Ransom's "Master's in the Garden Again"

Still Conrad's back is not uncurved
And here's an autumn on him *teasing*.

"Teasing" is odd for autumn, especially the autumn about to be served up, one of those savage understatements (like the "vexed" in "Bells for John Whiteside's Daughter"), or euphemisms which are directed toward the furies of pity.

In the final stanza, "Autumn days" (cf. Section ii of our new poem) the speaker gives up slyness, shifts of tone in the limited sense, becomes the most impersonal voice of all, lost in what it says—although phrasing and rhythm here are more barely idiomatic than elsewhere. The change is abrupt, and structurally the strongest thing in the poem—as if the first stanzas had been given only to afford us this sense of being brought up against the scene without recourse. The scene and its occupant are unchanged. Simply, they are now *seen*. Or, the voice has dropped its sham distance to transport us to the intimate position of no or absolute distance.

These lines are truly remarkable in their bareness of means. Two or three properties for the seasonal desolation, its extension in an allusive phrase ("the waters under the earth," which has also its flavor of a way of speech, a habit of feeling) and we have the immediate garden and its suggestion of the very limbo of matter's descent; the balance of "color" (an obvious generalization for the sensible) and "predilection" (the unexpected, concentratedly precise term for the ground in nature of the human) and there begins the assimilation to this scene of the man. A final image of a now impersonalized Conrad closes this movement and the poem:

Or a man's face as weathered as straw
By the summer's flare and the winter's flaw.

The face is not quite the man, but is an expressive attribute. Flare and flaw will do very well to speak for him inwardly. It will be a poor reader who is not respectful of the poem's reticence here, and ready to accept its propriety as one of those proprieties which it is the business of tone to prepare readers for and to sanction. Why then is this poem not one of Ransom's best?

Judgments such as that just implied will vary, and cannot be fully explained. Is it that the poem as conceived would be a subject more fruitful for a painter? It is not of course treated pictorially. Mr. Ransom has always been as sparingly descriptive as a poet can be, although he has been masterly at suggesting the visual in its repercussions. One way of indicating the impression of certain of his poems would be to say that such and such a pencil, penetrating at one stroke the actual of the grotesque and the harrowing, or of the ludicrous and the touching, could have drawn the mourners at this bed, the guests at this wedding. It is true that the best remembered of these evocations are given off in the course of a narrative movement, or the unfolding of a situation, and Conrad's is a still image. But then the author's poems *are* largely narrative, and the image postulated in "Painted Head," though so volatile in the movements of being it engenders, is yet more static than a man in a garden. Nor am I content to ascribe everything to the naked shift of tone (and metric) in the last lines. Yet this shift and Conrad's immobility, and still more, his lack of definition do contribute to a disrelation between the first stanzas of the poem and the final portion. The detail of the earlier lines recedes and we are left too much with Age and Death. The "general" of the poem is not fast in all its particulars as it is in comparable pieces: "Dead Boy," "Bells for John Whiteside's Daughter."

I have set down all this concerning "Conrad Sits in Twilight" because it constituted some sort of clue for me to the novel manner of the new poem. "Master's in the Garden Again" is concerned with some of its author's chief themes of experience and of speculation. It exploits, formally, the play of the comic and the pathetic, the terms of the domestic piece and the fable. But it manages all these in a way for him unprecedented, almost obverse to his usual practice. And though it ends by raising other questions, it begins by settling those raised in "Conrad Sits in Twilight."

Thus, if the directions of mockery there were puzzling and unplaceable, they are here embodied and patent. Conrad does act and speak, and at last is spoken for. The alternation of sections is reinforced and fully structural. The metric is the old native metric, easier to accommodate to the transposed passage. Mr. Ransom has used this metric before, but chiefly in its more rocking movement and for one kind of effect. Here it is put through more paces, from the doggerel alliterative to the broken and piercing, and with the sprinkled rhymes is made to change qualitatively from part to part, and this is very adroit. And lastly, if in the earlier poem the central voice (and so tone) did not work altogether sustainingly its role here is indeed diminished, intermittent.

On John Crowe Ransom's "Master's in the Garden Again"

From one view this poem is an abbreviated example of qualitative form, or musical form, a composition of rhythmic variations. Other examples that come most easily to mind are enlargements of the dramatic monologue: the speaker offers us such a range of experience, image and reflection that he is not too much with us as subjective sufferer nor too much thinned to mere mind, yet it would be hard to conceive the unity of such poems without him. Here we have something different. The speaker is only a chorus-prologue-narrator presenting us with a scene, interlude, and dumb-show.

There is something droll and folkish, crudely and immemorially traditional suggested, not only in this one-man chorus of all work, but in the poem's whole manner: something stilted and puppet-like in the opening colloquy; raw in the touch of the grotesque upon the painful in the pantomime; touching in the disjunctive strains of chorus.

The chorus is the most sophisticated poet and has the longest part and best lines. After the terse prologue the dialogue scene of Section i is comedy of manners and the stylized puppet-shrilling is an overtone of this. It is comedy of manners at a point where disguise frays indecently, and we hear the nervous archness of the woman's opening phrases break down into the grindingly inept, and the husband's irony snappishly overdone, edging into the vicious.

Is it the stock character frame (which I may have invented) which makes me see this pair so readily as man, woman, Adam, Eve, as levels or masks of reason? Woman is not here, as in other of the author's poems, the tenderly deluded, innocently wounded sensibility. As the underside of solicitude she embodies rather petty, greedily limited, practical reason. The action is to banish her temporarily so that a superior reason may find itself. Man is lordly in his unconscious assumption of himself as reason ("The health of a garden is reason's burden") and achieves absurdity in enunciating its dictates ("minding miasma"). The chorus-narrator in a thin aside calls him "the thinker" as in Section iii he mocks him with "Master." (This begins to remind us of "Old Man Playing with Children" in which folly or second childhood becomes wisdom; but the present poem could not contain the willful extravagance of statement there, nor, in its different management, resolve and poise implications so lightheartedly.)

Despite the impartiality of the comic vein, the reader is with the woman's banishment, and ready, as in the earlier poem, for the preparation of silence—

indeed, readier so that the effect of the break is deepened. The opening lines of Section ii (which adds only these and a final line of equal gravity to the transposed passage) are very good in giving duration to this silence. Time has passed. (Here one begins to feel a thickening sense of parody, as of our truncated, overburdened structures, fragmentations, dislocations, etc.) During the intermission what has happened? Peripety, a whole tragic action ("the show is of death"), recognition on the part of the hero, or just the offstage violence? In this section the chorus is traditionally enough describing the scene. But the scene as the order of nature is the antagonist and, as omnipotent, stands over the hero's defeat. We are now where we were at the end of "Conrad Sits in Twilight," except that that poem is complete, and a page break here would not deceive us. For here the unresolved lingers from the impassive opening couplet of the section. "Still Conrad's back has not uncurved" bears that curved back with some ring of pride but means too a shying as far back from acceptance as the recesses of infant omnipotence. The magic, or perhaps prayer, didn't work: "Nor the autumn's blow for a moment swerved." However, the hero is sitting out the moment of truth and we expect more of him. What? The happy, comic ending, heroic action, epiphany, food for choric wisdom? The elements so far given work on us "teasingly" (though perhaps only, or chiefly, if we have been brought to feel the mock-heroic, parody sense), and we could look to have any of these in a backhanded fashion. Perhaps that is what we do find, a little of each, in just that fashion, inside out, upside down.

That Conrad will trot in to supper is comic ending, reversed by coming first, especially since the preceding half-line foretells his action and undercuts it as sham "play" and its ground as "mood." For epiphany, then, we would next have reason in truer guise as moral sensibility and human champion. The chorus narrator in this crucial section splits up. Spoken as from within we have offended justice, a snatch of poignance, the pity of it. Then the pantomime, a heroic action, seen, is travestied in doggerel and with the insulting indulgence we have for a child's tantrum, and now too the inward voice of intent is made bluster. An image hovers above all this, grotesque, apoplectic, rigor mortis, for the accusing rage. Epitaphy? The last phrases are more true chorus and resolving. But how can we believe in this gay garden? Not as in the "olive garden for the nightingales" of the poet's "Painted Head."

On John Crowe Ransom's "Master's in the Garden Again"

For one thing the sequence grief-pathos, rage, gayety is emotionally strange. It would be easier to enter into this sequence through accepting the literal image simply: a man in the defect of age, transported to excess by a frost-bitten garden, purged in the frail round of senescent humors.* On the other hand, I should find the whole burden of the piece impossible to load upon Conrad as Conrad. This sense would for me put "Master's in the Garden Again" about out of the canon as all belabored to one harshness.

The last reversal, in the reading I incline toward, is this: *we* recognize the hero. He resolves his plight by a rudimentary mime. Other redemptive play-forms (manners and ceremony, ritual religion), which the author has set beside the play-form of art, show in this late garden as shrunken and malformed. We read the poem then as fable: a fable of the straits to which a noble art is fallen, and including in its parody aspect ("Have you known the fall of a year when it fell?" and more not here adumbrated) reminders as well of that art's self-conscious burden of history, and feeble origins "where all the ladders start."

As fable it is a wry one, with parody pervasive and reaching to the exegesis it prompts. But its poet-hero, with his fist-shakings at heaven, is after all an embittered romantic, remote from the classic temper and the olive garden which "Painted Head" (also, though so brief, managing an historic-modern perspective) at last postulated and celebrated. And, as fable it differs from any other of Ransom's poems developed figuratively. In others the literal level, clearly figurative and fabulous, returns us to the tenor of the actual by concentrating, enhancing and ordering the moral dimensions of behavior and of fact. Here, the literal level (Conrad) seems actual and solid, and as vehicle diminishes the human reach it adumbrates. Yet as vehicle the poem holds him in more acceptable relations than merely as old man.

And what of the dedication? Hardy made the garden the scene of a number of late poems. These were in the mode of pure pathos, and often achieved the pure dignity of pathos in the tragic scheme. The words "rage" and "gay" are apt to remind us of another poet of old age. I take it that these poets are invoked (if indeed both are) as geniuses of the shore, beyond the floods which would roll old fellows and old forms in the dust.

* I am omitting here the ambiguous use of "children," preferring, for a confluence of reasons, to take its sense as of "babes" in "Miriam Tazewell."

MURIEL RUKEYSER

This poem is a rewriting of another much earlier poem: it is quite different from the first in many ways, although some of the phrases are kept. John Crowe Ransom has done a strange thing, he has made an extension and a transformation. Even while the method is maintained. So that time and choice, which can bear the rhyme away, have with this poem borne it back again in a different life.

The poet has already been his own critic; and I, as reader, have been told what he thinks here, what he has preserved and what thrown away. Years after "Conrad in Twilight," its first life, the poem has taken on a second life whose meaning is based on—and contradicts—the first. "Master's in the Garden Again" speaks for a further stage of life. It is a declaration, and a celebration; it is offered to the reader as a transparency with a key. The transparency is here because we have that early matrix, much less in itself than this new poem, which Ransom describes as a "completely new version of the old and rather ignominious 'Conrad in Twilight'" in the Preface to his *Selected Poems,* which will have appeared by now, and whose proofs Knopf was good enough to send me. Ransom adds that his "greatest pleasure in preparing this edition came from this poem and one other." They mark a new period, after a long time without poems.

During the long gap there were essays; one of these, two rather, are the key to the poem, taken along with the dedication of "Master's in the Garden Again" to the memory of Thomas Hardy. The strength of the new poem is very close to the qualities of Hardy, Hardy old and seen by Ransom in "Old Age of an Eagle," an essay which first appeared in the *New Republic* in 1952. These qualities, established by admiration and a kind of identity declared and built, will be in the poem as it climbs and rouses past its dripping scene. But that comes later—although it is invoked by the dedication.

The poem sets the scene at once; although "Conrad in Twilight" jumped straight into dialogue, now we are given autumn ("Evening comes early"), the exchange (that is, true dialogue), and the man and woman, the lovers in bonds, conjugate. In the old days, the woman leapt right in, nagging:

Conrad, Conrad, aren't you old
To sit so late in your mouldy garden?

On John Crowe Ransom's "Master's in the Garden Again"

This time, Conrad is called both "dear man" and "surprise" (well, perhaps *he* is not called surprise, perhaps it is the warning voice of nagging practicality that is surprised by her own thoughts, but I think Conrad is dear man, and surprised, as he is later thinker and master and champion). He is mood; she is "intrusion." But we know more about him, more about her, more about the garden.

She calls him "bold" here, and one can live with that.

What is his boldness?

In the beginning, it is simply to stay in his garden. The garden, with the man and woman in it, we know from our own depth. Far back among explications, the *Zohar* gives us the Garden of Genesis as Gad-Eden, the Garden of Delight which is the City of God. Here it is, sodden, particular, contemporary, gone to muck and the end of autumn. Nothing "promises well." It is not Eden, it has a house in it. It is waiting its blow, and its blow will surely come.

It is possible to be put off early in this poem by what seems like bumpiness, coyness, dated diction. Ransom himself has warned us of this in other poems by other poets. The music he claims is one he has described in the Hardy essay: he uses the folk line, or dipodic line, with its symmetry and a syncopation in a line whose musical expectation is so strong that the pause which can be produced is in itself strong, too. This is a clear and country music on which Ransom counts, and he has provided it with two chief sounds to carry the range of this wide-ranging poem: the long ā established in *exchange* and *late* and carried through to the last sound of the last line, and the long ō that begins with *bold* and *cold* and takes us to *blow* and all the variant o's and ow's sounding out toward the end.

The new poem keeps the name Conrad for someone who may be an invention or a friend. The name takes almost all its elements from the poet's own name. Conrad answers with his gloomy boding; in his first incarnation, he was nursing his knees in the cold, and now he declares to her that he is; he asks his question about the falling blow ("Have you known. . . ?" he asks, and goes on, not waiting for an answer which indeed the woman does never make). And, as rational man, *he* answers her calling it "sodden garden" with

> "Indeed it's a garden, but if you will pardon,
> The health of a garden is reason's burden."

The sounds here are an echo of the crossed-out "Forest of Arden" whose wraith

On John Crowe Ransom's "Master's in the Garden Again"

he has said he is sitting in, in the first version of this poem, a lifetime ago.

The woman answers his mention of health with a "womanly" cautionary rounding back to the question of his own health, and a

"Come in from foul weather for pity's sake!"

Look at the first poem, "Conrad in Twilight." There is no woman here, although these questions are asked. Many of the hard words are kept, nagging words of deterioration, ill-health, ills of which damp and decline are reminders, asthma, neuralgia, goading and horrid.

"No," says the thinker. . . .

and he begins to pile up on her his moods. She is called more than "intrusion," of course, she's called "my loony," and he knows her loneliness. She is to go back in the house and wait. And she knows what will happen if she doesn't. In his own humorous, querulous, last-gasp effort to go beyond his mood, he tells her: he'll jump in the lake.

That is the end of her. The end of the dialogue. The end speech.

From now on all we have is acted out. In the first "Conrad" it was a matter of tea and slipper and a blazing log at home. In the old poem, autumn was "teasing" and the poem ended with a described autumn.

Here, in part ii of the new poem, we have another couplet setting the scene, which is the action of the man, a still, negative persevering in the face of what seemed to be only a warning of lateness, cold, damp, his own creakiness. But it darkens—

Nor the autumn's blow for an instant swerved

and then the described autumn, as it was the earlier poem,

Autumn days in our section
Are the most used-up thing on earth

and then the Biblical "or in the waters under the earth." Used-up is what the persevering is about, *that* is what she has been calling him under the names of solicitude, *that* is what he has been refusing to be, even when it looked as though

On John Crowe Ransom's "Master's in the Garden Again"

he could only be by sitting there. The black wet tatters of the year are here. Beyond them

> The show is of death. There is no defection.

Now a curious thing happens. We are beyond the old poem, and beyond the old life. There is something that is used-up, and the poet knows what it is. It is the old life itself. And there is something more. What comes next, in the bringing-together of gardens? What have these all turned into? What comes, once the show of death has been produced before us? It is produced, in full strength "no defection" and in full music, *show* being recognizable as a key sound in this poem.

Part iii begins with a magic statement, "He will play out his mood before he takes food." He has put away the life of the house up there with its food, its comforts and its mood-breaking. This is to be carried beyond the end. The one line is comparable to the couplets with which the other parts of the poem have begun, but they are shortened here to the brief magic. As it is said, the spell breaks, the weather breaks, the tragedies of the innocent arrive. The verse stands up, and bravery stands up. No more the world of nursing and neuralgia—or, if they are there, they are not central to this scene.

The dialogue is between man and the Power. The Hardy Power, the cruel weather, It with a capital I, and I with a capital all there is to deal with It. The children are gone, fallen, dead by suicide because they are too "menny," anyway lost. And no more the querulous

> "O did It lay them low,
> But we're a poor sinner just going to dinner."

The heart itself is transformed, no longer tell-tale heart but

> See the tell-tale art of the champion heart.

Now the incantation takes up speed and action, the sound begins to swing,

> Here's temple and brow, which frown like the law.
> If the arm lies low, yet the rage looks high.
> The accusing eye? that's a fierce round O.

On John Crowe Ransom's "Master's in the Garden Again"

> The offense was raw, says the fix in the jaw.
> We'll raise a rare row! We'll heave a brave blow!

Feeling has now been dealt with by assertion, domesticated, as Collingwood says. Ransom has spoken of "the metaphysical Powers arrayed against him"; here they are as one Power. The development of parallel feelings in this poem—no, conjugate feelings—lets me suspect that the wife has her chance for some parallel in the house, although it must come out of her "pity's sake" that works for his health as he sits out his mood for the health of his garden. There is her condemnation to the house, but he has come through; the garden's condemnation in the metaphor, although we know what winter is.

Ransom is not going to allow the metaphor to take over. His "that time of year thou may'st in me behold" is around him, being dealt with. But what happens? what is happening?

> A pantomime blow, if it damns him to do,
> A yell mumming too.

It has already "happened," though, in decision and in sound. And with the choice of the man, the garden has chosen. . . .

> But it's gay garden now,

and the acting-out, the singing, the making, which has done it to this garden, grants us a last invocation

> Play sweeter than pray, that the darkened be gay.

Here are the bravery, the irony, the honesty, the surprisingly banal moments, the music—and the maudlin, daily, saving life in Ransom's quickened poetry. I go back to early readings of his poems. The books of poetry at home were the Bible and Shakespeare, Longfellow and the sections in "The Book of Knowledge." Then I came to Untermeyer's anthologies and the living poets, and then, afternoons after school, read on the stairs at O'Malley's old bookshop in New York, the Oxford editions of poets, the leatherette Modern Library, Mosher's finely-printed paper books. Began to buy books with first money at about the time *Two Gentlemen in Bonds* came out, after the grace of *Chills and Fever*.

On John Crowe Ransom's "Master's in the Garden Again"

The narrow books, with their dark backs and their designs. The dooms of the equilibrists, the gallantry of Captain Carpenter, the harvesters, the girls. And the first poem of this garden, after all this lifetime with its poems, is transformed to the early and late of this second poem, with its darkness and play, its ease of irony as the poet moves along, full (as he said of Hardy) of "fierce folkish humor."

There are questions left. I left a friend's house the other day, and the door-man spoke to me. I was going across the river to read poems. "Oh, well, if it's poems," he said, "there's bound to be lots of questions." While the questions come, here the poem is—unswerving itself, in the poet's phrase "half mystical, perhaps half maudlin," saved by both and saving.

Afterthought: I am still haunted by what happens to the woman in the poem and to the vowels that deepen and deepen into the undersounds of the climax.

JOHN CROWE RANSOM

Now the Grateful Author

Three poet-critics have looked hard at my first poem. I mean the first made by my present Self, who has grown out of the several other Selves during the years of no poetry; made with all that awkwardness when one tries for the first time to fashion some difficult kind of thing. I am indebted to these critics because they have said what they thought about the poem, with sincerity and care. What can a poet do without critics to advise him what he is doing? and without critics to pass over in silence some of his favorite passages and by that silence tell him that he has not done what he thought he was doing? I can imagine that this latter testimony is one that happens often to poets who try to do only wonderful things, and discover from the general silence that poetry for them is tense, terse, and jerky, and that they do not address themselves to the general intelligence. It is well that this is a first poem.

Miss Rukeyser has gone right through the poem, defining the drift of its successive movements, and finally, with her unusual power of sympathy, responding approvingly. She cheers the author's spirits. There is a word of caution at the end, to say that one never finishes with the study of a poem, but no direful threat that other questions which may be raised about the poem cannot be answered so favorably.

Mr. Snodgrass has made a fighting defense of my poem, attending specifically to the vocabulary and verbalisms which he finds generic to the poet advanced in age, and happy to the point of overstatement at the success of the old poet trying his hand again. I have not met with so complete a champion turning up so unexpectedly. It makes me glad, and wary. As to the woman's deep involvement in the story, I keep thinking, How right he is there; he recognizes the bond that unites the man and the woman, the garden and the house, in perfect keeping with the author's understanding. One thing is missing in his study: the question of the success of the man's peculiar pantomime at the end, which is exactly the trouble-spot of the whole poem. Is it worth the bluster and the bother it has cost him, even if at last it can take place in the secrecy of his garden? Is it either probable or possible? Perhaps in the time and the space Mr. Snodgrass did not get round to it, but I cannot afford to think so.

On "Master's in the Garden Again"

Miss Adams is one of the most acute and intensive critics we have, very sure and exacting in testing the suitability of the verbal phrase and the detail of the action. Her own verse is a rare achievement for our time in its lyric purity. Ever so well she knows the few best of my early poems, and inclines to hold this late poem officially to their standard of performance. She stops fastidiously on the frequent harshness of the moral tone, the "broken spacings" and violent shifts in the narrative, the grotesquerie, the childishness of the final action, the comic note that may not have been intended. But she is willing not to make her judgment final, and that determines me to take plenty of time in coming to my own judgment. Her voice in this group is the indispensable complement to the others.

I thank especially Mr. Ostroff, our moderator, who accepted the poem while it was still unfinished, then assembled these bright and right persons to appraise it, and now asks me not to stint my reply in depth or in length.

My remarks will run at random. They will have to do wholly with some of the author's intentions, not his successes, about which I do not yet have an opinion.

The title which I gave to the poem (in place of the "Conrad Sits in Twilight" which topped the little old poem), and the dedication to Thomas Hardy, jumped into my consciousness simultaneously out of the memory of a slight but touching poem of his entitled "The Master and the Leaves." Its next-to-last stanza finishes the leaves' complaint, and the last stanza gives the master's reply:

III

We are turning yellow, Master,
    And soon we are turning red,
And faster then and faster
    Shall seek our rooty bed,
All wasted in disaster;
    But you lift not your head.

IV

—"I mark your early going,
    And that you'll soon be clay,
I have seen your summer showing
    As in my youthful day;

On "Master's in the Garden Again"

> But why I seem unknowing
> Is too sunk in to say."

My title therefore became "Master's in the Garden Again"; as he often was. But the date-line of the Hardy poem is 1917. At that time the poet was too dispirited by the World War, and perhaps too tired, to spend himself reiterating his old defiance against the Power that knows no special providence for Its creatures; he can only tell the leaves politely that he has seen what is happening to them. But it would have been indecent for me to pretend that Hardy is the master in the garden of my poem. The master—and hero—is still Conrad; and if there is any interest in this item I will say that to the best of my knowledge I had chosen that name, in the early 1920's, because it had been the pen-name of a brooding and intellectual Pole who wrote novels, and I happened to have been born in a town called Pulaski, about sixty miles from where I wrote. At any rate I would have preferred to have Hardy in my garden as he had been much earlier than the time of his own poems about the garden; let us say between the conclusion of his novels in the early 1890's and the turn of the century. That was when he was close on sixty years old, full of vigor as I suppose, and getting himself power-fully engaged upon his theological misadventure. The evidences would be in the astonishing Epic Drama of *The Dynasts,* and many small poems both before and after. I cannot deny that my imagination, while I was working on the pres-ent poem, would sometimes picture for me the aging but not yet aged Mr. T. H. sitting drooped on a wet stone in a prospect of fallen leaves, and maintaining his posture with only the slightest variation while he talked with his wife Emma, then brooded a while, and finally in his solitary rage made his play against the Immanent Will. It was a fleeting and pleasant vision but not suitable to Hardy's great dignity; though I could ask myself, Who is likely to know the peculiar habit or the ritual by which even a great poet raises and resolves his fury?

I must talk about that first stage in the poem, where Conrad seems harsh to his wife when she interrupts his revery. One of my governing motives in this composition was to try for certain formal effects, which would be prosodical ef-fects, all through the poem. I felt that the four-beat folk line, with its perfect two-plus-two symmetry, was capable of great versatility, so that in the three move-ments there might easily be as many effects. In the first movement the lines are end-rhymed as is common, but in irregular stanzas which assemble themselves in a very arbitrary way. That is to say that at the beginning I did what was quite irregular, but justified it by the characters I attributed to the man and the woman having their dialogue, and expected my readers to follow me though these had not been revealed. Conrad is a poet and his wife is not; he rhymes easily, but she has no knack for it. So the naughty man means to hear out her unrhymed lines, then cap them with a group of lines that supply rhyme-mates for hers, and for good measure some rhymed lines entirely his own. That is why her first address in two lines ending with *bold* and *garden* is followed by his stanza of five lines ending with *well, cold, fell, pardon, burden;* two separate rhymings for her *garden.* Her next sally has four lines ending with *muck, neck, asthma,* and *sake.* His reply is to assume that *muck* and *neck* may be put to her credit as lame rhymes (a little of his art having rubbed off on her) though probably their near-rhyming is perfectly accidental. He replies with four lines ending in *here, miasma, there,* and *lake.* The insult of the rhymes looks very rude of him; yet I thought of it as one of the conventions of their dialogue whenever they were having an argument. But in my obstinate economy of words I blundered here. I should have supplied an ampler leisure, and more and successively clearer examples of the rhyme game.

I had taken my cue from the charming but sophisticated French poet Jules Laforgue, to whom Mr. Eliot's prose criticism and early imitations had introduced me, and started off by trying to outdo him. But there are some genuine locutions in Laforgue's style. One of his best inventions was to match an intellectual man with the woman of his heart who was a sentimentalist; so that if the woman, for example, asks the man if he loves her still, he may reply with some completely irrelevant wisdom beyond her head. The invention works as a convention; it does not keep Laforgue's heroes from showing their real gallantry in action, when the occasion arises. Similarly Conrad, as when his first speech to his wife begins with a fierce pair of exclamations: "Woman! intrusion!" Or when he calls her his loony; this is mock-brutality, well understood between them. He is too polite to tell her to "go jump in the lake," and only threatens to do it himself if she will not leave him now; nor is she alarmed over that, if she has heard it many times before. It is only his final word that closes the argument; the master speaking. And on the other hand there seems to be some equally un-

On "Master's in the Garden Again"

flattering conventions of speech on her part. Conrad's two exclamations were only replies to those on her tongue when she entered the garden. "Conrad! dear man, surprise!" Indeed her playful language is more resented by Mr. Snodgrass, who is a man, than Conrad's. Possibly the convention which is her best weapon of attack is to assume the role of protecting Conrad's frail health, when it may well be that his health is very good, and never in his life has been impaired by neuralgia nor asthma. It is clear that I damaged my poem by making it take off from the ill-laid foundations of the old fragment, where the speaker or speakers make derogations against his failing age. In the early piece somebody says, "Aren't you old / To sit so late, etc." But in whipping the new poem into shape I changed *old* to *bold;* a word better befitting a hero. At the same time I changed one of the new phrases I had entered, *eldering lovers* becoming *conjugate lovers,* for two reasons probably: to keep the pair from seeming too senile for their duties, and—as Mr. Snodgrass has made me aware—because the latter word seemed more important as a precise and structural specification, eloquent only in the expectations it permitted.

Thinking of the rowdy persiflage of my conjugate lovers as a sporting and comic feature, I have the sense that their life together is good. I like to think of their marriage as still real, in the lawyers' sense of the word, meaning physical. Yet all will not be lost as they grow old. The diminishing desires of the flesh will be compensated by bonuses of extra companionship and affection. When they are not together, the garden and the house will be their respective spheres. But after the man's turn in the garden his appointment will be in the house. Mr. Snodgrass has said this almost precisely.

Now I skip over the second movement, which is only a static scene described by the author, noting only the last line: "The show is of death. There is no defection." The death mentioned means to refer to that of the leaves, of whom not one has survived, though they were the children "Who hurt no one where they shone in the sun." The author did not want to suggest the universal mortality to which Conrad himself, and all of us, are liable, and for which Conrad, like most of us at his time of life, is prepared. But that would be another poem. It is the dead leaves that matter now, and they are what he sorrows for. In this poem it is in the third movement that he rouses himself as the leaves' champion, and girds himself for heroic action. But he must fight for a lost cause; the leaves are gone already. So he will raise his hand and voice against the blind and brutal Power to punish him. Yet there is the most abject absurdity here. Conrad has no chance of hurting, nor of reaching, nor even of finding the awful Power; and Conrad knows it. Human justice is meted out ordinarily by tiny men against a tiny man, or a tiny hero against a tiny villain, but this case is different. In what fashion can Conrad play the hero even in his own estimation if he has to proceed against the unknown Power? He has been careful not to expose his enterprise to the public view. But another recourse suggested itself to the not impartial author.

The prosodical variation in this movement consists in abandoning the rhyme of lines with each other, and making them rhyme within themselves, the fourth or end beat with the second or middle beat. The rhyming becomes more immediate, therefore more audible; and more frequent too; altogether making perhaps for a richer music and a livelier substance. Furthermore, the lines fall into their proper groups structurally, logically, and we have the equivalent of the free paragraphs of a prose composition, or one in blank or free verse.

Now Conrad can take no real action against the Enemy, though I suppose we are all aware by now that he is going to perform a symbolic action which amounts only to pantomime. He will frown and look fierce, and grit his teeth, and at last he will raise his clenched fist toward Heaven and give a muffled yell of defiance. But let us not discount this operation in advance. What if the author will describe it in some special and stylized manner; is there a chance of his keeping the reader's attention and making the thing seem credible though strange? We know how much is done by sheer stylization when the story-teller would have us believe in his unsubstantial ghost, or some phantasy with many characters. But each case is too particular to generalize it. In the five lines of the pantomime where we see Conrad's features working in silhouette, and even in the final three lines which follow in the author's official voice, we have a very special prosodical variation upon the prosodical movement which I have described. All the sixteen rhyme-places, half in the middle and half at the ends, are supplied with long open vowels, which have no consonants after them or else silent consonants. Sixteen rhyming syllables, yes, sixteen monosyllables, fill those places, and show six different rhymes based on the following words, which are not given in the order in which they appear: *law, low, high, now, do, gay.* It used to be the understanding among poets that any two long open syllables at the right places would be construed as rhyming, but that is unnecessary here, where each one can find a rhyming partner, sometimes more than one. I shall not tell of the pain this pattern required of its composer, nor the joy when it began to work out. But it is pertinent to say that the authorial imagination works in two ways at the same time, and that the severity of the requirement produced finally lines that not only answered to the prosody but were more striking and unexpected than they might have been in the substance.

I do not know if the pantomime passage succeeded. But it pleased me that when it was finished the author's little epilogue or last word came into its three lines almost instantly, without sacrificing the pattern or the pertinence:

> A pantomime blow, if it damns him to do,
> A yell mumming too. But it's gay garden now,
> Play sweeter than pray, that the darkened be gay.

The garden is gay, if it can be gay, because the hero has performed his action, though it was only a symbolic action, in a sort of grand style, making something out of a barren occasion. And in the last line, with "Play sweeter than pray," the author has imagined himself as on the track of an incipient law for poetry, a way of distinguishing itself from theology when theology has failed the poet: to play the thing that we cannot pray.

So Conrad is purged and away to the house which expects him.

LOUISE BOGAN

PHILIP BOOTH

WILLIAM STAFFORD

RICHARD EBERHART

On RICHARD EBERHART'S

"*Am I My Neighbor's Keeper?*"

Richard Eberhart

AM I MY NEIGHBOR'S KEEPER?

The poetry of tragedy is never dead.
If it were not so I would not dream
On principles so deep they have no ending,
Nor on the ambiguity of what things ever seem.

The truth is his and shaped in veils of error,
Rich, unanswerable, the profound caught in plain air.
Centuries after tragedy sought out Socrates
Its inexplicable essence visits us in our lair,

Say here, on a remote New Hampshire farm.
The taciturn farmer disappeared in pre-dawn.
He had beaten his handyman, but no great harm.
Light spoke vengeance and bloodstains on the lawn.
His trussed corpse later under the dam
Gives to this day no answer, says I am.

LOUISE BOGAN

Richard Eberhart, from the beginning of his career, has often displayed that intense insight into reality which characterizes the poet whose gift is close to Blakean vision. This sort of insight works most frequently from a base of sharply apprehended reality, to rise toward levels where the fact at once dissolves and condenses into meaning. Eberhart's poem "The Groundhog" illustrates this power of transformation and transcendence very clearly indeed; and many of the poems of his early and middle period, including the extraordinary "The Fury of Aerial Bombardment," advance step by step from the observed fact to the resolving universal intimation.

And Eberhart, an assiduous writer, has been steadily engaged in experiments with form, over the years. He has been experimental within form—that is, he has worked inside poetry's conventional rules, modifying them within boundaries, instead of denying all formal precedent (as is the habit of many modern writers). This latter procedure can end only in monotony, since so many effects are passed over—effects truly fitted for the condensation of language and the production of "memorable speech." Eberhart's work has never become repetitive, although, of course, certain of his experiments, in the nature of things, have been less interesting than others. In the present instance he has experimented with the sonnet form.

Any experiment based on the sonnet form requires boldness. For the sonnet has peculiar and, it would at moments seem, magical and sacred powers. It is a form which cannot be attacked too rudely or be tampered with cynically. It does not yield to a frontal attack; under direct pressure it merely disappears. There have been eccentric sonnets written in various languages, ever since the Renaissance, but never one in which some adherence to the basic sonnet pattern does not hold. A succession of fourteen lines of prose cannot be named a sonnet; neither can thirteen lines of verse. Doggerel does not disguise well in this clear mirror; any falsity, whether of thought or emotion, together with any technical ineptitude, cannot be concealed. The sonnet, like the sonata form, has held to its classic organization throughout centuries of chance and change; through the varying demands made upon it by the prosodies of all Western European languages; through various revolutions of style; through innumerable shifts in taste.

On Richard Eberhart's "Am I My Neighbor's Keeper?"

It has managed to come through into contemporary expression practically un-marred; in fact, the sonnet in French, from Baudelaire through Mallarmé, helped to bring modern poetry into being. And during the last fifty years the sonnet has conquered the difficulties of a recalcitrant language (German) in which its effects heretofore had never strongly taken hold. Stefan George learned from Rossetti; Rilke, having translated both Louise Labé and Elizabeth Browning, brought his career to a triumphant close with the fifty-five *Sonnette an Orpheus*, written in 1922; and Bertolt Brecht has written "brilliant sonnets on themes from classical literature." In English, in our day, the sonnet has continued to be the most "concise and eloquent" lyric form: the dramatic stanza whose power has not been lost in the hands of Auden, Cummings, Roy Fuller, and others.

Since the first line of Eberhart's sonnet echoes the first line of a sonnet by Keats, perhaps the line of the sonnet's strongly continuing destiny should be briefly traced, at this point. What is the provenance of this strongly enduring design of the art of language? The sonnet did not originate in southern France, along with the many and varied lyric patterns springing from mediæval *langue d'oc*. So far as can be known, it came into being at the Sicilian court of the fabled Frederick Hohenstaufen, in the twelfth century. Dante altered its form; Petrarch gave it a patronymic. One authority has called the sonnet "one of the main via-ducts through which certain classical elements of the Renaissance flowed"—from Italy to France (the *Pleiade*) and from thence to England. The early, tentative sonnets of Wyatt and of the younger Surrey soon were transformed into the great sonnet sequences of the Elizabethans—of Spenser and Sidney and finally of Shakespeare and Donne. English poets changed the exigent Petrarchan octet and sestet into the more feasible (for the language) three quatrains and a couplet, but the pleasing (and dramatic) division (and contrast) between octet and sestet still held. This division allowed not only contrast but balance: statement and counter-statement; question and answer; and built-up climax. The English sonnet more or less disappeared after Milton, for a century and a half, but the Romantics brought it back, and it was enthusiastically practiced by Romantic poets, with the exception of Byron, who held it in scornful dislike. The Victorians continued to write sonnets in a rather desultory way, with the exception of Rossetti, who brought back a good deal of Idealistic and Italianate emotion into English. And

On Richard Eberhart's "Am I My Neighbor's Keeper?"

Meredith, in *Modern Love*, introduced the most successful variation ever invented, to the basic fourteen-line pattern.

The sonnet has learned to express, over the centuries, a wide variety of emotion; it can boast as well as plead, and describe the most delicate as well as the most powerful range of feeling. Its subject, in the dramatic nature of things, often has implicit reference to some major theme; or some fourteen-line block of strictly rhymed metrical lines is overarched by a quality of the numinous, or reinforced with passionate human hope or despair. The sonnet sequence—particularly those masterful examples written in Elizabethan English—can be structures bastioned at all four corners with the direct strength of the passions but at the same time blown upon, as it were, by the soft as well as the stern airs of heaven. The sonnet effect more often resembles the blow of a fist than an offering from an open hand. Impact is, frequently, all.

The sonnet, for full effectiveness, should establish its meter (traditionally, in English, iambic pentameter) firmly in its opening line. This meter, held to firmly for thirteen lines, gives to the fourteenth a decisive authority. The metrical pattern can be flexible, to a certain degree—lighter syllables coming in from time to time in anapest or dactyl, to increase speed; or heavier syllables moving slowly in repeated spondees. The sonnet, with Hopkins, yielded to true metrical innovations without being broken by them, to the syllabic overflow of "sprung rhythm": a meter made up of lines regular as to beat but exceedingly irregular in regard to syllable count. (Hopkins' sonnets are, for the most part, perfectly Petrarchan as regards rhyme.)

Eberhart has written "Am I My Neighbor's Keeper?" in a species of "sprung rhythm." And he has varied the number of *stresses* in the lines, as well as keeping the *syllable* count irregular. The first four lines (quatrain)—the poem is loosely Shakespearean in its rhyme-scheme—go according to no recognizable metrical pattern; the second quatrain begins with a line of eleven-syllable iambic pentameter, and then breaks over into a sort of alexandrine (iambic hexameter) design, although here again there is no metrical rule. At the beginning of the octet (line 9) the first line of absolutely regular iambic pentameter occurs—most effectively; and line 12 sustains it. And Eberhart's sense of one sonnet convention (the dramatic importance of the fourteenth and last line) comes into view, when he writes the fourteenth line in perfectly scannable iambic feet—five of them.

There is the constant likelihood that the final effect of a series of "sprung rhythm" lines will result, not in strength mounting on strength, but in weakness compounding weakness. Here, hair's breadth chances taken are irrevocable; the stumble remains a stumble. Eberhart does not wholly escape these dangers. His first four lines are largely wasted; the totally unmetrical variation on the line of Keats seems rather misjudged, and no line of direction is indicated. One tenet of sonnet-writing is illustrated here: no line, no stress, no word, no pause, can be wasted. It is an exigent form. There is no room in it to falter and halt.

From line 5 on, the Eberhart poem finds itself and moves on. It moves on not only metrically but in strength of concrete image. The first four lines are ineffectively abstract. The actual words used are extremely vague; and no images appear, to advance or clinch the meaning. With line 5 the poem begins to be enriched by the symbol, and by those condensing devices that give the part for the whole, and bind the general into the particular. At the beginning of the sestet, we are introduced, at last, to the strikingly particular: to actual description of a unique event. The poem goes over into a short narrative passage of six lines. The use of detail brings the poem into focus; and added "meaning," now of an *effective* abstract kind, comes into existence in the poem's final line.

Whether or not the sonnet can bear any load of actual narration is questionable. The weight of meditation, the powerful thrust of decision, the contrasts of shifting passions—these have been, and remain, the sonnet's chief materials. Eberhart has made an interesting try at introducing the anecdote to reinforce and illustrate a moment of philosophic speculation. That the poem finally *feels itself* a sonnet, its final movement toward the direct, the dramatic, the heightened (and heightening) convention, proves. After the first Keatsian line, it is more or less committed to the sonnet direction. But a good deal of time is wasted in search.

PHILIP BOOTH

I think I'd know "Am I My Neighbor's Keeper?" as an Eberhart poem even if Richard Eberhart hadn't signed it. Words like "veils," "unanswerable," and "the profound" are Eberhart's hallmark; and syntax like "but no great harm" is unmistakably his. Such language may, in itself, appear to veil what's finally profound in Eberhart's work; but the great originality of this present poem lies, dramatically, in how it *lifts* those veils of traditional language which surround the profound irrationality of its "inexplicable essence." The New Criticism has predisposed us to carefully inductive poems, rationally structured toward carefully limited conclusions. But like Eberhart's fine "The Fury of Aerial Bombardment," this new poem moves by *deduction,* and risks within itself a drama of deducing the specifically human relevance of its introductory abstractions. Innocently rational in form and first assertion as this poem is, it deduces and unveils (within its language) an irrational shadow which commits its poet to guilt. Something like this was Socrates' way of using language to question what language conceals; the way questions get raised within Eberhart's poem seem comparably individual.

Who else might title a perhaps sonnet with so open a variation on Cain's prime question? What less original poet might be so careless of critics as to double his debt, by drawing boldly on Keats for his opening line? In spite of its literate references, this is far from being an "academic" poem written, I suspect, as much on Eberhart's amateur pulse as with his intellectual courage. To ask, as Eberhart does, if he is his neighbor's keeper, is to extend Cain's blooded question toward answers of innocence or guilt beyond mere mindful brotherhood. Given the guilt implicit in any reference to Cain, there's something painfully ironic in adding to that reference an assertion derived in all innocence from Keats. But the problem of the poem is, as Stevens might say, how "to live in the world but outside of existing conceptions of it"; and Eberhart's variant paraphrases, individually and in juxtaposition, imply old moral concepts. Eberhart's veiled references, then, function to introduce moral possibilities which—his poem will discover—can't by any tradition be rationally resolved. Cain's question is ultimately a question of one's pulse, not of one's rational judgment; so does the poem's answer to that question become emotionally equivalent to the drama it de-

On Richard Eberhart's "Am I My Neighbor's Keeper?"

scribes and re-enacts. So was the murder the poem tells, I imagine, an equally irrational process of adrenalin building-up to release its commitment. Eberhart, after the fact, reflects quietly on the episode to which he has committed himself, but he deeply identifies with an act of vengeance beyond all points of reference or simple reason.

I probably have some special identification with this poem, as I grew up where Richard Eberhart now lives, and remember newspaper stories about the murder on which I assume his poem is based. Eberhart fictionalizes the location into New Hampshire, and it's probably a private irrelevance that I recall Bradford, Vermont as the actual locale of the murder of a dairy owner who had beaten one handyman too many. Whatever the literal geography, it's important to this poem's success that Eberhart finally grounds it in place and event. As it is, he compresses the narrative to his sense of its essence, perhaps to the point where certain dramatic facts are left out. As I think back on what I know of the murder, I think I'd be tempted—had I written the poem—to emphasize that the murder was finally unsolved, with nobody in Bradford about to give evidence, and the prime suspect finally set free. But Eberhart is usefully explicit about the details of the murder itself, and I take it he accepts as *implicit* the pivotal fact that guilt resides with what the court would call "a person or persons unknown." If I'm wrong about what Eberhart counts as implicit, I can only admit my sense of the poem's background as a self-defeating disadvantage. But I read-in nothing, I think, when I read Eberhart as answering his title-question with an acceptance of responsibility that involves the potential of guilt.

How (or whether) this "poetry of tragedy" may admit to guilt, yet survive, depends on how Eberhart answers his title-question. The rational question implies an innocently traditional *yes*. But that simple *yes* involves his man in *how* he may keep whatever neighbor. And to that second question, implicit within the first, the answer is complex, thickly ambivalent, and far from innocence. Eberhart's strange juxtaposition of his title-question and his assertive first line makes the poem difficult to discuss; the question and assertion seem, in retrospect, inextricably interrelated. I'm inclined to think that Eberhart *expects* his reader, moved into his first line, already to have answered the title-question with a glib affirmative. If this is so, then the reader is early trapped in imagining himself a kind of moral hero, worthy in his own right of Eberhart's implication that the "poetry of tragedy" survives by such men. But such glib rationalizing is a traditional trap, as the whole poem dramatizes. I find myself surprised, and moved, to discover as much. I can only think that my own critical predilections trapped me, as I first accepted the poem's most simple logic. Even in retrospect, I wonder that the poem's introductory assertion (compounded of title-question, implied answer, and first line) doesn't sentence the poem to immediate death. The proposition of the first line, in particular, seems too heroically abstract to admit of a tragic potential. But either to deny the assertion outright, or glibly to identify with it, is to deny the poem's deduction of its irrational complexities. (It is, in fact, to be already guilty of a kind of critical *hubris*.)

What is moving and remarkable about the poem is, I think, the complexity of involvement to which Eberhart was committed by writing it. If Eberhart perhaps began his poem with some notion of acting as intermediary between the world of classic tragedy and the world of the Bradford murder (only a journalistic "tragedy" at best), I think he found himself writing not only as an intermediary between the innocent rationality of his readers and the irrational murder, but as an intermediary between some several parts of himself. I think that Eberhart, in the writing-process of committing himself to an abstract proposition, discovered how the vengeance he began to consider irrationally committed him to realizations of guilt. "Am I My Neighbor's Keeper?" is a question for which Christian tradition demands, with the inevitability of Greek tragedy, the traditional answer, *I am*. And precisely according to the traditions of the Greek theatre, the drama of Eberhart's poem lies not in its predictable resolution, but in *how* he humanly arrives at it. A lesser poet might have contrived the poem's completion to satisfy the lesser demands of some simply rational structure. But Eberhart's present poem demands, beyond any rational tradition, that we share the guilt it ambiguously unveils. What is ambiguous? The murder's North Country issues involve neither States' Rights, a royal line of succession, nor a lynch mob; they're as simply human, universal, and classic as those which Eberhart brings to question. Yes. But Eberhart ambiguously commits himself to guilt (and traps us to commit ourselves) by *never defining to whom he most is neighbor*.

However unconsciously, the rational question of Eberhart's title involves a

On Richard Eberhart's "Am I My Neighbor's Keeper?"

dilemma of human choice which—as no man can rationally solve it—unveils for him the self-knowledge that his question has committed him to guilt. If Eberhart is neighbor to the taciturn farmer, keeping him safe from neighborly vengeance, he is accessory to the guilt of beating a hired man. If he is neighbor to the hired man, he becomes neighbor to his further neighbors in their vengeful guilt. Who is more guilty? The farmer who beats his handyman neighbor, or the neighbors who murder the farmer? There is guilt in both cases, and innocence in neither. That the handyman was beaten to "no great harm" (and that the "neighbor's" of the title is singular) seems to argue the greater guilt of the neighbors. But such a rationale nowhere in the poem absolves Eberhart from his self-discovered emotional complicity, nor does it resolve the "inexplicable essence" of his moral dilemma. Few poets and fewer critics have found right ways of dramatically realizing the relationship between "poetry" and "life"; but Eberhart's poem, as it unveils the human commitments posed by its language, demands recognition on just such terms. If, in "the ambiguity of what things ever seem," a man must (by the language of his traditions) commit himself to choice, the poem argues that he commits himself (in "life" as in a poem) to the tragic realization that his choice is both ambiguous and irrational.

If we fail to accept our choice in such events as commit us to acknowledge the ambiguous truth, Eberhart seems to say, we cannot experience the poetry which makes our tragedy bearable. "If it were not so," Eberhart (and we) "Would not dream / On principles so deep. . . ." But we do dream, in the traditions of Antigone, Hamlet, and Cordelia. And Eberhart realizes for us, in this poem, that such dreaming repeatedly involves us in those "veils of error" which hide the essential truth (however ambiguous it may be). Eberhart procrastinates like Hamlet in his octave, as well he might when faced with what is so richly "unanswerable." But he rationally recognizes such unanswerability as "the profound caught in plain air," and admits both poetry and tragedy to be that "inexplicable essence" which "visits us in our lair." The assertive octave turns on that key word, "lair," shadowed as it is with the image of Plato's cave.

If the language of the octave is, in effect, the shadow-language of abstract moral traditions, the language of the sestet specifies those moral choices by which men survive or die in the "plain air." "The truth" of such choices is only

On Richard Eberhart's "Am I My Neighbor's Keeper?"

"his" who, as murderer or murdered man, lies outside our shadowy knowledge. As the octave turns on "lair," the sestet turns to demonstrate the full involvement to which the octave (including its title-question) has committed itself, Eberhart, and us. Precisely as "tragedy sought out Socrates," we (in our traditional-rational lair) are sought out to deduce the irrational choices to which our mindful questions have committed us. Where might we (apparently as safe as Frost's drumlin woodchuck) be ever involved in tragic self-knowledge? Well, Eberhart seems to say, of a number of possible places, "Say here, on a remote New Hampshire farm." The immediate possibility is so rationally remote that only our blood can rise to its demand, pressured as we are by the traditions of the octave. All our glib identification with Socrates, all our early wisdom as self-assigned heroes, has collapsed on the octave's transitional comma. The veiled language of abstract shadows becomes a language that unveils those specific events to which, by deduction, we are morally committed.

There must still be at least one man, in Bradford, who will always know himself, and perhaps be known by his neighbors, by what he risked on an unlikely night. It's easy to think that Richard Eberhart, as one knows his sweating smile, could never be part of such up-country vengeance. Yet in ways equal to whatever risk of blood, Eberhart seems to me to have committed himself, through this new poem, to some of humanity's veiled and daily darkness. From traditionally rational assertions, he has deduced his own irrational involvement; and he involves us in that dilemma by *how* he unveils the specifics to which abstraction has committed him. As much is true even in the poem's least techniques. As Eberhart's *m* and *n* sounds compound in the last six lines, they're like cotton in a reader's mouth, as difficult to get rid of as guilt. "Farm," "pre-dawn," "handyman" and "harm" build with an irrational inevitability to "lawn": a climax to this series which terribly presents "light"—and prepares us for the plain fact of "later," when our guilt caught us under the dam. But even our guilt, ambiguous and irrational as it is, "gives to this day no answer." Eberhart's final "I am" is, in the context of the final couplet, an answer to the title-question only marginally related to it. In its ambiguous commitment to more than a single neighbor, it irrationally answers the dead (and all that is dead) with the tenuous self-knowledge of survival in spite of guilt. It is a climactic, and earned, margin of how irrationally, yet how meaningfully, "the poetry of tragedy" may ever unveil itself to survive. "Unanswerable" as the poem's prime question may be, in "this day" which is both a morning and an age, the question which the poem ultimately raises (and dramatizes) is the tragedy of commitments so irrationally ambiguous that there is no tradition by which to decide between them.

WILLIAM STAFFORD

No Answer to this Day

Richard Eberhart owns this poem; it is marked with his odd and endearing brands. Or you might say it has wounds: many of his poems are like ads for hiring the handicapped—"It makes sense; they have surprising strengths, and among these overlooked talents are sturdy qualities which could make you rich." So with this poem, it comes staggering up from a poor, slapdash beginning, and then parades in triumph, in acrobatic strength, as—caught in plain air—the profound corpse proclaims its tragic enigma: I am.

The echoes in the first stanza have an insidious appeal: if the reader veers to Keats in the first line—"The poetry of earth is never dead"—and to Longfellow in a more sidling way in line four—"mournful numbers . . . things are not what they seem"—then these responses hover in the mind disquietingly. The echoes insist; but a writer is sly—he knows you know and then goes on to use your simplicity. This wavering is an early issue in this poem—how to account for, defend, or indict the jangle of echoes presented almost to the point of parody, this sudden draft on Bartlett's *Familiar Quotations.* Confounding the readers could be just for fun. The juggling of passages can entertain; but two consistent displacements occur in this stanza, and the effect is to freeze the reader's response to something serious, but not necessarily to something convincing. One of the consistencies is that the echoes retain or increase their ominousness or portentousness; the first displacement in a quotation—not "poetry" of earth, but "tragedy" of earth—establishes the direction of displacement. Another consistency in the use of these echoes is that a rigor in reasoning is steadily implied—"If it were not so. . . ." The result of these elements—the serious turn and the formidable use of the passages—is that the reader of this stanza feels obliged to pay serious attention to some kind of case being asserted in terms of quickly mobilized allusions.

Does the reader willingly take up this job in this stanza? Can he confidently weave a positive course amid the richnesses and partial connections? The mind is able to adjust to such obligations, almost anywhere: you can sic your mind into a thicket of meaning and make it come out headed in any desired direction; but with this stanza the impulse is to hold the mind in leash and ask of the stanza that it first untangle, divest itself of gratuitous flippancies. Or put it this way: as

On Richard Eberhart's "Am I My Neighbor's Keeper?"

you are poised for commitment to a poem, either you receive inducements, hints of future pay-off, enticing concurrences in what you glimpse, or—and this is my experience with this poem—you receive signals which say, "Poor investment, cut your losses, stay free from maddening alliances." The contentions offered as truths and as consequences of truths do not immediately entice me; Aristotle would go dithering among these ambi-sequiturs, and my own mind, though indulgent with my vagrancies, is often austere about perceived delinquency in others' thought, unless I have been jollied into partnership first. No such persuasion is evident here, as the stanza jauntily asserts a non-exhaustive succession of big options. True, the jauntiness catches the attention, and high spirits command some allegiance; but this engaging quality is more than canceled by grandiosity in phrases like "principles so deep." So, to tell the truth (an impulse to be indulged on occasions like this, among friends), the first stanza ends without much momentum for me; and only a habit of leaning forward when I read carried me into the second stanza. (My first sight of this poem came when I was holding *The Saturday Review* beside me, snatching a few minutes of reading while waiting for a family dinner to begin.)

The second stanza, however, made me late for dinner: good influences begin to dominate. What is it that calls us to commitment on such occasions? For me it was not any of the more elaborate realizations I now have the urge to expound, but it was a general sense of development in the main ingredients of the poem. For instance, later I might hark back and like "shaped in veils of error," and I do so hark back; but at first reading it was along in the second line of the second stanza that my antennae began to quiver with positive signals, and particularly with "the profound caught in plain air." Is it in the phrasing that inducement comes? I believe not, or at least not primarily. This phrasing begins to catch up resonance with the rest of the poem, and with a rich, vibrating word I had read at the beginning—"Eberhart." Little gongs begin to sound all the way back to some occasion in college when I stood, neglecting my lessons, snatching a look at an early poem by this writer: aerial bombardments begin to come at me again through this plain air.

The poem has begun to breathe. Reading "Centuries after tragedy sought out Socrates" I unleash what has been withheld before; and from now on my efforts are seconding the poem; what were stumblings before are now occasions

On Richard Eberhart's "Am I My Neighbor's Keeper?"

for leaping, and coming upon "inexplicable" in the next line I no longer abide with ditherings from Aristotle or anyone else and merely accept the word tentatively, and then am glad, treasuring up a retrospective validation of "unanswerable" which had irked me two lines earlier, but which now reverberates. Still, all is not smooth in acceptance: "lair" at the end of the line sets my teeth on edge—such a reached-for word, so odd. I experience a wave of dis-allegiance, mixed with envy of a person who has friends so powerful they may defend him and probably (I grant this in a flash to my cringing self) vindicate him, even, for using this insulting offhand word. But my hesitations and my flickering thoughts of Eberhart's commando friends turn to allegiance again as the sound of *lair* modulates in a trapeze-lilt move into the new stanza, without a full pause, and onto the location and the clenching of the poem: "Say here."

The poem is thriving. It could be carpentered out to the ending and could suffer much, and still not fail. Or so I tell myself in the momentum of my delight. And at this point, just when smug recognition has been elicited, a further bonus occurs, and the writer firmly proves his ascendancy. The place where this happens for me may mark an unusual reaction, but I do experience something exotic and good in the phrase "but no great harm." There is unexpected magnanimity in the ending of the line, a turn of consideration which would not have occurred to me, and I get a sense of associating with a person whose moral judgments have a scope and freedom I could never without his help understand. At this point I learn the difference between the fine latent possibilities in the poem and my own mean performance as a reader. Hitherto I had not attained the perspective of tragedy, but had been reacting in terms of local encounters: for the duration of the earlier lines my parochial responses allied me with the murderer; his impulses would be my impulses. My local resentments subside even as in a wave of welcomed ambiguities light speaks vengeance and the day receives its enigmatic message, the dammed corpse. "No great harm" has at first puzzled me and then broken in on my tame progression; the phrase opens a larger view that accepts without loss of balance the jolts which would precipitate thoughtless action in people like me.

The last line detains the reader. The form of the poem enables the last two words to link to the first two words of the title; and of course the last two words are also expressions from the corpse: both the speaker in the poem and the corpse assert that last positive statement, and it is disturbing, coming from either of them. The ending comes trailing a cloud of sound reinforcements from earlier rhymes, and it has its firm, fundamental echo of other emphatic assertions of I am.

A tour through the poem, part by part, has built a certain kind of accumulated effect; as in many other Eberhart poems the effect is dominantly moral. Here is a writer whose natural topic is something about what ought to be; this poem openly carries a moral thesis, and the parts enforce the issue throughout— truth, error, light, dark, harm, vengeance, question, answer, Socrates. So steady an intention deserves to be recognized in estimates of the poem.

Those brands or wounds or endearing handicaps noted at first now connect with this moral direction: as the serious intent of the poem emerges the reader begins to accept convictions about the importance of the end, and the writer's manner indicates that he too is involved in something so important that short-term sacrifices do not detain him. It is hard to specify these awkwardnesses, and ungrateful, too; and furthermore each reader might find extenuating circumstances for any cited passage. But I appeal to other readers—do you also read the poem with the persistent sense of its powerful ungracefulness? For me the clotted syllables, jerry-built comparisons, flat subject-verb-object sentences take on validating effects. The consequence is this: we begin to understand that we are pursuing serious topics; we have a straight purpose; we must close with important things and not waver; we have a thirst for righteousness which impels us hurriedly through trivial emergencies in the lines.

Richard Eberhart's poetry has this power of conviction. His open, blunt moves are appropriate for dealing with topics which deserve our precipitate attention. The manner and the content say he is trying to give to this day an answer; and it is part of the appeal of this poem that it takes a definite stance about important things.

This kind of poem, though, and all tragedy as intensified experience of what cannot be avoided, and all literary confrontation which welcomes enigma as a literary device—these efforts bear contradiction within them. At the end of "Am I My Neighbor's Keeper?" we receive intense commitment to the idea of involvement, but we gain that intensity at the cost of a realization that there is no way to *be* so. The stance is heroic; the literary effect is intense; but the social effect is paralyzing, just as the enigmas of violence in much current literature are paralyzing: Hemingway and Faulkner are prototypes of this kind of intense futility. Indicated moves in the processes of doing good are blurred for the purpose of artistic effect. Eberhart's last line celebrates that kind of shuddering confrontation which delivers the tough, heroic—dead-end—response.

So—the topic of this poem is that of being concerned; the intensification achieved is by way of offering a particular instance with many reinforcing parts that reverberate our feelings—but then shut out impulses toward effective alleviation. In the process of realizing to the full the human helplessness which makes the poem live, the human intentions implied by the title are neglected and in a sense denied.

A sharp depiction of what should cause concern, along with a demonstration of what appear to be unanswerable obstacles to overcoming the situation, is the contemporary pattern in literature. The enigma is welcomed as a literary device. Puzzles which cannot be solved are posed against would-be solvers; human frailty is triumphantly demonstrated. Tough reality demands abjection—reality is strife, suffering, martyrdom. You prove you're real by failing.

Richard Eberhart illuminates this tradition, and he intermittently provides magnificent struggles against it; but what if we all are being immobilized by the devastating effectiveness of aesthetic power in religion and tragedy? My impulse is to struggle against being too much impressed by "no great harm" and other such temporary relaxations which just prepare me for the impending, artistic violence. There is great harm, or at least quite a bit of harm. A good keeper makes the open, easy, small moves which alleviate. Not forgiveness, but restraint in the first place, is the indicated need. Tragedy sought out Socrates, alas; but youth not trained to smugness need not be corrupted in order to be cured by brilliant—and enervating—paradoxes.

Put the other way round: the human condition permits little, helpful moves, by non-heroic people. Richard Eberhart's work often provides sustenance and exhilaration for such people. The static confronting of tragedy, however, in this poem, reduces the kind of value Mr. Eberhart prevalently offers.

Remember—if what I hint is treason I do not assert it loudly or with a flung gauntlet. Besides, am I this keeper's brother? Yes. I am.

RICHARD EBERHART

Looking at the original manuscript of "Am I My Neighbor's Keeper?," I see it is dated in pencil at the top of the left of the page, January 5, 1962. I forget what time of day it was. There are eighteen and a half lines in pencil, some of them somewhat reworked.

The poem was begun because I felt an urge to say something about an event, or series of events, which occurred in this region several years ago, of which I had read. The poem was apparently stimulated because of reading a current newspaper account of the happenings.

At the beginning the poem's final form was unknown. That is, it was not a preconceived poem as to form. It is a poem written in deliberation, with care toward exactitude of expression. It is unlike most of my poems, or what I like to think are most of my best poems, in the rationality of its inception and execution. I like to think that some of my best poems result, as in fact some have, from immediacy of inspiration. They burst into life spontaneously. To say it perhaps more accurately, they result from an upwelling into consciousness of a poetical system at once present to the imagination and available to immediate execution, from an unpredicated and unpredictable mood—perhaps of reverie or of memory, probably of both and of other elements—a state of more than ordinary perceptiveness and ability.

I have believed that some of my best poems have been given to me, as I have said elsewhere, as a gift of the gods. They are a laying-on of spiritual power or order, power of spirit, something given, not something sought or rationally tried for. I do not say that these poems are irrational for they plainly are not. I believe that the rational will could not bring them into being, but that, rather, the personality, at unpredictable times due, probably, to subtle and complex causes, becomes the vehicle for poetry. These times must be those of unusual harmony of nature. I suspect that these times, when the creative act is as easy as leaves coming to a tree, may be the source of what Keats called Negative Capability. I have tried to fathom what he meant and even now have only a general notion. I have never read a satisfying explanation of what he meant, although there are a good number of explanations on record. It must be, though, that this passive state is a negation, or negative side of what would be purposive action were one wholly acting, committed to purpose immediately impinging on the world. But here, in these negative states, there is the action of pen or pencil on paper, so that the poem becomes a surrogate for positive action.

It is only negative in one sense for, paradoxically, there may be more life in the creative act making the poem, and in the poem made (a poem which might conceivably live for hundreds of years), than there is in positive, so-called "real" action and its results. This state of creation has fascinated me but I have never been able to express to my satisfaction its meaning or essence. And I should say states, for no two states of being could be alike. And it is not certain in these states that a good poem will result, or that one would write a poem which one subsequently would publish.

My point is that the ordinary experiences of real life often rise to the mind some time (perhaps months, even years) after they have taken place, when one is in a mood of extraordinary receptivity, with an ability all their own to become poems which, startlingly enough, do not require the change of more than a line after their writing—if even that. Often the so-called real experience is a substratum upon which the imagination builds a new construction, the meaning of the poem in some cases almost unrelated to the original actual experience thought to be known in the real world. We are concerned here with the working of the psyche, which I consider to be mysterious. Poetry is on the lap of the gods while one is holding pen or pencil to paper.

Returning to the poem in question—which was conceived without the title, which was added later—I had written about eight lines, with some reworkings, in this deliberate, prose-like poetic use of the rational evaluative mind, when it probably occurred to me that there could be two quatrains, then a concluding six lines to make it a sonnet. The point is that this poem did not begin as a sonnet but became one. By breaking the quatrains it would look less like a sonnet.

I have nothing against the sonnet as a form of poetry. In my *Collected Poems* there is only one example of this form, a poem entitled "Burden," written very early. Thus I am not addicted to the sonnet form. Furthermore, I have partaken of a doctrine of William Carlos Williams that the sonnet is a dead form which should not be used if you feel you have exciting life within you. He held years ago that it was static, too rigid, fixed, a dead art form. I have been given to sometimes passionate acceptance of dicta passionately held by my colleagues.

On "Am I My Neighbor's Keeper?"

Williams on the sonnet was a case in point. I accepted his notion, although I was in no danger of writing a sonnet myself. About the time of my first book (1930) I had had a passionate outburst of sonnets, hoping to write as many as Shakespeare, in a youthful, high-spirited and misguided state, but my passion ran out at thirty-one sonnets. Only one or two of these were printed in magazines, none in a book. From that time I left the sonnet field.

Incidentally, I also learned from Dr. Williams his lesson on the badness, even the social as certainly the psychological harm of any kind of inversion. I took that preachment and practiced what he preached. However, I would like to point out a curious fact, which shows the ambivalence of poets even when they hold strong views. Since Dr. Williams was so dead set against the sonnet, as an archaic and non-viable form of poetry, you would think that he would never applaud in print a sonneteer. Yet he wrote introductory, laudatory words for a book of new sonnets by Dr. Merrill Moore, now deceased, who wrote more sonnets, I believe, than any man, far out-doing Petrarch in quantity.

Merrill Moore showed considerable invention in altering the accepted sonnet form. He did not on all occasions limit himself to fourteen lines. His line-breaks were ingenious. His grammar, caesurae, and punctuation were sometimes original. He tried to put everything of the world as he saw it into his sonnets and was said to have written at least one every day from his teens. Sometimes he would dash one off between changes of the traffic lights on the way to his psychiatric office on Commonwealth Avenue. His understanding of old Boston ladies and gentlemen was acute and is fixed in sonnets he wrote about them and other metropolitan types. I thought better of Dr. Williams for applauding his colleague than if he had refused to write introductory remarks due to a too-rigid anti-sonnet motivation.

The first line of my poem was written "The poetry of tragedy is never ended." The last word was changed to "dead" because the third line concluded with "ending." I was thinking of the first line of Keats' sonnet "On the Grasshopper and Cricket," which begins "The poetry of earth is never dead" (December 30, 1816). I wanted the idea of the poetry of earth but had in mind something much more stern than Keats' poem, which is only pleasant. As a matter of fact, I could not recall the rest of his lines, but the first had stayed with me for decades. It is characteristic of English poetry that sometimes single lines may stay in the memory while a series of lines or a whole poem do not. Sometimes a series of lines stays, but not the whole poem.

I do not intend to comment on every line of the poem. In the second quatrain I first wrote "Centuries after tragedy-seeking Socrates." I felt that this was not right and subsequently emended the line to read "Centuries after tragedy sought out Socrates." Even the wisdom of Socrates cannot avail to unseat tragedy.

The particularities of the sestet are in contrast to the generalizations in the first two quatrains. The principle of the first line is exemplified in the narration at the end. There is an overtone, or so I felt, that the first line is true even after the bleak ending of the poem. The paradox of death keeps the idea alive. I feel, but do not know whether others should, a contributory subtlety in a pun on damn, meaning damnation, in the word dam. The statement at the end not only announces the final bleakness of the tragic situation but has, perhaps, the overtone that if the murdered man could speak he would do so, although he could only do so now in the mute form of a corpse. The line "Light spoke vengeance and bloodstains on the lawn" was first written "When light came, there were bloodstains on the lawn." The details of the substantive event were taken from a newspaper account of the actual occurrence, as I said at the beginning. Such being the case, this poem is not typical of my practice.

The reader may wish to know what I think is typical of my practice, if this sonnet is not. There are fine distinctions in types of imagination at work in the making of poems. Perhaps one does not or cannot know what is typical of his methods, which change with time, and take the perspective of a disinterested critic to determine.

I like to think of a passage from Plato which speaks for what the Greeks called the divine madness. Plato's meaning is plain and convincing. He says,

> For all good poets, epic as well as lyric, compose their beautiful poems not by art, but because they are inspired and possessed. And as the Corybantian revellers when they dance are not in their right mind, so the lyric poets are not in their right mind when they are composing their beautiful strains; but when falling under the power of music and meter they are inspired and possessed; like Bacchic maidens who draw milk and honey from the rivers when they are under the influence of Dionysus but not when they are in their right mind. And the soul of the lyric poet does the same, as they themselves say; for they tell us that they

On "Am I My Neighbor's Keeper?"

> bring songs from honeyed fountains, culling them out of the gardens and dells
> of the Muses; they, like the bees, winging their way from flower to flower. And
> this is true. For the poet is a light and winged and holy thing, and there is no
> invention in him until he has been inspired and is out of his senses, and the
> mind is no longer in him: when he has not attained to this state, he is powerless
> and is unable to utter his oracles.*

This is one kind of dogma about poetry. I am sympathetic to this point of view
and know that some of my poems have sprung into being under the Platonic
aegis and auspice. I respect this theory of inspiration because it is beyond and
above conscious will. Therefore, a poem composed as the reception of a "gift of
the gods" would seem to be of a higher origin and nature than a poem composed
by taking thought, and then taking care.

Some of my poems which I think of as coming under this theory of creation
are "Now Is the Air Made of Chiming Balls," "If I Could Only Live at the
Pitch That Is Near Madness," "1934," "Go to the Shrine That's on a Tree,"
"Only in the Dream," and possibly also, but perhaps less purely, poems like
"Maze," "For a Lamb," "The Groundhog," "In a Hard Intellectual Light," "In
Prisons of Established Craze," "Light from Above," and "Vast Light."

On the other hand, I grew up in the convictions of ambiguity, ambivalence,
and irony as central to poetry and cannot rationally accept Plato's last words
"when he has not attained to this state, he is powerless and is unable to utter his
oracles." Leaving aside the old-fashioned notion of oracles, this is a special sort of
pleading which has no absolute truth. It may have a relative truth. I can more
readily imagine the truth of the first half of Plato's last sentence than I can that
of the second half.

A poet is not powerless and unable to create when his mind is very much
with him. It may be that he may be most powerful when least "inspired and . . .
out of his senses" in Plato's ideology. Modern effects of ambiguity, ambivalence,
and irony would seem to be controlled by a conscious use of the mind, by will,
not to be created by the divine madness of Plato. I could adduce numbers of my
poems which would evade the exclusiveness of Plato's dictum. "Am I My Neighbor's Keeper?" is certainly one of them. Plato is talking about pure poetry, which

* *The Dialogues of Plato*, "Ion," translated by B. Jowett (Random House, 1937).

is rare. Most poetry has the impurity of the whole warring and loving human nature of man.

The foregoing was written before Mr. Ostroff sent me the criticisms of Louise Bogan, Philip Booth, and William Stafford. Their critiques are quite different, as would be expected, and only one of the poet-critics, Mr. Booth, happened to know the actual event which motivated the poem.

Miss Bogan spends over half of her article on a historical consideration of the sonnet as an art form. She seems to be somewhat afraid of it. She writes, "For the sonnet has peculiar and, it would at moments seem, magical and sacred powers." She does not adumbrate these powers. I admire her respect for the form. She says "A succession of fourteen lines of prose cannot be named a sonnet; neither can thirteen lines of verse." I take a more liberal view and believe new wine can be poured into old bottles. Roy Fuller, whom she mentions, has written a most effective series of poems, entitled "To X" (*Shenandoah,* Spring, 1963), each of thirteen lines, which have the controlled artistry of a *tour de force,* and have the feel and look of sonnets, although Miss Bogan would deny the allegation. His poems are in two quatrains with a concluding passage of five rather than six lines. The reader is invited to study his intricate rhyme scheme. There is the further device, employed effectively with occasional subtle variation, of a repetition of lines two and eight and a repetition of lines seven and thirteen. Mr. Fuller maintains this graceful and artful mode through a series of twenty-one "sonnets," a splendid success in enlivening and altering the sonnet form for contemporary pleasure. I gladly accept Miss Bogan's animadversions on my own sonnet, which are well reasoned and sincerely made.

Both of the other critiques penetrate the poem differently.

Mr. Booth's reading is deep. He sees the poem as a system of mutual guilt, the guilt of the protagonist, the guilt of the neighbor or neighbors, the guilt of the author, and the guilt of the reader.

He is aware of the subtleties of the ramifications of all the possibilities in these contexts. He admits that as the murder was unresolved, the problems of the poem are unresolved, if not unresolvable. The protagonist is his neighbor's keeper, ironically, in that he will keep him in his place. The murderer or murderers are the protagonist's keeper or keepers in that they kept him deepest of all, as a trussed corpse under the dam. Mr. Booth may not sufficiently point up the grammar of the last two lines, which state that the corpse, or the fact of the corpse, says that "I am." But he perceives that this has other than literal connotations. He also, while implicating him, which is human and reasonable, absolves the author in favor of the impersonality of poetry. He writes, the author "ambiguously commits himself to guilt (and traps us to commit ourselves) by *never defining to whom he most is neighbor.*" He sees that the problem goes back to Cain and Abel, stating that the "veils of error" hide "the essential truth."

He equates irrationality with ambiguity at the end, saying "the question which the poem ultimately raises (and dramatizes) is the tragedy of commitments so irrationally ambiguous that there is no tradition by which to decide between them." Why irrationally ambiguous? Why not rationally ambiguous? But he may be right, since reason cannot pierce the veil of this mystery. In suggesting that irrationality also may not, he gives the reader a deep sense of the mysteries behind the poem.

Where Mr. Booth deals principally with ideas, Mr. Stafford is more personal and lets the reader intimately in on his experience in reading the poem. This approach is engaging; he does not hold back, but gives himself sturdily to his feelings; he gives the reader the pleasures of his own self-discovery. Noting Keats, he also suggests Longfellow's "mournful numbers . . . things are not what they seem," which I should not have thought of. His prose is almost racy in spots—"you can sic your mind into a thicket of meaning and make it come out headed in almost any direction." He has fine phrases like "gratuitous flippancies," "maddening alliances," "big options" and uses enticing terms like "dithering," "jauntiness," and "grandiosity." Students should enjoy his confessional manner: "(My first sight of this poem came when I was holding *The Saturday Review* beside me, snatching a few minutes of reading while waiting for a family dinner to begin.)" The next sentence reads, "The second stanza, however, made me late for dinner . . ."

He goes on to narrate the circumstances and see-sawings of his immersion in the poem, a humane and enjoyable kind of literary criticism. The reader is won to him as he explains how he was won to the poem. And when he has the humanity to announce his own possible "mean performance as a reader" the author also renders up his recognition of the unlikelihood of writing a perfect poem.

He sees nice points: "The form of the poem enables the last two words to link to the first two words of the title." He says outright "both the speaker in the poem and the corpse assert that last positive statement, and it is disturbing, coming from either of them."

He moves to moral considerations and to the idea of concern, and then generalizes from this poem as a limited type to want some other answers from contemporary literature. His last few paragraphs are stimulating, but not altogether clear to me. I wish he would expand them into a general essay on modern poetry. Criticism has to keep its eye on the work being criticized. Any reader can see that this is not a heroic poem. Goethe was sensible when he said that for criticism to be just the critic should state the author's intention and judge the work according to how well he had fulfilled that intention.

We have here three different types of critical commentary. Miss Bogan's deals with a kind of poem and this poem as an example of the kind. Mr. Booth penetrates the poem deeply and gives the most objective account of its properties. Mr. Stafford gives the reader a lively personalized experience of reading the poem, extending his appreciation to what sort of poetry in our modern world he would like to see.

On rereading Mr. Stafford's last few paragraphs I believe he had misread the poem. He does not seem to consider the conditions absolute, which they are. If the condition of murder is absolute (since Cain), there is no way of alleviation; there is no "restraint," in his sense, which would cause people to hold back from action; all are involved; and thus this is a tragic poem.

The recognition of tragedy is its own reward ("Was man made stupid to see his own stupidity?"). By recognition one could hope man would be better. But the idea of poetry as propaganda to do good is not the idea behind this poem. Against certain ideas, which are absolute, there are no relative solutions. Tragedy is one of these absolute ideas. For instance, if the beating of a handyman had not become a problem perhaps one could conclude that certain social restraints were operant. "No great harm" indicates that within the poem the suggestion is that the protagonist should have been able to get away with it. This itself is a big question. But the neighbor or neighbors took over and by committing murder on the protagonist (there is even a theory that he committed suicide and trussed himself) raised the situation to the absolute that began with Cain.

On "Am I My Neighbor's Keeper?"

There is no use having any heroic ideas about this poem. If Stafford wants heroism, which Booth saw was not in question, and which I dream of too in other contexts, he won't find it in such a situation as this and cannot validly criticize the poem for being something which it plainly is not. It is not propaganda, it is art.

GEORGE P. ELLIOTT

KARL SHAPIRO

STEPHEN SPENDER

W. H. AUDEN

On W. H. AUDEN'S

"*A Change of Air*"

W. H. Auden

A CHANGE OF AIR

Corns, heartburn, sinus headaches, such minor ailments
Tell of estrangement between your name and you,
Suggest a change of air: heed them, but let
The modesty of their discomfort warn you
Against the flashy errands of your dreams.

To grow a sailor's beard, don monkish garb,
Or trade in an agglutinative tongue
With a stone-age culture would be mollycoddling:
To go elsewhere is to abstain from movement;
A side-step, a short one, will convey you thither.

Although its chaffinches, maybe, have learned
The dialect of another river-basin,
A fault transformed the local building stone,
It has a priest, a post-mistress, an usher,
Its children know they are not to beg from strangers.

Within its average elsewhereishness
Your name is as a mirror answers, yourself
How you behave in shops, the tips you give;
It sides with neither, being outside both,
But welcomes both with healing disregard.

Nor when you both return here (you will, of course),
Where luck and instinct originally brought you,
Will it salute your reconciliation
With farewell rites, or populate your absence
With reverent and irreverent anecdote.

No study of your public reappearance
Will show, as judgment on a cure demands,
A sudden change in love, ideas or diet;
Your sojourn elsewhere will remain a wordless
Hiatus in your voluble biography.

Fanatic scholarship at most may prove
That you resigned from a Committee, unearth
A letter from the Grand-Duke to his cousin,
Remarking, among more important gossip,
That you seem less amusing than you were.

GEORGE P. ELLIOTT

A poem of speculation on a difficult part of the actual world is apt to be hard to understand at first reading. When it comes from a mind as quick, various, and quirky as Auden's, it must be read more than once to be read at all. In "A Change of Air," which is such a commentary poem, there are two immediate perplexities. Who is "you"? What does "it" in the middle three stanzas refer to? Now one may be agile enough to decide after the first reading that "you" is a very important government official—a prime minister or a secretary of state, someone of that sort—and that "it" must refer to "thither" in line ten, which refers in turn to the unspecified place where "you" are to go for a change of air. Even so, there will be a few more readings before the parts of the poem settle into order in the reader's mind, for this is not a poem held like the meat of a nut in a shell of puzzle. The difficulty native to speculative poetry is owing to the nature of the truth, which is the main thing such poetry aims to say to a reader. To be worth learning, a truth must be hard to learn, either because it is of itself hard to grasp or because its location is difficult of access; and some truths, because they cannot be completely stated, can be learned only imperfectly, temporarily, partially. In "A Change of Air" the generic difficulty is put to specific use, by being so built into the structure of the poem itself that there never comes a time when one can state exactly what the poem is about.

This is the less to be expected since the poem is as much prose as verse. The rhythmic unit is as much the phrase or clause as it is the metrical foot or the line, as much the sentence as the stanza; every statement is in itself clear enough; images, figures, and symbols neither obscure the paraphrasable meaning nor siphon energy away from it; the words are those of intellectual discourse. When at every moment you are clear about where you are, it is strange to discover aftterward that you are not quite sure where you have been.

To be sure, the poem is also as much verse as prose. Prosodically this is not one of Auden's virtuoso pieces (surely he is the master craftsman of the present age), but the foot, the line, the stanza are all solidly there. The movement is characteristic of Auden's speculative, commentary verse: a very complicated shuffling, loping, side-stepping dance, much imitated in this generation but never imitated successfully. It is usually best when, as here, its variations are worked out on a strong prosodic structure. For example, if the first three lines of the fourth stanza had been printed as free verse—say in lines measured by rhetorical pauses —then the iambic foundation of the verses' dance would hardly have been felt by the reader, at least not in a way that would matter; also, he would have missed the special liveliness of meaning which is given to the following words by virtue of their being joined by pentameter in the same line, "Your name is as a mirror answers, yourself," a joining which would have felt unpleasantly artificial for any other than a prosodic reason. Each of the five-line stanzas consists of one self-contained sentence, with no more stanzaic enjambment of meaning than of syntax, and each of the seven sentence-stanzas is a necessary part of the rational structure of the argument. In other words, the poem is not mysterious because the dance is irrational and ambiguous.

In what does the mystery reside? Before answering this question, I had better suggest what I mean by the mystery anyway. To help do this, I will contrast "A Change of Air" with one of Auden's earliest commentary poems, #29 in his first book *Poems* (1930), "Consider this and in our time / As the hawk sees it or the helmeted airman" (reprinted in *Collected Poetry*, 1945, as "Consider," with the first part of the third paragraph omitted). The reasons for the later poem's total superiority over the earlier one, which it in some ways resembles, indicate something about its special quality.

(Not that "A Change of Air" is without flaws. The first word seems to be there more for its power to surprise than for its truth: I doubt that there is any sense in which corns can "tell of estrangement between your name and you," as there is some psychosomatic sense in which heartburn and sinus headaches may be thought to do so; since there is no possible magic in the making of corns, any magical use they are put to, of this sort, is merely whimsical. In line 5, "errands" seems less than the right word, though in another context dreams as errand-bearers would be a good idea. The parenthesis in the first line of the fifth stanza, "(you will, of course)," is a bit easy and expectable, especially to anyone who knows Auden's poetry well. But none of these flaws is serious enough to harm the poem.)

"Consider" also is difficult to understand, but before long one suspects that

On W. H. Auden's "A Change of Air"

that puzzle probably contains nothing of much substance and certainly hides no mystery. The obscurity of this line does not seem to be worth the trouble of cracking: "In Cornwall, Mendip, or the Pennine moors." Nothing in the poem explains why these three geographical names are joined, nor does their being joined illuminate anything in the poem; it is cryptic for the sake of being cryptic, to mark the in-group off from all those others, the brash young gang from the bosses. The first paragraph is apparently addressed to an unspecified, generalized reader. The second paragraph (". . . supreme Antagonist") is addressed to the devil, who like the God of the next and more celebrated poem, "Sir, no man's enemy," owes his existence to rhetorical convenience. The first part of the third paragraph ("Financier") is addressed, as many of Auden's speculative poems are, to a person of importance in society, a type that is scarcely at all an individual either in situation or in traits of personality. The dominant tone of the poem is threatening: "the insufficient units / Dangerous, easy, in furs, in uniforms"; "mobilize the powerful forces latent / In soils that make the farmer brutal / In the infected sinus, and the eyes of stoats"; "It is later than you think"; and, the last two lines, "To disintegrate on an instant in the explosion of mania / Or lapse for ever into a classic fatigue." Finally, though one neither knows nor wants to know all the references in the poem, one does know exactly what it intends to do: to bully the "you" of the third paragraph, a type not far from the "you" of "A Change of Air." The intelligence of observation and comment and the prosodic skill of the original, 1930 "Consider" are put to a service which is immediately exciting but finally ignoble. The 1945 version, by omitting the financier, makes the object of the threat vague and generalized, and the poem loses much even of its initial excitement.

The aim of "A Change of Air" is quieter—to understand the "you," not to shove him around and gloat over him. He is still not happy, and he is still bothered by sinus trouble; but he is seen by a wiser poet, by the poet in a wiser way. He is seen as recognizing both his social responsibilities and the division in himself brought about by his position. He is seen as a man—a man who has some idea of what is wrong with him and of how to heal himself. Just because he is apprehended as a person, he is seen as mysterious; and the poet does not violate his mystery by shoving him into a type and then threatening the type with ob-

On W. H. Auden's "A Change of Air"

literation, mostly for the malicious joy of threatening. Instead, he makes mystery essential to the poem just as it is essential to the "you"—that is, to this sort of man as the poet is now apprehending him.

The questions provoked by a first reading of the poem (Who is "you"? Where is "it" he goes to for a change of air?) become again, after the lesser difficulties have vanished with understanding and familiarity, the questions about which the reader's imagination plays. But now, instead of being as-yet-unexplained perplexities about the poem, they point to not-to-be-explained mysteries in the actual world.

The "you," the reader has learned, is a man of consequence in worldly affairs. But, just because the reference of "you" is uncertain and indeterminable in the first five stanzas, "you" can be every citizen. You need not be a Minister to need a change of air—to have fantasies of disappearing into outlandish disguises, to find a split between your self and your name, to seek the "healing disregard" of a world of ordinary civilized decency. Yet the "you" is indeed a special case; he is not only a heightened form of the general, but also a case peculiar to his own high position. He will not remain identifiable as every man.

The core of the strangeness—and the special wonder of the poem—is the nature of the "it" into which "you" can retire for a while. Here are the words which refer to it: "a change of air"; "A side-step, a short one, will convey you thither"; all of the middle three stanzas, especially "elsewherishness" and "healing disregard" in the central stanza; "Your sojourn elsewhere will remain a wordless / Hiatus in your voluble biography." The clue is in the paradoxical line in stanza 2, "To go elsewhere is to abstain from movement," and its sequel "A side-step, a short one, will convey you thither." And the "you" who is seen as able to sidestep into that elsewherishness which is not elsewhere need not be just a VIP; in some degree he can be every man in danger of being cut off from his name, his public self, by worldly concerns. You—you the VIP, you every civilized man, you the reader—can refresh yourself by going into the city of your average life in a different way for a while.

When Harun al-Rashid wanted to go among his people, he could not take his name with him. What is this poem's not-elsewhere city—it has post-mistress, priest, and usher, "Its children know they are not to beg from strangers"—which cordially

GEORGE P. ELLIOTT
On W. H. Auden's "A Change of Air"

leaves a VIP and his name alone to come together as they wish and makes no to-do over his returning to the "here" from which he came? The tact of the poem is not to say, and I think it unmannerly of an exegete to try to define the secret of a poem much more explicitly than its creator has felt called upon to do—especially when the poem itself is a sort of exegesis of a part of the mysterious world.

KARL SHAPIRO

Nobody in his right mind is going to horse around with an Auden poem—even a blackboard poem like this one, written with one hand tied behind him. Talk about *an* Auden poem is anyhow irrelevant; he is a poet of issues and the issues are big. He is his own anthology, the typical poet of the age, the Explainer, and all that. He really is all that. He is lots of other things, one of the few masters of modern speech, one of the great practitioners of English prosody, a true custodian of the tradition. In the Serious World he is already *aere perennius,* something which is not absolutely certain about Eliot, for instance.

Baudelaire was a great furniture salesman and the twentieth century is still buying and selling his Effects.

> *Des meubles luisants,*
> *Polis par les ans,*
> *Décoreraient notre chambre* . . .

He was also the pseudo-traveler or travel agent.

The travel agent never goes anywhere and is apparently happy sighing through the brochures. This voyage of Baudelaire's which he never took—never intended to take—is one of the great topics of modern poetic conversation. But B after all was on short tether; A is not. Baudelaire made an ideology out of his fear of travel and his hatred of the home town (Paris). We inherit his hatred and his fears. But Auden has the ambience of a fish and is a regular Vasco da Gama. The voyage of B has long since become an affair of psychoanalysts. The voyage of A was a quest and ended successfully in the chapel. B was ashamed of his touristic sensibility and lampooned it, while A covered all the ground and found it wanting. In between was Rimbaud, the last of the voyagers to really go Elsewhere. Nowadays going Elsewhere is as easy as falling off a log.

To go elsewhere is to abstain from movement. One might as well stay Here. Travel poetry is the poetry of our time; we take Baudelaire's voyage after making very sure that the furnishings will not upset us when we arrive at Elsewhere. Nice shiny old furniture, maybe scented with the perfume of the locale, but really just like mother's old bedroom at home.

For all practical purposes, Place has ceased to exist. A change of air is about all that is left of the voyage, minor therapy or getting a tan in January. One would think that all searches are over and done with, that poets are as blank as scientists, searching out there for something to discover. Like newspapers. Auden of course is not talking about any of this but about fame. And yet he would not be chatting about fame if there were still someplace to go, some quest to be fulfilled. On the other hand, the voyage in the old romantic days was the classic way to find one-self (fame and fortune) or putting oneself back together again (broken heart). This dissociation of name and self in Auden's poem is a very minor form of ennui, almost not worth bothering about. This is a very balanced poem that pivots in the middle. In the pivotal stanza there is a wishful thought that the poet's fame might live a life of its own, whether the poet is taking his fame for a walk or has left it home in the drawer. It is always surprising to surprise oneself in a shop window.

I think it was Robert Browning who said his name over and over until he reached the plane of illumination—the moment before the fit so often described by epileptics. Browning was the farthest thing from an epileptic, and we have no illuminati among modern poets, only consciousness addicts and intelligent poets. Intelligent poets are extremely rare and Auden is one of them. Perhaps it is the voyage to the land of intelligence which makes modern poetry so peculiar. In any case, this concern about name and self pulls the rug out from under poetry. If there is one question the poet is not allowed to ask it is Who am I? (There goes ninety per cent of poetry.)

Name and fame are interchangeables (in this poem I read "name" almost as a misprint). To say one's own name (except with prigs) requires psychological ef-fort. To say one's own name is a kind of sin; it is for others to say. In fact, to see oneself in a mirror takes a great deal of skill and a very high degree of conscious-ness. There are no end of platitudes on the subject, beginning with Narcissus. Auden wrote once

> How beautiful it is
> that eye-on-the-object look

and paid homage to the first collector of sea-shells, the first maker of flints. Alas for the poet, whose objects are necessarily the products of his own psyche. Fool as he will with words they are only *his* words. In the craftsmanship of Art there is no real objectivity. Isn't consciousness the opposite of poetry? Isn't it when the poet is forced to be conscious that he cracks? Even Valéry, a self-created monster of consciousness, treated his art as *donnée*.

As far as poetry is concerned, there is no "average elsewherishness" except perhaps for Sunday poets. Your fame (name) can't live its own life but can only do what you do. No poet really believes that he behaves normally in a shop; he behaves either famously or like an escaped felon. Properly speaking, he doesn't behave at all—he is behaved by. Yet there are those blessed moments of relief when one pretends to experience a change of air.

> Your sojourn elsewhere will remain a wordless
> Hiatus in your voluble biography.

Depending on what you wrote there.

A poet never confuses his fame with the fame of his poems, it seems to me. It is the others who do that (they have no choice). Nothing is more remote from the poet than what he has already published; I daresay nothing is more painful to him than reading his old poems before an audience. Nothing is more puzzling to him than those old poems. Consequently he is the least equipped to say what was intended. Practically everything a poet says about his work has a special irrelevance. As for tinkering with old poems, as Yeats and Auden do, perhaps that is the only way the poet can stand to read his old works.

Elsewhere is the place where the poet lays down on the job. But characteristically this is what the poet never can do. When he is not "converting" he is dead. It is better to be Wordsworth writing all that drivel than to take a change of air. As for corns, heartburn, etc., those are the minor ailments of people of the Serious World, not poets. Poets have a different psychosomatology. This poem of Auden's is probably addressed to, say, a famous historian.

STEPHEN SPENDER

What strikes me immediately about "A Change of Air" is that it is a return in subject and manner to the early "think" poems of Auden. When I say early I mean the pre-1930 Auden who wrote occasionally poems about time, change, etc., as well as the famous ones about love.

For example, there is a poem ending with the lines:

On neither side let foot slip over
Invading Always, exploring Never,
For this is hate and this is fear.

On narrowness stand, for sunlight is
Brightness only on surfaces;
No angel, no traitor, but peace.

The influence of Robert Graves' "O love be fed with apples while you may" is so heavy in the early poem as to lay the young Auden open to reproach for cribbing (compare the last line of the Auden quoted above with the last line of the Graves poem, "With the grave's narrowness, though not its peace," and this is apparent). Perhaps on account of an unconscious memory of the earlier poems of this kind, "A Change of Air" is also Gravesian, with abstractions used to create an effect of concretely felt atmosphere in a line like "Within its average elsewhereishness" which at once sounds "philosophic" and like the dull gray weather of the place (which is also a metaphysical place) evoked in the preceding stanza.

Subject, theme and treatment of these make this poem almost a paraphrase of the early Auden. The idea expressed in a good many of these early poems is that it is wise not to be drawn into the drama of opposite, extreme positions, but to make cool intellectual decisions undeluded by the neurotic tug of self-dramatizing alternatives. It is remakable how frequently in these early poems the preposition "between" occurs. For example:

. . . poised *between* shocking falls on razor edge
Has taught himself this balancing subterfuge. . .

Between attention and attention
   The first and last decision

On W. H. Auden's "A Change of Air"

Is mortal distraction
  Of earth and air.

Upon this line *between* adventure
Prolong the meeting out of good nature
Obvious in each agreeable feature.

And where "between" is not stated there are nevertheless choices stated as between "fear" and "reserve," "no" and "yes," "love" and "hate." The point repeatedly made is that although there are real choices in life, the dramatic acting-out
of choices is neurotic and dangerous. It means *becoming* one of the alternatives
of feeling offered, being drawn onto a circumference when you ought to stay
calmly at the center of your own being. You ought to make choices, but you
ought not to become the emotionally colored extremes of action in which they disguise themselves.

"A Change of Air," then, expresses one of Auden's earliest preoccupations.
The poet says that occasions arise which suggest that a dramatic change has taken
place in your nature, you experience a sense of conversion, there is "estrangement
between your name and you." The delusory aspect of this is that it suggests that
you ought to behave in some way which projects into your external role in society
the change within. You think you should grow a beard, become a monk, or live a
life of primitive simplicity among primitive people. All this is mollycoddling.

The answer that Auden provides for the question raised by the first two
stanzas—how am I to realize the change?—is double and its doubleness depends
on the distinction made in the first stanza between "name" and "you"—which
one might also call "mask" and "being." It is that you should resist the flashy
temptation to alter your "name" by dramatic action. You should, however, alter
your being; but in a way which so far from adding glamor to your "name" will
either go unremarked or may make you appear dull and boring (because in choosing being rather than name, you have withdrawn from your "name" qualities
which please and astonish other people).

Of course, a difference between the early and late Auden is that in the early
work choice meant choosing yourself as a rational, psychoanalyzed, uninhibited,
released individual capable of loving and being loved according to behavior patterns derived from Viennese psychologists. Today being is transformed by enter-

On W. H. Auden's "A Change of Air"

ing into orthodox Christian traditional patterns of living: different from that of modern society perhaps by their deeper, more significant and ancient ordinariness than by their extraordinariness. The people among whom you live and move hardly notice the change: or if they do it seems that you have become duller.

Auden seems to be writing here a bit autobiographically: about his own return to the Anglican church, about the reaction of some friends, colleagues and critics to his absorption in theology.

A curious thing about the poem is that Auden—perhaps deliberately—seems to make little effort to challenge the reaction of those who comment "you seem less amusing than you were" by demonstrating (as Eliot does, for example in the opening section of "Burnt Norton") that his conversion, his orthodoxy, have resulted in any intense inner excitement. If one applies the simple test of writing out the sixth stanza as prose it seems not only a little flat even as prose, but prosaic in sentiment.

> No study of your public reappearance will show, as judgment on a cure demands, a sudden change in love, ideas or diet; your sojourn elsewhere will remain a wordless hiatus in your voluble biography.

In fact, the last two stanzas seem tired, thrown away almost. The first two stanzas have distinction and neatness, the third stanza has some of the quality of Auden at his best, suggesting that he really does inhabit a wonderful inner mental landscape of stones, and gray weather, and local customs.

Auden writes a great variety of poems, and "A Change of Air" is, it seems to me, an example of one of those types which I have called above the "think" poem. It is really an essay or note for a spiritual journal written by a man who has the habit of animadverting in verse. That in writing this poem he reverts to a very early manner (that in which he was influenced by Laura Riding and Robert Graves) oddly suggests that in rather casual and marginal notes of this kind he has not taken the immense pains to transform his style and form which he applies to his more ambitious later poetry.

There is advantage in the poetic form in an "essay" of this kind if it is used with precision and distinction which makes it clearer even than prose. The poetic intensity is lowered to that degree that there is a kind of joke implicit in its being a poem at all. As the passage I have printed above in prose demonstrates, it is written as it were on both sides of a dividing line between poetry and prose, some-times placidly remaining the same as it would be if actually written in prose, but sometimes rising to an entry on the side of the line which is poetry. "Corns, heart-burn, sinus headaches, such minor ailments" could be the first line of an entry in a medical textbook. In the next line, "Tell of estrangement between your name and you," the writing works as poetry, and Auden keeps up throughout the poem this play between the prose and the poetry.

The uncomfortableness I feel after reading the poem twenty times or more is that all the same the amount of poetry we are given is a bit stingy: and there is not that distinction between the prose "scientific" jargon ("agglutinative tongue," "dialect of another river-basin") which occurs in the early Auden, for ex-ample in "Sir, no man's enemy," a poem stuffed with psychoanalytic jargon, which leads up to the shining poetry of the line "new styles of architecture, a change of heart." It is a bit disconcerting that in this poem the meaning is clear whereas the grammar creates mystification. One knows so well what the poet means that one jumps at the meaning which is not as defined as it should be in the words. Thus what "its" refers to in the first line of the third stanza is not clear in the language, only by reference to the general drift of the argument. "It's" evidently refers to a noun which is indicated by "thither," the last word of the second stanza: but "thither" itself refers to "elsewhere"—which is also an adverb. A possessive pronoun can refer to a noun, or a noun clause, but not to an adverb. This gives the third stanza an air of mystification which is purely and only verbal: since one concludes from the sense of the third stanza that the place which is "elsewhere" and "thither" is a village where there are "a priest, a post-mistress, an usher." In the first line of the fourth stanza, there is another "its," this time clearly referring to the place which has now been indicated, but em-phasizing one's sense that the first "its" is slovenly. A further mystification is added by the line "It sides with neither, being outside both" (also in the fourth stanza). To what does "it" refer? Grammatically, I think, there is no clear answer, for it might either connect with the noun-clause referred to by "its" in the first lines of the third and the fourth stanza, or it might refer to "your name." How-ever in the second and third lines of the fourth stanza the distinction is made between "your name" and "yourself." "Your name is as a mirror answers" and "yourself [is] how you behave in shops." Thus it "which sides with neither" cannot be one of these alternates. It must be the village with the priest and post-mistress.

Having registered these objections, I nonetheless feel that this is a charming poem, a kind of poetic wet-blanket applied to self-dramatizing emotional changes. Not everyone will agree with the sentiment expressed. However it is difficult to argue about this, because some changes are dramatic and some are not. It is difficult to think that the conversion of Saint Paul, for example, would respond to the cool analysis provided by this poem. But for most people's inward conversions, the warning that they should not dramatize them is salutary.

W. H. AUDEN

I am not sure that I know what an author is supposed to do when he "replies" to his critics. If he agrees with what they have written, he has nothing to say except thank-you: if he disagrees, he cannot, except on some point of historical or technical fact, refute them for, as any reader "reads" a poem, so, for him, that poem is.

Let me begin, at least, by thanking Messrs. Elliott, Shapiro and Spender for their kindness in taking the trouble, not only to read "A Change of Air," but also —they are busy men with more important things to do—to write about it.

I must confess to feeling a little sad—am I to blame?—that none of them seems to have spotted the kind of poem it is, namely, a parable. Mr. Elliott nearly did, for he saw the *You* of the poem could be identified neither with one particular individual nor with a generalized Everyman. And Mr. Shapiro, in his account of how he feels in shops, a feeling which, I can assure him, is not shared by all poets, reveals that he has read the poem as it is intended to be read. In calling it a parable, I mean that the answer to the question "Who is the *You* in this poem?" is as follows: if Mr. Elliott is reading it, *You* is Mr. Elliott; if Mr. Shapiro, Mr. Shapiro; if Mr. Spender, Mr. Spender; and so on. *You's* age, sex, social status, profession and persona-ego problem are those of whoever happens to be reading the poem.

It, by the way, always and, I should have imagined, obviously refers to *Elsewhere.* Mr. Spender in the role of grammarian is a new Mr. Spender to me. The syntactical status of all the position words, *here, there, somewhere, nowhere, elsewhere,* is ambiguous. For example, if I write on the back of a picture-postcard, *Here is where I am staying, here* is certainly a noun, and if I say *I shan't go to Rome; I shall go elsewhere* (or *somewhere else*), it seems to me more logical to think of *elsewhere* as a noun signifying the antithetical place to *Rome* than as an adverb qualifying the verb *go.* If Mr. Spender argues that, in order to give it the status of a noun, I ought to say *I shall go to elsewhere,* is he seriously prepared to assert that, in the phrase *I shall go home, home* is an adverb? In any case, whatever his own grammatical fads may be, it passes my comprehension that he should not have instantly recognized that, in my poem, *elsewhere* is a noun. How, otherwise, could I have used the abstract noun *elsewhereishness* which presupposes both a noun *elsewhere* and an adjective *elsewhereish?* So much for misplaced pedantry.

As is the case with most poems, the germ of "A Change of Air" was a real historical event. I had been translating Goethe's *Italienische Reise* and was fascinated by the circumstances under which it began, how, without telling his friends, Goethe suddenly bolted from Carlsbad to Italy under an assumed name: his Weimar persona, his epistolary love-affair with Charlotta von Stein, etc., had become intolerable to him. For some time I considered writing a poem specifically about Goethe, but decided against it for two reasons. I had in the past written a number of poems about historical characters and wanted to do something different this time: then, Goethe's actual flight into "elsewhere" was much too dramatic to suit the basic theme of my intended poem, the contrast between a person's inner and outer biography. It is, surely, a general experience that those events in a person's life which to other people seem decisive and with which biographers are concerned are never the same as those moments which he himself (or she, herself) knows to have been the crucial ones: the inner life is undramatic and unmanifestable in realistic terms.

I set out, therefore, to try and write a poem in which it would be impossible for a reader to be distracted from its personal relevance to himself by thinking of Goethe or, even more mistakenly, of me. One relic of the never-written poem remains, the Grand Duke in the last stanza. There exists a letter written by the Grand Duke of Weimar, though not to a cousin, in which he complains that, since his return from Italy, Goethe has become, not less amusing, but more aloof —the old intimacy is gone. I debated removing him, but came to the conclusion that, since no reader of mine was likely to know a real Grand Duke personally, he would do as a parabolic figure standing for Society, Literary Critics, etc.

One of the problems in writing a parable is finding images which will be devoid of any too-specific historical or geographical associations for the reader, but at the same time be concrete enough to hold his interest. Thus, when, in the second stanza, I had to find images for bogus, overdramatic breaks with the past, I thought, as a poet well might, of Rimbaud, but I was resolved that the reader shouldn't. At the same time, I had to find a flight-image which was historically possible. It is possible for anybody "To trade in an agglutinative tongue/With a stone-age culture" but, to do so, he must go to Greenland, not Abyssinia.

There is one, only one, autobiographical detail in the poem and I couldn't help smiling at Mr. Elliott's objection to it. Evidently, he has never had the misfortune to suffer, as I do, from corns. (I have never had heartburn or a sinus-headache in my life.) If he had, he would know, firstly, that, for their victim, they are anything but "whimsical" and, secondly, he would be only too familiar with their psychosomatic whims. (For years they tormented my right foot; then they suddenly transferred their attentions to my left.)

I think it was a little naughty of Mr. Spender to play that old trick of printing five lines as prose because, in the case of unrhymed iambically-based pentameters in which the line-end pauses play an unusually important rhythmical role, almost any passage can be made to sound "prosy" by this procedure. I am glad, however, that he did, because it gives me an excuse for talking about my current aesthetic-technical preoccupations. Here I feel sure of my ground. A poet's explication of his poems is no more authoritative than anybody else's and may well be less but, on the subject of what, so far as his own writing is concerned, he sees the aesthetic-technical problems to be—whether or not he has solved them is another matter—he alone can speak with authority.

On various occasions I have expressed my dislike of persons who hold some Theory of Poetry to which they demand that all poems shall conform, and I will repeat it here. At the same time, every poet has to ask himself what kinds of poetry, given his temperament and talent, it is authentic for him to write, and what kinds are not, and, in reading other poets, he has to distinguish between their merits, which may be very great, and their influence upon himself, which may be pernicious. It was not the fault of Yeats or Rilke that I allowed myself to be seduced by them into writing poems which were false to my personal and poetic nature.

Well, then, my problem is this. In so much "serious" poetry—poetry, that is to say, which is neither pure playful song nor comic—I find an element of "theatre," of exaggerated gesture and fuss, of indifference to the naked truth, which, as I get older, increasingly revolts me. This element is mercifully absent from what is conventionally called good prose. In reading the latter, one is only conscious of the truth of what is being said, and it is this consciousness which I would like what I write to arouse in a reader *first*. Before he is aware of any other qualities it may have, I want his reaction to be: "That's true" or, better still,

On "A Change of Air"

"That's true: now, why didn't I think of it for myself?" To secure this effect I am prepared to sacrifice a great many poetic pleasures and excitements. At the same time, I want what I write to be poetry as Robert Frost defines it, namely, untranslatable speech. Normally, when we read prose, we are not consciously aware of *how* it is saying what it says, of either the rhythmical value of the syllables or of each word as a unique entity with unique overtones: in poetry— this is its greatest glory—we are continually made aware of them. The ideal at which I aim is a style which shall combine the drab sober truthfulness of prose with a poetic uniqueness of expression so that, if a reader should try to translate a passage into French, say, or Italian or German, he will find that this cannot be done without loss of rhythmical values and precise shades of meaning. (Can Mr. Spender, for example, in the stanza of which he complains, give me two German words which have not only the same general meaning but also the same overtones as *sojourn* and *voluble?*)

Whatever else it may or may not be, I want every poem I write to be a hymn in praise of the English language: hence my fascination with certain speech-rhythms which can only occur in an uninflected language rich in monosyllables, my fondness for peculiar words with no equivalents in other tongues, and my deliberate avoidance of that kind of visual imagery which has no basis in verbal experience and can therefore be translated without loss.

Every poet has his dream reader: mine keeps a look-out for curious prosodic fauna like bacchics and choriambs. (One of my minor pleasures in life is trying to make George Saintsbury turn in his grave.) When, for example, he reads the line

Hiatus in your voluble biography

I imagine him saying: "Wait a moment. Surely, this line is a foot too long. Oh, now I see! Mr. Auden is scanning the last three syllables of *biography* as a dactyl, so that it would rhyme not with *be* but with *geography*. Daring in an unrhymed poem, but legal." Age dulls many faculties, but it should grant an increased sensitivity of ear and, to be frank, I am rather vain about mine.

One more little point concerning the last line of the poem:

That you seem less amusing than you were.

W. H. AUDEN
On "A Change of Air"

In my experience, wit requires a combination of imagination, moral courage and unhappiness. All three are essential: an unimaginative or a cowardly or a happy person is seldom very amusing. The reader of "A Change of Air" who has had a successful sojourn elsewhere and reintegrated his persona with his ego need not suppose that he has become duller in mind or more afraid of life or even—God save the soul of Stephen Spender!—an Anglican: he has only to imagine that he has become happy.

ADRIENNE RICH

DONALD JUSTICE

WILLIAM DICKEY

KARL SHAPIRO

On KARL SHAPIRO'S

The Bourgeois Poet

Karl Shapiro

From THE BOURGEOIS POET

14*

They held a celebration for you, Charles, in Iowa. I was asked but I regretted. It was the hundredth birthday of your book, your proper Christian book called *Flowers of Evil*. (Or is it THE *Flowers of Evil?* I never know.) And in that hymnal, how well you made yourself in the image of Poe—Poe with a cross, that's what you are, adored of the gangster age. In fact, aren't you a children's poet? Aren't you the Lewis Carroll of small vice? Your shabby Wonderland of pus and giant nipple, your cats and jewels and cheap perfumes, your licking Lesbians and make-believe Black Mass, O purulence of Original Sin. And always playing it safe in the end, like Disneyland. So many safety devices, pulleys, cranks, classical alexandrines. It's Iowa for you, restless spirit, where elderly ladies embezzle millions in the *acte gratuite*. You'll need no naturalization papers here. I loved you once, and Delacroix and Berlioz in my gangster age. The little boy in me loved you all, O solemn Charles, so photogenic. And this is my flower for your anniversary. I fashioned it of Mexican tin and black nail polish, little French Swinburne burning in Iowa City.

* Sections 14, 15, and 16 of a series of poems from Mr. Shapiro's work-in-progress, *The Bourgeois Poet*, as printed in the May, 1962 issue of *College English*.

15

The bourgeois poet closes the door of his study and lights his pipe. Why am I in this box, he says to himself, although it is exactly as he planned. The bourgeois poet sits down at his inoffensive desk—a door with legs, a door turned table—and almost approves the careful disarray of books, papers, magazines and such artefacts as thumbtacks. The bourgeois poet is already out of matches and gets up. It is too early in the morning for any definite emotion and the B.P. smokes. It is beautiful in the midlands: green fields and tawny fields, sorghum the color of red morocco bindings, distant new neighborhoods, cleanly and treeless, and the Veterans Hospital fronted with a shimmering Indian Summer tree. The Beep feels seasonal, placid as a melon, neat as a child's football lying under the tree, waiting for whose hands to pick it up.

Condemned to write a long bad poem in middleclass magic, what have we done? Condemned to sniff the skull of classicism. Paah!

Who are those poets in homburg hats? Who sent that lumbering drunk an invitation? The one with the cape. The one with the high voltage in his veins. Who talks prosody; what is this riffraff?

Condemned to win the world-wide prize in the winter of life. Condemned to endless promotion.

A woman enters the room behind my back. The poet I am talking to bursts into peacocks. The Celtic genius visits the stockyards. He chats hysterically with the president of the beeves, who describes discreetly what he would do to quell a prison riot. The president wears puttees in his panelled office and affects torn elbows.

Condemned to grimace in the picture pages. Condemned to his very own image. Delay the design as long as possible. Nothing spontaneous.

The poem condemned to wear black, be quoted in churches, versatile as Greek. Condemned to remain unsung by criminals.

ADRIENNE RICH

The title, first: I assume it intends to shock and discomfit the incipient reader as the poet has already long ago been shocked and discomfited by himself and the landscape of which he is a part. There is little doubt that Shapiro's long poem-in-progress was primarily conceived in terms of "This is what I am" rather than "This is what They are." We are entering a spiritual autobiography, not, as with *Howl*, an attack on the Others; Shapiro knows he's been no angel-faced hipster in the Negro streets. The poem is to be first of all the record of a facing of self.

In every public and most private facings of self there is an element of vanity. A man who exposes himself at his worst says implicitly: I have at least this virtue of honesty, I have at least done away with illusions. Implicitly, too: the rest of you are still rotting in the illusions I have cast away. Further, in the particular confrontation of *The Bourgeois Poet*: You let me become what I am, you, America, bourgeois society, publicity, blandishments of reputation, lecture platform, Pulitzers, etc. I swallow the life you force-fed me, but I swallow it protestingly. Here is the protest, the poem: the evidence that I am not wholly bought. I put myself on trial, and thereby cut myself loose from the rest even though my *curriculum vitae* reads like theirs.

In this the poem takes great risks, and does not always transcend them. I would like to have written about the sections chosen for discussion here with the whole more vividly in my head; I have encountered parts of it here and there during the past year and a half, responding with different intensities. There were sections that seemed to me merely a wail in the old exhausted intonations: we had been through it all before, heard it all so often, how American culture stifles its artists with foundation grants and professorships, how we are all "condemned to endless promotion," tamed and emasculated by prosperity, inflation of reputations, writers' conferences, the exigencies of careers, domesticity. But there came, for some, a time when the chief necessity was to drive on inward, leave the magazines unread, stop taking literary prizes seriously, stop listening to the noises of the culture, if only because its literal impertinence and ultimate impermanence began to come clear. If you are praised for your mediocrities and your best goes misread, the inevitable bitterness *can* turn to relief, with the recognition that the culture only has to matter when personal vanity, boredom and confusion force you to listen to it, exploding in wasteful anger on predictable occasions.

Shapiro, too, has driven inward in this poem, I think—not in all of it, not with equal conviction everywhere. My impression, from the memory of parts read earlier, is that the poem is getting better, that sections of it which seemed to me mere flailings of impotent anger and self-humiliation were a preliminary spasm, a kind of rhetorical nausea; and that Shapiro has since begun writing the real poem, getting often at a kind of savage beauty and precision of which mere anger is incapable.

The language reveals something. It is not simply a difference in rhetoric that makes the difference between a work like *Howl* and a work like *Leaves of Grass*, between poetry that may be read aloud convincingly yet flattens out on the page, and poetry that is incandescent with detail and loving precision. The language of Whitman is potent because it is created as experience, not as a reaction or defense against experience. Similarly, Shapiro rejects in Section 14 the Baudelaire of, say, "Femmes Damnées" or "Au Lecteur"; but there is also the Baudelaire of "Le Cygne," "Les Petites Vieilles" or *"Je n'ai pas oublié, voisine de la ville. . . ."* Shapiro's more recent (to my knowledge) sections of *The Bourgeois Poet* have, even in their most dreamlike and private moments, a new conviction of language. I am thinking of passages like the one in which the landlord hangs the chandelier in the empty house; the "angel with patent-leather wings who rows himself toward our distant star"; the cracking-plant that "sails on through the delicate Oklahoma night, flying the thousand flags of Laputa"; the woman shopping for a nightgown to wear in the hospital ("There should be colors weak as tears, silks with no memory of blood.")

This in general. There are exceptions, returns to the mode of obsession, or unexplored resentment. To me, Section 15 is one such. It reads like a piece from a novel of academic life, one of those predictable and lassitude-engendering novels which fail through a fanatical attention to types and a monolithic absence of character. "The bourgeois poet sits down at his inoffensive desk—a door with legs, a door turned table—and almost approves the careful disarray of books, papers, magazines and such artefacts as thumbtacks." The door turned table is a stroke of wit and poetry, marred by the routine summary of its routine litter. It may all be true—the pipe, the Midwestern suburb, the inoffensive desk—but it is tiresome. The poet editing *Poetry* in an office next door to the Chicago Models Club, in another section, is more intensely present and alive there than he is in this stale true confession.

If self-castigation and attacks on inoffensiveness and "Fame, you wall-eyed bitch" were the chief matter of *The Bourgeois Poet* it would be, in fact, "a long bad poem in middleclass magic." I have the feeling (not most from the sections here officially under discussion) that Shapiro is working into something more, a poem about America which will tell us more than we already know. The passages on the Nashville Parthenon, or a Tulsa or Baltimore night, or contrasting a Kansas gas station with one on the Côte d'Azur, suggest that he is developing a new mode of confronting America in himself, and himself in America. He has chosen a loose, flexible and inclusive form, the prose-poem founded on memories of iambic meter. Now and then whole sentences are iambic pentameter lines, but almost never do they force themselves into an obvious metricality; the rhythms work, are at one with the language most of the time. When, as more and more often, Shapiro insists on the physical, peculiar concreteness of his vision, he dispels completely my private reservations about the prose-poem in English.

I've attempted no fine analysis of specific sections: I can't react to this kind of poem in terms of *explication de texte*. It seems to me that the poem as a whole is going to be a moral experience if it is anything. For a poet, in any case, language is always a form of moral behavior: it is through a constant revising and purifying of his speech that he goes through his private analysis, his boycott, his freedom-ride, his regeneration. This work is still going on in *The Bourgeois Poet*, sometimes with stunning success. But I am troubled at the end of Section 16 by "The poem . . . condemned to remain unsung by criminals." I think in a phrase like this Shapiro is borrowing Genet-like language values without meaning them; it is a beautiful-*sounding* line which holds me off. I don't believe Shapiro thinks that criminals in his America sing any kind of poetry; the criminal here is just another opposite number to the offensively inoffensive English professor. We all think and feel in these terms at times. I single out this final phrase only to illustrate the need for relentlessness in accomplishing the kind of task Shapiro has undertaken.

DONALD JUSTICE

What is the opposite of the sonnet Dr. Williams signed the death certificate for? Mr. Shapiro's answer comes with a logic as disarmingly simple and as charmingly absurd as anything in Poe: "a million-word prose-poem." We are to examine three specimens from this work-in-progress, and we are aware of risks, aside from ignorance, which make it sporting. Any critical reading, especially an exegetical one, by stopping down the natural time of a poem, by lingering and worrying at and over and around, tends to manufacture puzzles where none exist, where certainly none were meant. With poems as open-faced and bare-handed as these, the temptation is irresistible. Let me just apologize in advance for the violation and get on with it.

About all that is really necessary to understand these poems and to begin to like them is to forget, if one can, Mr. Shapiro's early poems, fine and formal as they were, except insofar as they may hang as a backdrop against which the new man, with poems and polemics, sets up his rostrum. Mr. Shapiro is like other American writers with early successes behind them, who having flown high and well with instruments want to try what it's like flying blind, with the seat of the pants. To go no further than his immediate contemporaries, we have the similar cases of Robert Lowell (with *Life Studies*) and John Berryman (with Henry's mad-songs). About the time he must have been working on these poems, Mr. Shapiro published in *Poetry* for June, 1961, a lecture-essay called "The Farmer and the Poet," on which I will be drawing from time to time, since it makes even more clear than *In Defense of Ignorance* the platform from which Mr. Shapiro now addresses us in these prose-poems.

There he draws a distinction between "the biological view" of poetry, in which he believes, and "the historical view," which our culture has adopted. "The one is natural and uses nature as its standard; the other is artificial and uses history, tradition, civilization, and the machine as its standard. The one is variable, informal, expansive; the other static, formal, and constrictive. The one is joyous, spontaneous, adaptable; the other full of despair, anxiety, obscurity, and legal prohibition." The attractions of a million-word prose-poem must include its allowing for "the biological view." "Variable, informal, expansive," it will let you do anything; you are flying blind. (That is, excepting for the French prose-poem, going back to Baudelaire and Rimbaud, and perhaps unclassifiably prophetic and anti-formal writers like Miller and Lawrence.) Perse once asked the poet why he did not write more prose-poems like the early and fine "The Dirty Word"; the reply was that it was hard to break a thousand-year-old-habit. But "The Dirty Word" was more artful, more insistent in its rhythms, more French in spirit than these new prose-poems; the habit is breaking.

14

The general attitude and feeling of all three poems is, I think, clear enough, but so much in them depends on reading the tone right that the details are sometimes tricky. There are not many thematic clusters in the parts of *The Bourgeois Poet* so far published, but the three before us do form such a group. There is a passage in "The Farmer and the Poet" which affords a clue to the not-very-mysterious question of their grouping (it may be only a tentative arrangement but it seems right) as well as to Mr. Shapiro's choice of Baudelaire as an example. "Frequently," writes Mr. Shapiro, "the natural poet falls into the religious perversion because he has cut himself off from the natural functioning of poetic man. Such a poet takes cover behind the doctrine of the 'mask'; he is indeed a freak. A good recent example is Charles Baudelaire. Baudelaire is the prototype of the modern poet, the true poet who ends up betraying poetry to the authority of religion and of culture. His poetry is grounded on the hatred of mankind . . . . And he finishes in the arms of the church and of mother."

The celebration may seem a convenient fantasy of the poet's, but it did in fact take place: May, 1957, Iowa City, the state university. Paul Engle arranged for it. French scholars and critics read short papers in the afternoon—Fowlie, Shattuck, Ruff, etc.; a soprano sang verses of Baudelaire's set by various French composers; a booklet of poems, printed by Cummington Press, was distributed; a lithograph of Baudelaire had been commissioned; afterwards, there was a big dinner at the Amanas, in a restaurant operated by a former big-league relief pitcher, a toast by the French consul, a blonde drum-majorette whirling on the grass, and a fire-station glee-club singing (the last two items incidental bonuses). I go into such detail not simply because I was there but to suggest some of the pleasant absurdity of the occasion, which in reality was of quite another kind than that which the poem exposes.

The first sentence of the poem establishes that kind clearly enough, I think, merely by bringing into juxtaposition the name of the poet and the name of the place: *Charles* (with its tone of familiarity, of fellow-feeling between poets, of some condescension perhaps mingling with a mildly compassionate shrug or sigh at this latest among all the absurdities of life) and *Iowa* (with its standard associations of healthy-American-rural-provincial, all that is opposite to the cultured decadence of Baudelaire's Paris). Out of this contrast develops the attitude the poem wants to express, but it is a development which twists around on itself, with small surprises along the way. The familiarity and apparent sympathy with "Charles" continues, but with "proper Christian book" some of the condescension expected toward *place* begins to turn on *poet* instead. Coupled with the title of Baudelaire's book, "proper Christian book" gives a funny contrast in itself, the sort of thing a prose-poet must feel lucky to discover, where the natural absurdity of language and fact reveals itself simply by being uttered. It is like saying: Who would think of writing a "proper Christian book" and giving it the ludicrously inappropriate title of *Flowers of Evil?* But the Catholic critics nowadays tell us that is what it is, and we remember Baudelaire's sad last days, some of his letters: "The book starts from a Catholic idea, but it is a consideration of another kind . . . ."

What is the point of the parenthetical quibble about the correct title? It seems wasted to me. In over-all rhythm, as postponing for a moment the attack on Baudelaire as "the Lewis Carroll of small vice" (the wittiest shot in the poem), it's okay, but aside from the fact that Mr. Shapiro elsewhere in *The Bourgeois Poet* assigns the article to the title without hesitation, this pose of ignorance (more attractive to the poet than to his reader) seems a mere piece of rhetorical strategy, another way of separating himself from the pretensions of both occasion and poet.

With the next sentence the broadsides against Baudelaire begin in earnest. "The gangster age" is the age of teen-agers, ours perhaps insofar as we are ruled by the j.d. set. (From another prose-poem: "The sixteeners are all playing gangster.") This interpretation is borne out by the childhood references that follow: "children's poet," "Lewis Carroll," "shabby Wonderland," "Disneyland"—all linked with the period-horrors Baudelaire cultivated in his poems, which seem to Mr. Shapiro childish now. (Here, I think, is a soft spot in the poem, a dullish, standard list, not redeemed by the rhetoric of the final phrase or the slight alliterations—"licking Lesbians and make-believe Black Mass"—or its falling out by phrase into balanced rhythms of 6/4/6/4.) "Safety devices, pulleys, cranks, classical alexandrines" is like a series in Pope: one incongruous-seeming element, which is shown by placement not to be incongruous after all: this is a small volley fired from the poet's anti-formalist foxhole.

The colloquial idiom of "It's Iowa for you" is like the sentence a comical judge hands down—"It's Devil's Island for *you*." The poet here sentences the "restless spirit" to exile; the elevated, faintly religious phrase might well be a translation of something in Baudelaire himself, something he might have called one of the *femmes damnées* or the little old ladies of Paris, or himself. Although in exile, you won't feel out of place there, the poet adds with mock reassurance: Burnice Geiger's 1961 embezzlement from the Sheldon (Iowa) National Bank of $2,126,859 (I looked it up) is as gratuitous an act as something in Gide, as French as the untranslated slogan itself. By this means, a little too quickly perhaps, the contraries with which the poem began, Baudelaire and Iowa, are reconciled, though not quite in the way the celebration itself may have hoped to do. "You'll need no naturalization papers here" draws out the point more convincingly.

Then, a partial turn in feeling: "I loved you once"—undercut perhaps just slightly by the names of the Romantic painter and composer, and a little more so by the rhetorical and rhythmical anti-climax of "in my gangster age." (Winchell would have punctuated this with ellipsis points.) A similar effect follows: some flow of feeling in the first part of the next sentence, undercut slightly by "solemn," more so by "so photogenic," which implies posing. "Little boy" and "solemn" play against one another too: all that pomposity, how childish it was!—A dart for another literary balloon. (Mr. Shapiro, be it noted, made at least two skillful and devoted translations from Baudelaire in his youth.)

To offer a poem as a gift is a custom: Baudelaire's *Je te donne ces vers*. This prose-poem—not a sonnet, no classical alexandrines, but Baudelaire himself was a pioneer in the prose-poem—is the poet's centennial offering. Considering the attitudes of the poem, it is appropriately if figuratively made of the cheap metal of exotic and perhaps religious souvenirs got up for tourists or the poor, adorned with a nail polish so garishly decadent I've never seen any of its kind (despite my residence in now-decadent Iowa).

The unkindest cut is saved for the last phrase: *little* downgrades, though I hope it humanizes too; *Swinburne*—well, we know about Swinburne, but had thought he had got hold of the wrong Baudelaire; *burning*—a double suggestion of the gem-like flame of the aesthetic life and the roasting of souls in a Catholic hell. (Now that I recall it, the centennial day in Iowa was hot, as late spring days are likely to be, so perhaps *burning* works a third way, too.) Obviously it picks up the sound from *Swinburne*; perhaps, given the attitude, there is even a faint hint of swindle, though I doubt it. *Burning* may be the most loaded word in the poem, but it is too plain and innocent in appearance to violate the style.

In 14, then, the poet removes himself from the artificial literary life and the artificial culture-poet both, and does so with a good deal of sharpness and nasty humor.

15

A quiet poem. The tone is more attractive to me than the tone of 14; there Mr. Shapiro's literary attitude demanded of him the stance (rhetorical or real) of superiority or disdain, modified only in part by the last few sentences. I suppose I've been trained, by just the criticism the poet feels has warped the age, to prefer a rhetoric of self-mockery, though gentle, to mockery of others, or perhaps it is only human nature, not criticism which so inclines me—what does Aristotle's *Rhetoric* have to say on this point?

Some of the words are, I think, just adjectives, there because this is a prose-poem and not "pure" prose, or because the poem, being brief, more like a snapshot than a movie, does not have time to develop a narrative that would make the details clear without the coloring of adjectives. "Inoffensive" desk, for instance: yet that it has "legs" and has "turned" table makes something out of this, as if it were a domesticated pet, perhaps a turtle, helpless on its back, and therefore just the desk for the Beep, an attractively inoffensive person (one might think). The Bourgeois Poet, shortened by successive stages of good-natured self-mockery to B.P. (like V.I.P.) and finally to Beep (like Vip—honking his own horn, too?), cultivates the paradoxical role of the bourgeois, as opposed to the commonplace

On Karl Shapiro's "The Bourgeois Poet"

of the "freak"-poet. Seen here on the verge, perhaps, of composition (or life itself?)—"It is too early in the morning for any definite emotion"—it is clear that he has withdrawn from the wild and whirling literary life of the capitals of culture (see 14 and, even more, 16) to "the midlands": no Baudelaire, he. If at this stage of a work-in-progress we can make any structural interferences at all, this must be the significance of placing 15 between the Baudelaire piece and the literary-life piece, the centerpiece of a triptych, health between two sicknesses.

Even so, the beauty of nature in the midlands is seen, through his eyes, as faintly literary, "the color of red morocco bindings." "Morocco," just as a piece of diction, is nice in context here, but what associations are intended? The books in the Beep's study are richly bound, a natural and fitting hue? Or, things in nature take on a bookish cast seen through even a non-literary poet's eyes? Nature will be his book? I can't tell.

So accepting, so affirmative in a quiet way is his vision that suburbia, for once, is made to sound fine, "cleanly and treeless," a freshly positive feeling given by this adjective-pair to the denuded landscapes of greedy contractors. Even an official government building, with the aid of one "shimmering" tree, becomes part of this (unofficially) poetic landscape.

The usual poetic richnesses are saved for the last sentence, which seems especially rich by a contrast, partly of content and partly of figuration, with the plainness and flatness of all that precedes it. By shape, the melon and the football are figures for the poet's heart, ripe now and ready to be sported with, probably by a stranger, perhaps the Muse, a chance to which the poet is content to commit himself.

I do not quite understand why I assume the time of the poem to be early autumn, the beginning of a new academic season for the Beep: is it only "Indian Summer" and the football? Or does an autumnal mood pervade the whole paragraph, a feeling of pleasantly lazy expectancy, of things about to begin, which I, as one who also teaches in a university, arbitrarily associate with late Septembers? At any rate, life here, even in the midlands, even (or especially) to the bourgeois poet, is ready to happen; the poem is ready to be composed or so this carefully undramatic glimpse of the poet at the not-work which may be work suggests.

16

Everyone who hangs around literature long enough picks up a store of anec-dotes about poets, whether he listens or not: Brinnin's *Dylan Thomas in America* is the kind of thing I mean, and it is from Mr. Shapiro's own store that the details of 16 seem to come. I can't put names to the people who pass phantasmagorically before the camera's eye here, can't think I was meant to; the theme is general, and the right names won't matter so much as the right feel. For that, one last passage from "The Farmer and the Poet" ought to help: "The history of modern poetry is the history of fright and subsequent madness . . . . Success itself has become a terror to the artist; this which should be his ultimate reward is his ulti-mate nightmare. Fame has become the curse of poets, literally the poisoned cup of a Dylan Thomas. All in the name of traditional acceptability, all in the name of the law of history or the law of churches and armies."

The poem is organized as variations on a rhetorical base ("Condemned to . . ."), as Allen Ginsberg says he used "who" in *Howl*, or as Whitman used parallelisms for structure; the alternating paragraphs are literary anecdotage, fragmented. Then, as a coda, a shift from what the poet is condemned to by his culture to what the poem itself is condemned to.

The "long bad poem" is, of course, the epic, honored by literary tradition as the highest or second highest in the critical hierarchy of forms; but now it is to be written, not for the aristocracy or, better, the peasants, but for the middleclass. (Even so, I can't see my neighbors reading *The Cantos* or *Paterson*.) "Magic" unavoidably, for me, calls up Yeats, an irrelevance, I imagine. The "skull of classicism" is in bad odor with Mr. Shapiro: sniffing is a doggy kind of smelling around. The thought of what Americans would be like if the classics had a wide circulation troubles Mr. Shapiro's sleep, but not in the same way as it did Pound's. We are condemned to "the historical view" of poetry.

The second paragraph, comic and bitter, offers cinematic glimpses of our poets as public figures—the bad results of the critical attitude of paragraph 1—at a literary party, perhaps at Mrs. Stevenson's, perhaps in the offices of *Poetry*, some banquet back in the early 50's, when Mr. Shapiro was editor of that magazine. Homburg hats: to me (from ads) the mark of the executive, the upper class, the

On Karl Shapiro's "The Bourgeois Poet"

public figure, never worn, I take it, by "natural" poets. The "lumbering drunk," the "one with the cape," "the poet with high voltage in his veins"—all this in the tone of a hostess, or a bemused natural poet, regarding this collection of poets who are culture-freaks. "Who talks prosody" may mean that nobody does; if any-one does it might have been, back in those days, Mr. Shapiro himself, author of *Essay on Rime,* compiler of *A Bibliography of Modern Prosody.* Concerned at least with the honest techniques of his craft rather than the public show he makes, is this poet to be preferred to the variety of public creatures? If so, the semicolon includes the prosodist among the riffraff, setting him off, favorably, from the wearers of homburgs and capes. (Eliot, for instance, the villain of *In Defense of Ignorance,* affects ignorance regarding prosody.) But probably I senti-mentalize, and riffraff includes all; from the hostess' point of view it should.

Statistics would probably show the average age of winners of the Nobel Prize as very advanced indeed. The winner of the world-wide prize might be anyone, Yeats, Pasternak, Eliot; not Tolstoy, who, as Mr. Shapiro relates else-where, "when a group of writers sent him an apology for failing to secure the Nobel Prize for him . . . answered that he was grateful *not to have to accept this distinction.*" With "endless promotion" one thinks of Pasternak, who kept his dignity; of Faulkner, who—in my opinion—didn't. But who can blame anyone? It is the culture's fault, its constant pressure, as Mr. Shapiro here persuades me.

With the next paragraph we return to the party, or another in the endless round of literary teas, cocktail parties, banquets. To burst into peacocks must be to use colorful language, in order perhaps to impress the woman entering the room; possibly to flap one's arms about excitedly, to preen. Here it is both unex-pected during a presumably quiet conversation and, after all, predictable, since this is a poet and thus, as our culture reads him, an extravagant personality. The Celtic genius? Almost certainly Thomas (a Chicago friend tells me this is a local Thomas anecdote), but for a while I thought it might be Yeats, in 1914, after the first *Poetry* banquet, though Harriet Monroe tells only of helping Yeats to escape the reporters so as to visit privately a medium in Edgewater: my waver-ing will suggest, anyhow, the generalizing tendency of the anecdotal here. The poet is, of course, hysterical; the businessman, "president of the beeves" (implica-tion: one of the beeves himself, elected by his fellows), is discreet. But—and this is the twist—given to violent, authoritarian topics and, in the midst of the opulent fittings of his office (through whose windows one ought to be able to hear the lowing of the common herd that elected him), as much given to affectation as the poet. (Puttees: authoritarian, fascist; torn sleeves: fake-humble, countrified, man of action.) So culture stamps us all.

Having followed the prescriptions of the culture, the poet is condemned to success. Pictures, trying to smile, in the tabloids; and, worst fate of all, becoming what he imagines himself to be. In a more personal prose-poem about literary fame, Mr. Shapiro puts it this way: "The word 'image' is now in government . . . once I kissed Fame (mouth like an ass hole)." "Delay the design as long as possible. Nothing spontaneous" puts me in mind of Pound, of whom Mr. Shapiro has written: "In America, a hero of culture, such as Ezra Pound, is held up by a reactionary Press as a culture hero. The State backs the artist, so long as the artist backs the State." (Incidentally, remembering St. Elizabeth's, I find this remark curious.)

The last paragraph shifts to the poem itself, which, like the poet, is condemned to conversion into a useful object, so as to be displayed by and to serve the culture: to be dignified in black, in fact, to go in mourning, not to be "joyous, spontaneous, adaptable" as a "natural" poem would be; used in the service of religious authority (if not yet armies); to be as infinitely translatable and classic and exotic as Greek (perhaps beyond its intended use). Eliot, whose conversion is still a wound in the liberal intellectual's memory, is, I feel certain, evoked here.

The last sentence strikes a Romantic pose. Insofar as the "criminals" who do not sing our poems are anti-social types, those for whom a bad society could find no use, the sentiment of this last sentence fits; otherwise I am dubious. I suppose the "natural" poems of a Whitman would be sung by criminals, but not the unnatural poems of Eliot, Pound, and that lot; on the other hand, I've never heard Whitman quoted, much less sung, by criminals. (A convict recently sent me some of his poems: they were strict quatrains in praise of nature's beauties.) Still, the healthy poem would presumably be sung by the healthy man, who in our time might find himself in jail. Finally, the word *criminals* liberates the current of suggestion buried throughout in *condemned*: the poet and the poem, as weapons of culture, are committed to the culture-prison. Remotely, one may take this as the "protest" version of the almost stock quasi-religious figure of our culture as a hospital, where everyone is sick. How this relates to the notion of the

On Karl Shapiro's "The Bourgeois Poet"

good gray bourgeois poet himself, as a substitute ideal for the freak-poet, I can't say; I don't think it does, but among the million words we have to look forward to, inconsistencies like this may even become a principle. In any case, I can't see that it harms this particular poem, where it makes an only mildly cockeyed sense.

If I miss things in these poems, it is the wildness I feel they need to serve Mr. Shapiro's new purpose. Do I like 16 best only because it is the most nearly formal? Perhaps. But it may be that it is also the wildest: that, surely, is a winning combination.

WILLIAM DICKEY

I have read now thirty-two sections of *The Bourgeois Poet:* those which have appeared in *College English, Poetry,* and *The Kenyon Review.* Obviously that's not enough to serve as a basis for any sure comment on the poem; nothing will be until the whole work is available. I don't know at present what order the groups of sections come in or what intermediate material may be intended to connect them. I cannot yet have a clear idea of the shape of the poem, or even of its size. Since it consists of a series of episodes, rather than having a continuous narrative or dramatic line, the poem seems at the moment illimitable; there is no reason why things ought not to keep going until either the poet or the poem tires.

This lack of limitation is the strongest initial impression the poem gives. We find ourselves moved everywhere in space: Baltimore, Chicago, Tulsa, Amsterdam, Papeete. We are shifted in time, though not to as great an extent. We are confronted with a great diversity of figures: Baudelaire and Miss Cohen, de Sade and the editor of *The Kenyon Review.* And we observe a great variety in poetical method and in tone: from the surrealistic to the representational, from heightened lyric to diminished prose.

Faced with such a multiplicity of subjects and attitudes, the reader might easily conclude that the poem is a casual succession of illuminations, connected only by the fact that they are observed by or experienced by a single man. Further readings, though, will suggest the presence of certain controls on the succession, controls which consist of recurrent images and metaphors (like the image of gangsters), recurrent concerns (like the relationship of experience and art), and recurrent techniques (juxtaposition of extremes, for one instance, ironic diminution for another). In the light of these recurrences, perhaps I can suggest a pattern of intention in the poem.

Any such pattern must center upon the "I" who observes and comments throughout the sections, and is their single continuous figure. Some definition of this "I" is already made in the poem's title. He is to be regarded in social terms: the word "bourgeois" must involve us with such terminology. He is concerned with aesthetic considerations, since he is a poet. He is himself an example of the juxtapositions I mentioned above, since the concepts of "bourgeois" and "poet" are not those we customarily expect to find together; they are disparate rather

On Karl Shapiro's "The Bourgeois Poet"

than harmonious. Finally, "I" is in some sense to be regarded ironically; both the juxtaposition and the usual connotative weighting given to "bourgeois" dispose of the possibility of a tragic or wholly noble figure.

There is a further aspect of "I" which the title does not suggest; he is involved with experience as a man, as a poet, and also as a member of a particular generation, who feels himself opposed to, or at least separated from, the generation that follows. It is this triple order of experience which the succession of illuminations is intended to make clear; each of them produces a scene, realistic or allegorical, which either by plain statement or by implication should further our understanding of one or more of the three possibilities.

For the man, the poet, the member of his generation, the poem presents a central conflict between a world of single, direct, instinctive action, and a world of double realization with its ironic possibilities. The first world is represented by images of gangsters and of war. Among the business tycoons, the figures of power, "policy is decided by word of mouth like gangsters." The teen-agers, the new generation, "are all playing gangsters," as, on another occasion, the children play soldiers. The failure of false organization poets is that they cannot come into touch with directness; they are "condemned to remain unsung by criminals." The poet proudly remembers the Queen Mary as a troopship: "gray from stem to stern, all ports and windows blocked, the monster zigzagging from Boston to the Sydney Heads."

But if the world of directness has its attractions, it still can be final only for children, for those who have not been forced to recognize the double world. War and criminality are reduced to miniature, to games: "Today we play on the gray wooden battleship" or "in another part of the town there is a miniature court like a toy." Between these miniature outgrown violences and the wholly wooden unspontaneous acceptances made by the organization poets—on this slippery ground between complete rejection of social pattern and complete subservience to it—the bourgeois poet will be required to live. He will find the peacetime voyage unlike the wartime one: "Ah, this is different, says Miss Cohen: we are paying for this."

This payment, which is a recognition, is both good and bad. It involves the necessity of seeing incongruities: not only Baudelaire in Iowa, but a concrete replica of the Parthenon in Nashville and a French gas station which "is a thing of beauty, shiny and blasphemous as a cenotaph." It involves concealments and

On Karl Shapiro's "The Bourgeois Poet"

betrayals, the discovery "that your favorite poet is a homosexual" after which you must "close the door of your mind on those love letters. Beware of the poisons of pronouns." It shows a California where "you look down on promised advertisements of green come true, green for the eating, money-green. . . ." But at the same time that recognition shows discontinuity, it allows the possibility of new combinations, so that the Tulsa cracking-plant becomes a "candlelit city of small gas flames by the thousands" or at the climax of the stripper's act "our faces light up with intelligence."

Such an explanation of *The Bourgeois Poet* is admittedly tentative and incomplete. There are passages I find difficult to relate to the explanation (in some instances because I find them difficult to understand). But I don't think the poem anywhere contradicts the reading I've given, and I think that reading is particularly useful with respect to the three sections of the poem that are the immediate subject of this symposium.

Of these three sections, the first and third represent the unbalanced extremes mentioned above. In social terms, the first shows complete rebellion, the third complete acceptance. In aesthetic terms, one might think of the first as content without form (and consequently without the perspective that can bring about understanding), and of the third as form without content, the dramatic figure of the poet being substituted for the fact of the poem. In neither case, to borrow Miss Cohen's phrase, is anything being paid for. Baudelaire and the children save themselves by never taking responsibility for their acts, the poets in homburg hats by never acting genuinely or significantly.

This contrast seems apparent enough not to need further comment. What may be noted, though, is that the method of the first and third sections, though they begin from different sources (the first identifiable as real, the third allegorical or imaginary), is essentially the same. In each case the language, the succession of images, is vivid, rapid and excitable: "Wonderland of pus and giant nipple" or "chats hysterically with the president of the beeves." And in each case the excitement of the language plays against a succession of diminutions, so that the incongruity of the juxtapositions makes it doubly impossible for us to accept the attitudes described. The diminutions are dense and continuous. From the moment Baudelaire is addressed as Charles, some of his distant black stature is gone.

WILLIAM DICKEY
On Karl Shapiro's "The Bourgeois Poet"

Locating him in Iowa continues the process: he is deprived of the setting that might contain and justify his work. The polite social-secretary tone of "I was asked but I regretted" (with the double sense of "regretted" operative), the cozy word "birthday" instead of the stiffer "anniversary," the use of "proper Christian book" (terror and blasphemy may be Christian enough, but it is hard to think of them as proper, sitting in rocking chairs, lips pursed), the uncertainty as to the book's title—each of these serves to scatter the unified impression which would be necessary if we wished to take Baudelaire seriously. The language builds up violently through "licking Lesbians" and "purulence" only to stop, bleakly and prosaically, at Disneyland. Similar incongruities, perhaps a little less marked, take place with "middleclass magic," with "Celtic genius" over against "stockyards," with "president" and "beeves." The tolling repetition of "condemned" functions in the same way, given the feebleness of the condemnations: "to grimace in the picture pages." (I momentarily admire the poet bursting into peacocks; it seems an amiable thing to do, but I am afraid it's only one more example of groundless extravagance.)

The attitudes of both these sections, then, are unambiguous and denunciatory, their technique is single-minded and insistent, their language highly charged. The second section, which in my reading represents the balance between the two simplistic and undesirable extremes, is restrained in its language, ironic, double-valued, using much lighter connotations and much more delicate effects.

I have mentioned the incongruity inherent in the phrase "bourgeois poet." Here that phrase is farther removed from romantic stature, diminished first to "B.P." (an advertising figure? "B.P.'s wife wears B.H. Wragge?") and then to "Beep" (a compound of Alben Barkley and an auto horn, a mere noise). The effect is to diminish the personal importance of the poet. It is impossible for a Beep to wear a cape or celebrate a Black Mass, impossible for the figure of the poet to intrude upon or substitute itself for the poetry.

And if the poet cannot intrude, neither can any adventitious collection of dramatic objects. No "cats and jewels and cheap perfumes," not even a desk with Gothic battlements—merely a door, merely thumbtacks which cannot even wound once they have been identified as "artefacts."

The structure of this section is tripartite: figure, vision, response. The first

part (the first five sentences) is not only muted in language but ironically balanced: the poet asks himself a question, but it is not a real one; the possibility of drama that might arise ("Why am I in this box?" he screamed) is instantly refused. The desk is inoffensive, the disarray careful (and hence as much an array as a disarray). The poet has no advance commitments, no absolutes to be hewn to; it is too early for emotion.

Up to this point there is nothing in the section to engage our sympathy particularly; the ironic balance has been too careful. It is the substance of the next sentence which constitutes the right and sympathetic vision, sympathetic because it is a vision of beauty, right because it admits the different kinds of elements of which the beauty is constituted. We are given the Indian Summer tree (the strongest of the images of beauty in the sentence) not in isolation, but against the Veterans Hospital (the least beautiful of the images). We are required to compare background and foreground, to compare precisely ("the color of red morocco bindings"), and to see without exaggerating either the thing seen or the person doing the seeing.

The final sentence of the section, the response to the vision (if my terms are not too violent for the quietness of the occasion) reduces the figure of the poet still farther, first through the use of "Beep," then through the comparison to a melon (still organic, at least), then down to the child's football. The poet is reduced to an object, divorced from any requirement to admire himself; placid and neat, he waits to perform his function, to be used.

The irony has by no means disappeared in this sentence, but it has doubled upon itself. If it takes, as I suggested earlier, a sense of ironic discontinuity to be able to reduce the figures of the poet to the image of a football, that sense may be what gives one the freedom to observe new congruities, to see that when appearance is reduced to its least dimension, reality may find it possible to expand.

"Why must grown people listen to rhymes?" Shapiro asked in the Engle-Langland anthology, *Poet's Choice*. "Why must meters be tapped out on nursery drums? Why hasn't America won the battle of Iambic Five? When are we going to grow up?"

The form of *The Bourgeois Poet* constitutes Shapiro's answer to these questions, an attempt to find a kind of language which will be poetic without depend-

On Karl Shapiro's "The Bourgeois Poet"

ing on traditional metric. Any evaluation of the poem, then, must consider not only the subject matter, the balances and juxtapositions, but also whether or not the language is convincing as poetry, whether it is as memorable as good poetry that uses the conventions of metric and rhyme.

The first of these requirements Shapiro seems to me to have met. The language of *The Bourgeois Poet* is distinguished from the language of prose in several ways: by the density of image, the frequency of metaphor, the intensity of sound relationship ("your licking Lesbians and make-believe Black Mass"), the presence of repetitive units of duration which provide some equivalents for lines and stanzas, and by the use within the smaller units of a considerable amount of metrical language.

Image, metaphor and sound relationship do not need to be demonstrated in the three sections of the poem considered here; the extent to which they are used is self-evident. The use of units and of metric language, however, may require discussion.

The largest unit employed is, of course, the numbered section. These sections are not identical in length, but neither are they wildly various: a section of three lines is not followed by a section of a hundred. Indeed, there are no sections that small or that large. Some kind of pattern of section length might be shown in the seven sections of the poem printed in *Kenyon*; they range from eighteen to twenty-six lines. For those printed in *College English* the range is somewhat wider, but the principle remains the same: one is conscious of units which are more similar than dissimilar in duration. The idea of a repetitive structure operating in time, the same idea which governs the stanzas of *The Faerie Queene* or the cantos of *The Divine Comedy*, has been established for *The Bourgeois Poet*.

Within this unit structure two other repetitions can be found. Some of the sections, like the third of those considered here, are broken into short paragraphs which again show similarities of duration. Thus each of the "condemned" paragraphs is about equal in length; only the two paragraphs which vary the rhetorical pattern change the duration to any extent. Finally, the principle of repetition extends to sentences or phrases. Breath pauses often fall about the same distance apart, sometimes so much so that the sense of a sequence of poetic lines can be heard within the paragraph structure.

This sense of the line is likely to be reinforced by Shapiro's retention of metrical elements in single sentences and sometimes in successions of sentences. Let me reset the first sentences of the Baudelaire in Iowa section:

> They held a celebration for you, Charles,
> in Iowa. I was asked but I regretted.
> It was the hundredth birthday of your book,
> your proper Christian book called *Flowers of Evil.*

Allowing two feminine endings, one anapest, and one trochee (none of which is an unusual variation), I see no problem in scanning those lines as iambic pentameter. Other phrases and sentences are similarly amenable to scansion. My point is not that Shapiro is cheating on us, that *The Bourgeois Poet* is metrical verse in a thin disguise (the old whore chased off the streets and now calling out the window). Clearly the Baudelaire section *as a whole* cannot be regularly scanned, though parts of it can be. What Shapiro is doing is allowing the principle of metrical repetition (the alternation of accented and unaccented syllables) to begin a development, then cutting that development off before it can become continuous or dominant. The sound of a succession of lines is sometimes very clearly there; sometimes it is muted or inaudible. Thus, though the language of *The Bourgeois Poet* may have the appearance of prose, and though it contains prosaic elements and organizations, it is more tightly governed in time, more aware of the repetition of units, than prose language customarily is.

Given the breadth of subject Shapiro wants to treat, and the variety of attitudes and tones present in the poem, this language seems flexible and useful. It is I think true that a regular metric will tend to enforce on a long poem a greater singleness of tone than Shapiro desires here, that blank verse, say, possesses an inertia that pulls the poem back toward the level of diction with which it began. By means of the section breaks, the differences in kind and intensity of the various illuminations, and the insistence or relaxation of the repetitive elements, Shapiro escapes that inertia; his language will carry him anywhere he wants to go.

But such a language and such a structure do have two possible drawbacks. One of them I mentioned at the beginning of this discussion: it is the question of whether the poem will hold together sufficiently to appear one thing, rather than a collection of loosely relevant parts. Though I have tried to find unifying attitudes in the poem, I do not yet feel it to be structurally clear and inevitable.

WILLIAM DICKEY

On Karl Shapiro's "The Bourgeois Poet"

Still, I have no right to judge these matters in a poem I have not seen entire.

The second possible drawback is easier to discuss now. Is the language of the poem memorable? The one clear advantage of metric and rhyme is that they make it easier to remember language, to keep in mind an exact sequence of words rather than a more general impression of an idea or a scene. The difference in the way we remember prose and poetry is caught up in this distinction. We say "Do you remember Madame Bovary in the carriage?" or "Do you remember Dick Diver making the sign of the cross over the beach?" But we seldom repeat the passage verbatim, and when we try to, I am afraid we often quote it wrong. With metrical poetry, we are more often inclined to remember the exact passage, and if we try to misquote it too flagrantly, the requirements of the metric and rhyme will point out to us where we are wrong.

I do not think the language of *The Bourgeois Poet* is likely to prove memorable in quite this way. For all of its intensity, for all the striking quality of its images, I think I will remember it more diffusely than I do the language of Enobarbus describing Cleopatra or the language of Pope describing Atticus. I can sympathize very strongly with Shapiro's desire to find a contemporary poetic language. I think he has found one, but one that is still less adequate than metrical language in this particular respect.

Those are my responses to *The Bourgeois Poet;* such of them, at least, as I can now define. There are places where I would quarrel with the poem's execution: brief passages that strike me as too prosaic or as artificially naïve. But I do not think one can help being impressed by the diversity, the size and the seriousness of the intention, or by the number of scenes that do focus exactly, that do illuminate. And what strikes me as even more impressive is the acceptance and understanding of moral responsibility that shows so clearly in the three sections under discussion, that is so intimately involved in the working-out of the initially paradoxical title. A bourgeois poet? Nonsense! Poets are creatures of the air, feeding on honeydew or absinthe, toying with ethereal milkmaids or hallucinatory drugs. This easy and dramatic evasion Shapiro refuses to accept. In our world, the bourgeois poet, maintaining his difficult balance, is a real, ironic and admirable figure; it is important that Shapiro's intention to deal honestly with him be encouraged and understood.

KARL SHAPIRO

It practically abashes me to see the care and accuracy and understanding of my critics. I want to put my hand out and cry: No, no, you are too serious; life isn't like that, etc. I want to say: It's *only* poetry (if it's that)!

For me there is still the vulgarity of the word, a good dose of Bad Taste in every line. One must defend Bad Poetry, scramble the standards, take a long new look at the art *from the bottom up*.

Ted Roethke dubbed me the Bourgeois Poet. He catalyzed me on the spot. To me the name was equivalent to a ten-year psychoanalysis—something I hope never to afford. It was the admiring contempt with which he said it that did the trick. I ought to dedicate the book to his memory.

Adrienne Rich is right. The poem is just a documentary. One can be inside and outside such a poem at the same time. Much of the poem is phony (bourgeois), in bad faith, or even phony-bourgeois. It is not elevated to a style. Sometimes it must display the staggering banality of institutionalized life itself. Miss Rich has the impression that the poem is getting better. This I would take as a danger signal. Better or worse is beside the point.

My editor at Random House said: The only limits to a book like this seem to be physiological. Right again. (What other limits are there?)

Naturally, I am pleased when Adrienne Rich singles out fine phrases or images. And disappointed. One might almost come out with a new fine phrase: the phoniness of the immortal phrase. Hackneyed Latin. It is no longer a question of saying that my bad is better than your good, but that my bad is as good as my good. To stop this eternal aesthetic moralizing is a big order.

I am grateful that she saved me the trouble of explaining that many of the lines are wholly in iambic pentameter. Everyone agrees that there is no such in English, but whatever it is that passes under that name is a prominent characteristic of poetry in English, like a nose. In any case, I use the iambic pentameter as a foot, not as a line. We must, as Williams tried so hard to make clear, stop using the line as a nose. Once and for all, away with the horse-faced English poem.

One objection I have to record: *moral* and *purify* are not in my dictionary.

KARL SHAPIRO

On "The Bourgeois Poet"

We want a poetry that is neither moral nor immoral nor amoral. Unmoral is good enough.

I admire all three poets for their metrical manners. Still, I am smug enough to say about my early poems: I used to be able to do that quite well, as Picasso must have said to his canvas a million times: You're damn right I can "draw." And then proceed not to.

It pleased me to see my essay about the farmer and poet brought up by Donald Justice and also the state of poetry in Iowa. It's all the same battle in different sectors. And it's a delight to have the reminder of the great Iowa embezzlements, though I rather doubt the gratuituousness of those latter-day train robberies. (I forget what the poem said.) The embezzlements were excellent but were tainted with morality. Here's how to be a banker, said the embezzlers— doing some nostalgic bronco-busting. Yet it was good for Iowa; there's spirit in the old girl yet.

"Condemned to remain unsung by criminals" is taken from Sade, more or less. The only natural man is the criminal. To get off the dead surface of this cliché is another titanic task. Sadistically speaking, the poet is the self-condemned. Society has nothing to do with it. There is a lot of "social protest" in *The Bourgeois Poet,* but not really. It only sounds like that because social protest is one of the favorite bourgeois poses. One votes to pretend to be voting. Whereas true political action always takes place outside of politics, as poetry takes place outside Literature. Literature being the educational placenta of the poet, or something like that.

Mr. Dickey wonders about the order of the poems in the final work. So does my publisher. So do I. Most books of poems, curiously, do have an order. At one point I literally did the Jackson Pollack or *I Ching* trick: I dropped the pages from the top of a ladder and picked them up at random. There is no order, thematic or chronological. At the very last, however, when it was time to submit the manuscript, or after the first editorial objection to the disorder, I chickened out. The manuscript is now a triptych, one section more prone to autobiography, another more prone to sounding-off, one specializing in the erotic, so to say. And each section ends with a Long Poem. I tried to avoid the Long Poem, but (as poets say with glandular humility) it *came.*

214

On "The Bourgeois Poet"

"Illimitable" is the right word, as William Dickey says. Illimitable, irrational, and irresponsible. Wheresoever there is a convention it must be traduced or at least libelled. The conventions in my poem are used hypocritically. I'm no Lautréamont or Rimbaud obviously; being bourgeois *enough* I am fed and fêted by the bourgeois raven. This raven quoths: Evermore. Which is the bourgeois word for Tenure.

Practically anything one says about his own poem is going to be held against him. Even the profoundest insights from the artist about his work are chit-chat.

An objection to Mr. Dickey's remark ("an attempt to find a kind of language which will be poetic without depending on the traditional metric"). *Poetic* is a fighting word. The aim is to find the poetry without traditional poetic faking. What I am after is the anti-poem, not simply the anti-poetic. A student from Africa heard me read some of the sections and asked whether there was supposed to be a point to the poems. The answer was no. Rather there should be a falling-off, a let-down, even a disappointment and unfulfillment. It is the poem of the absurd, poem in which the aesthetic is only a trace of memory in the cloud-chamber. It must be meaningless above all, since we have preached Poetry straight into the ground. The formlessness should make you dizzy, nauseated, and give you vertigo. (I don't think I've perfected that.)

Dickey iambicked me, as Spender did Auden.* But you can also iambic the telephone book.

Is the Whole "structurally clear and inevitable"? I hope not. A structure is only a point of view.

Is the language memorable? It is faulty if it is, at least in this case. Like the dyes from coal-tar, as Lawrence said.

But the critics all did well by me, giving me the benefit of the doubt, etc.

At random about the "prose-poem." When you can no longer distinguish between poetry and prose it then becomes possible but not probable to write poetry. What we have always called poetry—almost always—is a hood over the

---

* An allusion to Stephen Spender's essay in the symposium on W. H. Auden's "A Change of Air."

On "The Bourgeois Poet"

truth. Admittedly the ritual is a protective device, like dark goggles for welders or the physician's lead apron. Poets who go at poetry bare-eyed and apronless are naturally expendable. Why they try to shield the audience I'll never know.

The French "prose-poem" was an attempt to break through the lie. It worked now and then but the French are fatally afflicted with their own cleverness. Very quickly their prose-poem became just another French Work of Art. I begin one of the sections of *The Bourgeois Poet* with a satire on French-poetry-always-going-itself-one-better. As for English poetry, it is so loyal to English poetry that every modern English poem seems to resemble a *carmen figuratum* of the island.

And don't think because I have "discovered the prose-poem" that there will be no more cakes and ale, or early Grand Rapids Chiffonier. All forms of poetry should exist simultaneously, yet there should be the form that encompasses the rest, a form that is capable of shifting its contours radically and with ease. Wallace Stevens was French; Robert Frost, British; but we still have the examples of Williams and Pound for a starter.

The vocation of poet in America has about it a delicious absurdity. The paradox itself is enough to turn the veriest clod into a poet. Our poetry should be as crude, vulgar, thick-skinned, lumpish, arrogant, immature, and sado-masochistic as These States themselves. Once we get onto the wave-length of the language we'll have it. As a matter of fact, we do have it. Or rather, everybody has it except the poets.

A parting reminder. Practically every writer who amounts to a hill of Iowa beans has started out as a poet—*and ended up as a novelist.* (Yes, Virginia, I'm writing a novel.)

Now who is going to be man enough not to write a novel?

1935 *The Dog Beneath the Skin* (W. H. Auden and Christopher Isherwood), Random House, New York, 161 pp.

1936 *The Dog Beneath the Skin* (W. H. Auden and Christopher Isherwood), Faber & Faber, London, 180 pp.

1936 *The Ascent of F6* (W. H. Auden and Christopher Isherwood), Faber & Faber, London, 123 pp.

1938 *On the Frontier* (W. H. Auden and Christopher Isherwood), Random House, New York, 120 pp.

1939 *On the Frontier* (W. H. Auden and Christopher Isherwood), Faber & Faber, London, 120 pp.

1951 *The Rake's Progress: Opera in Three Acts* (libretto by W. H. Auden and Chester Kallman, music by I. Stravinsky), Boosey & Hawkes, London & New York, 60 pp.

1961 *Elegy for Young Lovers: Opera in Three Acts* (libretto by W. H. Auden and Chester Kallman), Schott Music Corp., New York, 63 pp.

TRANSLATED AND/OR EDITED

1935 *The Poet's Tongue* (ed. by W. H. Auden and John Garrett), G. Bell & Sons, London, 222 pp.

1938 *Oxford Book of Light Verse*, Clarendon Press, Oxford, 553 pp.

1944 *A Selection from the Poems of Alfred, Lord Tennyson*, Doubleday, Doran, Garden City, N.Y., 268 pp.

1946 *Henry James*, Scribner's Sons, New York, 501 pp.

1948 *Portable Greek Reader*, Viking Press, New York, 726 pp.

1950 *Poets of the English Language*, 5 vols., Viking Press, New York.

1955 *Kierkegaard* (ed. by W. H. Auden), Cassell, London, 184 pp.

1956 *The Criterion Book of Modern American Verse*, Criterion Books, New York.

1956 *The Faber Book of Modern American Verse*, Faber & Faber, London.

1956 *Magic Flute* (Mozart) (libretto trans. by W. H. Auden and Chester Kallman).

1957 *The Knights of the Round Table* (Jean Cocteau) (tr. by W. H. Auden).

1961 *Van Gogh: a Self-Portrait* (letters of Van Gogh), New York Graphic Society, Greenwich, Conn., 389 pp.

1962 *The Viking Book of Aphorisms* (sel. by W. H. Auden and Louis Kronenberger), Viking Press, New York, 405 pp.

ROBERT BELOOF (b. 1923)

Mr. Beloof was educated at Haverford College, Middlebury College, and Northwestern University. During World War II he was a conscientious objector. Since 1948 he has taught at the University of California at Berkeley. He has been the Robert Frost Poetry Fellow at Bread Loaf, and in 1958 was Fulbright Professor of American Literature in Milan. At present he is on appointment to the Institute for the Creative Arts at the University of California.

POETRY

1956   *The One-Eyed Gunner and other Portraits,* Villiers, London.

JOHN BERRYMAN (b. 1914)

Mr. Berryman was educated at Columbia University and Clare College of Cambridge University. He has taught at Wayne State University, Harvard, Princeton, the University of Cincinnati, the University of Washington, the University of Minnesota, the University of California at Berkeley, and Brown University. Honors and awards for his poetry include the Shelley Memorial Award of the Poetry Society of America, and a National Institute of Arts and Letters Poetry Award.

POETRY

1942   *Poems,* New Directions, Norfolk, Conn., 25 pp.
1948   *The Dispossessed,* W. Sloane Associates, New York, 103 pp.
1956   *Homage to Mistress Bradstreet,* Farrar, Straus & Cudahy, New York.
1959   "   "   "   "   , Faber & Faber, London, 111 pp.
1959   *His Thought Made Pockets & the Plane Buckt,* C. Fredericks, Pawlet, Vermont, 11 pp.

PROSE

1950   *Stephen Crane,* W. Sloane Associates, New York, 347 pp.

LOUISE BOGAN (b. 1897)

Miss Bogan has taught at the University of Washington and the University of Chicago, and served as Poetry Consultant to the Library of Congress. For some years she reviewed poetry for *The New Yorker* magazine. Her honors and awards include two Guggenheim Fellowships (1933 and 1937), the Bollingen Prize for Poetry (1955), an honorary Litt.D. from the Western College for Women in Oxford, Ohio (1956), and an Award for Distinguished Accomplishment from the American Academy of Poets (1959). In 1944 she was made a Fellow in American Letters of the Library of Congress.

POETRY

1923   *Body of This Death*, R. M. McBride & Co., New York, 30 pp.
1929   *Dark Summer*, Scribner's Sons, New York, 72 pp.
1937   *The Sleeping Fury*, Scribner's Sons, New York, 42 pp.
1941   *Poems and New Poems*, Scribner's Sons, New York, 116 pp.
1954   *Collected Poems, 1923–53*, Noonday Press, New York, 126 pp.

PROSE

1951   *Achievement in American Poetry, 1900–1950*, H. Regnery Co., Chicago, 157 pp.
1955   *Selected Criticism*, Noonday Press, New York, 404 pp.

PHILIP BOOTH (b. 1925)

Mr. Booth has taught at Wellesley College and at Syracuse University, where he is presently Associate Professor of English. He has also taught at the Boston College Writers' Conference and at the Tufts Poetry Workshop. Among his honors and awards are the Lamont Poetry Prize of the American Academy of Poets (1955) and the Guggenheim Fellowship (1958).

POETRY

1955   *Letter from a Distant Land*, Viking Press, New York, 87 pp.
1961   *The Islanders*, Viking Press, New York, 79 pp.

BABETTE DEUTSCH (b. 1895)

Babette Deutsch (Mrs. Avrahm Yarmolinsky) was educated at Barnard College and Columbia University. She was for a short time secretary to Thorstein Veblen at the New School for Social Research in New York, where she also taught poetry. She has served on the faculty of Queens College and, until recently, as a lecturer at the School of General Studies of Columbia University. She is a member of the National Institute of Arts and Letters, and has won various honors and awards for her poetry. For two years, Miss Deutsch was Director of the Poetry Center of the YMHA in New York.

Notes and Bibliography

In 1946 she was given an honorary D.Litt. from Columbia for her accomplishment in American Letters.

POETRY

1919   *Banners,* Geo. H. Doran Co., New York, 104 pp.
1925   *Honey Out of the Rock,* D. Appleton & Co., New York and London, 129 pp.
1930   *Fire for the Night,* J. Cape & H. Smith, New York, 77 pp.
1931   *Epistle to Prometheus,* J. Cape & H. Smith, New York, 95 pp.
1939   *One Part Love,* Oxford, New York, 86 pp.
1944   *Take Them, Stranger,* H. Holt & Co., New York, 72 pp.
1954   *Animal, Vegetable, Mineral,* E. P. Dutton, New York, 59 pp.
1959   *Coming of Age: New and Selected Poems,* Indiana Univ. Press, Blooming-
        ton, 160 pp.
1959   *Coming of Age: New and Selected Poems,* Oxford Univ. Press, London,
        160 pp.
1963   *Collected Poems, 1919–1962,* Indiana Univ. Press, Bloomington.

PROSE

1926   *A Brittle Heaven,* Greenberg, New York.
1927   *In Such a Night,* John Day, New York.
1929   *Potable Gold: Some Notes on Poetry and This Age,* W. W. Norton & Co.,
        New York, 96 pp.
1933   *Mask of Silenus,* Simon & Schuster, New York, 249 pp.
1935   *This Modern Poetry,* W. W. Norton & Co., New York, 284 pp.
1940   *Heroes of the Kalevala, Finland's Saga,* J. Messner, New York, 238 pp.
1942   *Rogue's Legacy; A Life of François Villon,* Coward-McCann, New York.
1952   *Poetry in Our Time,* Doubleday, Garden City, N.Y., 411 pp.
1957   *Poetry Handbook,* Funk & Wagnalls, New York, 177 pp.
1962   "   "   (revised and enlarged), Funk & Wagnalls, New York.
1963   *Poetry in Our Time* (revised and enlarged), Doubleday Anchor Books, Gar-
        den City, N.Y., 457 pp.

EDITED AND/OR TRANSLATED

1920   *The Twelve* (Alexander Blok) (ed. and trans. by B. Deutsch and Avrahm
        Yarmolinsky), W. Huebsch, New York.
1923   *Contemporary Germany Poetry* (ed. and trans. by B. Deutsch and Avrahm
        Yarmolinsky), Harcourt, Brace, New York, 201 pp.
1923   *Modern Russian Poetry* (ed. and trans. by B. Deutsch and Avrahm Yarmo-
        linsky), John Lane, London, 181 pp.

1927   *Russian Poetry* (ed. and trans. by B. Deutsch and Avrahm Yarmolinsky), International Publishers, New York, 254 pp.

1941   *Poems from The Book of Hours* (Rilke's *Das Studenbuch*) (ed. and trans. by B. Deutsch).

JUVENILE

1941   *Walt Whitman, Builder for America,* J. Messner, New York, 278 pp.

1942   *The Welcome,* Harper & Bros., New York and London, 197 pp.

1946   *The Reader's Shakespeare,* J. Messner, New York, 510 pp.

1952   *Tales of Faraway Folk* (Babette Deutsch and Avrahm Yarmolinsky), Harper, New York, 68 pp.

1963   *More Tales of Faraway Folk* (B. Deutsch and Avrahm Yarmolinsky), Harper, New York, 93 pp.

1964   *The Steel Flea,* Harper, New York, 56 pp.

WILLIAM DICKEY (b. 1928)

Mr. Dickey was educated at Reed College, Harvard, the University of Iowa, and Jesus College, Oxford. He has taught at Cornell University, Denison University, and San Francisco State College, where he is at present. He has won the Yale Prize for Younger Poets and the Union League Poetry Prize. Mr. Dickey was a Fulbright Fellow in England in 1959.

POETRY

1959   *Of the Festivity,* Yale Univ. Press, New Haven, 47 pp.

1963   *Interpreter's House,* Ohio State Univ. Press, Columbus, 94 pp.

RICHARD EBERHART (b. 1904)

Mr. Eberhart was educated at Dartmouth College and at Cambridge University. He has taught at the University of Washington, University of Connecticut, Wheaton College, and Princeton. Since 1956 he has been Poet in Residence at Dartmouth College. As a young man he spent a year as tutor to the son of the King of Siam. During World War II he served in the U.S. Navy as a gunnery instructor. He has served as Consultant in Poetry at the Library of Congress. His awards include the Shelley Memorial Award, the National Institute of Arts and Letters Poetry Award, and the Bollingen Prize. He was recently awarded an honorary D.Litt. from Dartmouth.

POETRY

1930	*A Bravery of Earth*, J. Cape, London, 128 pp.
1936	*Reading the Spirit*, Chatto & Windus, London, 79 pp.
	" " " , Oxford, New York, 79 pp.
1942	*Song and Idea*, Oxford, New York, 55 pp.
1944	*Poems, New and Selected*, New Directions, Norfolk, Conn., 30 pp.
1947	*Burr Oaks*, Oxford, New York, 68 pp.
1949	*Brotherhood of Men*, Banyan Press, Pawlet, Vermont, 11 pp.
1950	*An Herb Basket*, Cummington Press, Cummington, Mass., 8 pp.
1951	*Selected Poems*, Oxford, New York, 127 pp.
1953	*Undercliff: Poems, 1946–53*, Oxford, New York, 127 pp.
1957	*Great Praises*, Oxford, New York, 72 pp.
1957	*The Oak*, Pine Tree Press, Hanover, N.H., 4 pp.
1960	*Collected Poems, 1930–60*, Chatto & Windus, London, 228 pp.
	" " " , Oxford, New York, 228 pp.
1962	*Collected Verse Plays*, Univ. of North Carolina Press, Chapel Hill, 167 pp.
1964	*The Quarry*, Oxford, New York.
1964	" " , Chatto & Windus, London.

PROSE

1944	*Free Gunner's Handbook* (compiled by Richard Eberhart), Aviation Free Gunnery Training Unit.

EDITED

1945	*War and the Poet* (by Richard Eberhart and Selden Rodman), Devin-Adair Co., New York, 240 pp.
1958	*Thirteen Dartmouth Poems*, Dartmouth Press, Hanover, N.H.
1962	*Forty Dartmouth Poems*, Dartmouth Press, Hanover, N.H., 51 pp.

GEORGE P. ELLIOTT (b. 1918)

Mr. Elliott was educated at the University of California at Berkeley. He has taught at Cornell University, Barnard College, St. Mary's, the University of Iowa, the University of California, and Syracuse University, where he is at present. His awards for writing include the Hudson Review Fellowship (1956), the Guggenheim Fellowship (1961), and a Ford Foundation Fellowship (1964).

POETRY

1961   *Fever and Chills,* The Stone Wall Press, Iowa City, 34 pp.

PROSE

1958   *Parktilden Village,* Beacon Press, Boston, 200 pp.
1961   *Among the Dangs,* Holt, Rinehart and Winston, New York, 255 pp.
1962   *David Knudsen,* Random House, New York, 339 pp.

EDITED

1956   *Fifteen Modern American Poets,* Rinehart, New York, 315 pp.

ROBERT HORAN (b. 1922)

Mr. Horan attended the University of California at Berkeley. He has been a dancer with Martha Graham, and worked for a time as secretary to Gian-Carlo Menotti. For some years he taught at the University of California at Berkeley. His honors and awards include the Yale Younger Poets Prize and a National Institute of Arts and Letters Poetry Award.

1948   *A Beginning* (Yale Series of Younger Poets) Yale Univ. Press, New Haven, 87 pp.

DONALD JUSTICE (b. 1925)

Mr. Justice was educated at the University of Miami, North Carolina University, Stanford University, and the University of Iowa. He has taught at the University of Missouri, Hamline University, and the University of Iowa, where he is at present. Among his awards and fellowships are a Rockefeller Fellowship (1954), the Lamont Poetry Award of the American Academy of Poets (1959), and a Ford Fellowship (1964).

POETRY

1960   *The Summer Anniversaries,* Wesleyan Univ. Press, Middletown, Conn., 49 pp.
1963   *A Local Storm,* The Stone Wall Press, Iowa City, Iowa.

Notes and Bibliography

EDITED

1960   *The Collected Poems of Weldon Kees,* The Stone Wall Press, Iowa City, Iowa.

STANLEY KUNITZ (b. 1905)

Mr. Kunitz is a graduate of Harvard. He worked for a publishing company for some years, until World War II, in which he served as a sergeant in the U.S. Army. He has taught at Bennington College, the New School for Social Research, the University of Washington, and Brandeis University. He was Director of the Poetry Center of the YMHA in New York for several years. His awards for poetry include a two-year Ford Foundation Fellowship, the National Institute of Arts and Letters Poetry Award, and, in 1959, the Pulitzer Prize.

POETRY

1930   *Intellectual Things,* Doubleday, Doran & Co., New York, 63 pp.
1944   *Passport to the War,* H. Holt & Co., New York, 60 pp.
1958   *Selected Poems, 1928–58,* Little, Brown, Boston, 116 pp.

EDITED

1932   *Living Authors,* H. W. Wilson Co., New York, 466 pp.
1933   *Authors Today and Yesterday,* H. W. Wilson Co., New York, 726 pp.
1934   *The Junior Book of Authors,* H. W. Wilson Co., New York, 400 pp.
1936   *British Authors of the 19th Century,* H. W. Wilson Co., New York, 677 pp.
1938   *American Authors, 1600–1900,* H. W. Wilson Co., New York, 846 pp.
1942   *Twentieth Century Authors,* H. W. Wilson Co., New York, 1577 pp.
1951   *The Junior Book of Authors* (rev. ed.), H. W. Wilson Co., New York.
1952   *British Authors Before 1800* (by S. Kunitz and Howard Haycroft), H. W. Wilson Co., New York, 584 pp.
1955   *Twentieth Century Authors–First Supplement,* H. W. Wilson Co., New York.

ROBERT LOWELL (b. 1917)

Mr. Lowell was educated at Harvard and Kenyon Colleges, and has taught at both institutions and at Boston University. He was a conscientious objector in World War II. In 1947 he was made Poetry Consultant at the Library of Congress. Among the many awards and honors Mr. Lowell has received for his poetry are a special award from the National Institute of Arts and Letters, a Guggenheim Fellowship, and both the Pulitzer Prize (1947) and the National Book Award (1960).

POETRY

1944   *Land of Unlikeness*, Cummington Press, Cummington, Mass., 43 pp.

1946   *Lord Weary's Castle*, Harcourt, Brace, New York, 69 pp.

1950   *Poems, 1938–1949*, Faber & Faber, London, 102 pp.

1951   *The Mills of the Kavanaughs*, Harcourt, Brace, New York, 55 pp.

1959   *Life Studies*, Farrar, Straus & Cudahy, New York, 40 pp.

TRANSLATED AND EDITED

1961   *Imitations*, Farrar, Straus & Cudahy, New York, 149 pp.

1961   *Phèdre* (Racine), Farrar, Straus & Cudahy, New York, 213 pp.

JOSEPHINE MILES (b. 1911)

Miss Miles received her undergraduate education at the University of California at Los Angeles and her Ph.D. at the University of California at Berkeley, where she has been Professor of English since 1952. Her honors include the Shelley Memorial Award (1935), a Guggenheim Fellowship (1948), and a National Institute of Arts and Letters Poetry Award (1956).

POETRY

1939   *Lines at Intersections*, Macmillan, New York, 58 pp.

1941   *Poems on Several Occasions*, New Directions, Norfolk, Conn., 32 pp.

1946   *Local Measures*, Reynal & Hitchcock, New York, 62 pp.

1955   *Prefabrications*, Indiana Univ. Press, Bloomington, 90 pp.

1960   *Poems, 1930–1960*, Indiana Univ. Press, Bloomington, 160 pp.

PROSE

1942   *Wordsworth and the Vocabulary of Emotion*, Univ. of California Press, Berkeley and Los Angeles, 181 pp.

1942   *Pathetic Fallacy in the 19th Century*, Univ. of California Press, Berkeley and Los Angeles, 304 pp.

1946   *The Vocabulary of Poetry; Three Studies*, Univ. of California Press, Berkeley and Los Angeles.

1951   *The Continuity of Poetic Language; Studies in English Poetry from the 1540's to the 1940's*, Univ. of California Press, Berkeley and Los Angeles, 542 pp.

Notes and Bibliography

1957   *Eras and Modes in English Poetry,* Univ. of California Press, Berkeley, 233 pp.

1960   *Renaissance, Eighteenth Century and Modern Language in English Poetry; A Tabular View,* Univ. of California Press, Berkeley, 73 pp.

EDITED

1948   *Criticism; the Foundations of Modern Literary Judgment* (by J. Miles, M. Schorer, G. McKenzie), Harcourt, Brace, New York, 553 pp.

1958   *Criticism; the Foundations of Modern Literary Judgment* (rev. ed.), Harcourt, Brace, New York.

1959   *The Poem; a Critical Anthology,* Prentice-Hall, Englewood Cliffs, N.J., 553 pp.

1961   *Classic Essays in English,* Little, Brown, Boston, 360 pp.

1961   *The Ways of the Poem* (shorter version of *The Poem; a Critical Anthology*), Prentice-Hall, Englewood Cliffs, N.J., 440 pp.

JOHN FREDERICK NIMS (b. 1913)

Mr. Nims was educated at De Paul University, Notre Dame University, and the University of Chicago. He has been on the faculty at Notre Dame since 1939. He has also served, for a year, as editor of *Poetry Magazine,* and is a regular member of the faculty of the Bread Loaf School of Writing. Mr. Nims has won several grants and awards for his literary work. In 1959 he held the Smith-Mundt Professorship at the University of Madrid.

POETRY

1947   *The Iron Pastoral,* W. Sloane Associates, New York, 86 pp.

1950   *A Fountain in Kentucky, and Other Poems,* W. Sloane Associates, New York, 72 pp.

1960   *Knowledge of the Evening; Poems, 1950–1960,* Rutgers Univ. Press, New Brunswick, N.J., 96 pp.

TRANSLATED

1959   *The Poems of St. John of the Cross,* Grove Press, New York.

1959   *Andromache* (Euripides), Grove Press, New York.

JOHN CROWE RANSOM (b. 1888)

Mr. Ransom was educated at Vanderbilt University and at Christ Church, Oxford (where he was a Rhodes Scholar in 1913). He served as a field artillery officer in World War I. He has taught at Vanderbilt University and at Kenyon College where he founded *The Kenyon Review,* which he edited from 1939 until his retirement in 1958. Since his retirement Mr. Ransom has been extremely active in writing and in lecturing and reading at various colleges and universities throughout the United States. His honors include the Guggenheim Fellowship (1931), the Bollingen Prize (1951), an American Institute of Arts and Letters Poetry Award (1951), the Gold Medal of Brandeis University (1958), the American Academy of Poets Award for Distinguished Achievement (1962), and the National Book Award (1964).

POETRY

1919	*Poems About God,* H. Holt & Co., New York, 76 pp.
1924	*Chills and Fever,* A. A. Knopf, New York, 95 pp.
1924	*Grace After Meat,* L. and V. Wool, London, 57 pp.
1927	*Two Gentlemen in Bonds,* A. A. Knopf, New York, 87 pp.
1945	*Selected Poems,* A. A. Knopf, New York, 75 pp.
1955	*Poems and Essays,* Vintage Books, New York, 185 pp.
1964	*Selected Poems* (revised and enlarged), A. A. Knopf, New York.

PROSE

1930	*God Without Thunder; an Unorthodox Defense of Orthodoxy,* Harcourt, Brace, New York, 334 pp.
1935	*The World's Body,* Scribner's Sons, New York and London, 350 pp.
1941	*The New Criticism,* New Directions, Norfolk, Conn., 339 pp.
1943	*A College Primer of Writing,* H. Holt & Co., New York, 137 pp.

EDITED

1935	*Topics for Freshman Writing,* H. Holt & Co., New York, 519 pp.
1951	*The Kenyon Critics,* World Publishing Co., Cleveland, 345 pp.
1961	*Selected Poems of Thomas Hardy,* Macmillan, New York.

ADRIENNE RICH (b. 1929)

Miss Rich (Mrs. Alfred Conrad) was educated at Radcliffe. She has been given a Guggenheim Fellowship (1959) and the Amy Lowell Travelling Fellowship (1962), among other awards for her poetry.

POETRY

1951   *A Change of World,* Yale Univ. Press, New Haven, 85 pp.

1955   *Diamond Cutters, and Other Poems,* Harper, New York, 119 pp.

1963   *Snapshots of a Daughter-in-Law; Poems, 1954–1962,* Harper & Row, New York, 71 pp.

THEODORE ROETHKE (1908–1963)

Mr. Roethke was educated at the University of Michigan and at Harvard. He taught at Lafayette College, Pennsylvania State University, Bennington College, and, from 1947 until his death, at the University of Washington. Among the many honors and awards given him for his poetry were a Guggenheim Fellowship (1945), an American Academy of Arts and Letters Award (1952), a Ford Foundation Fellowship (1952–54), the Pulitzer Prize (1954), the Bollingen Prize (1959), and the National Book Award (1959).

POETRY

1941   *Open House,* A. A. Knopf, New York, 70 pp.

1948   *The Lost Son,* Doubleday, Garden City, N.Y., 64 pp.

1951   *Praise to the End!* Doubleday, Garden City, N.Y., 89 pp.

1953   *The Waking: Poems, 1933–53,* Doubleday, Garden City, N.Y., 120 pp.

1957   *Words for the Wind,* Secker & Warburg, London, 200 pp.

1961   " " " " , Indiana Univ. Press, Bloomington, 212 pp.

1961   *I am! Says the Lamb,* Doubleday, Garden City, N.Y., 70 pp.

MURIEL RUKEYSER (b. 1913)

Miss Rukeyser was educated at Vassar and Columbia. She has worked as a journalist, was in Spain during the Spanish Civil War, and has travelled widely. She holds an honorary D.Litt. from Rutgers. Among other awards she has received for her poetry are a Guggenheim Fellowship and a Poetry Award from the American Academy of Arts and Letters.

POETRY

1935   *Theory of Flight,* Yale Univ. Press, New Haven, 86 pp.

1938   *U.S. 1,* Corvici, Friede, New York, 147 pp.

1939   *A Turning Wind,* Viking Press, New York, 120 pp.

1942   *Wake Island,* Doubleday, Doran & Co., Garden City, N.Y., 16 pp.

1944   *Beast in View,* Doubleday, Doran & Co., Garden City, N.Y., 98 pp.

1949   *Elegies,* New Directions, Norfolk, Conn., 82 pp.

1949   *Orpheus,* Centaur Press, San Francisco, 30 pp.

1951   *Selected Poems,* New Directions, New York, 111 pp.

1958   *Body of Waking,* Harper, New York, 118 pp.

1962   *Waterlily Fire; Poems, 1935–62,* Macmillan, New York, 200 pp.

PROSE AND DRAMA

1942   *Willard Gibbs: American Genius,* Doubleday, Doran & Co., Garden City, N.Y., 465 pp.

1949   *The Life of Poetry,* Current Books, New York, 232 pp.

1957   *One Life,* Simon & Schuster, New York, 330 pp.

1961   *The Colors of the Day* (drama), Vassar Centennial Series, Poughkeepsie, N.Y., 62 pp.

TRANSLATED

1948   *The Green Wave* (trans. of 6 poems by Octavio Paz and of rari from the Marquesas by Moa Tetua and others), Doubleday, Garden City, N.Y., 95 pp.

1963   *Selected Poems of Octavio Paz,* Indiana Univ. Press, Bloomington.

1963   *Sun Stone* (poems by Octavio Paz), New Directions, New York, 47 pp.

JUVENILE

1955   *Come Back, Paul,* Harper, New York.

KARL SHAPIRO (b. 1913)

Mr. Shapiro was educated at the University of Virginia and Johns Hopkins University. During World War II he served with the U.S. Army in the Pacific area. He has taught at Johns Hopkins, Loyola University, the University of Iowa, the University of California at both Berkeley and Davis, and at the University of Nebraska, where he is presently Professor of English. He edited *Poetry Magazine* from 1950 to 1956, and since then has been editor of *The Prairie Schooner*. He has received various awards for his poetry, among them the Pulitzer Prize (1945) and a Guggenheim Fellowship (1953).

POETRY

1935   *Poems,* Waverly Press, Baltimore, 64 pp.

1942   *Person, Place and Thing,* Reynal & Hitchcock, New York, 88 pp.

1942   *The Place of Love,* The Bradley Printers, Malvern, Australia, 78 pp.

1944   *V-Letter, and Other Poems,* Reynal & Hitchcock, New York, 63 pp.

1945   *Essay on Rime,* Reynal & Hitchcock, New York, 72 pp.

1947   " " " , Secker & Warburg, London, 64 pp.

1947   *Trial of a Poet,* and Other Poems, Reynal & Hitchcock, New York, 81 pp.

1953   *Poems, 1940–53,* Random House, New York, 161 pp.

1958   *Poems of a Jew,* Random House, New York, 70 pp.

PROSE

1953   *Beyond Criticism* (lectures), Univ. of Nebraska Press, Lincoln, 73 pp.

1960   *In Defense of Ignorance* (addresses, essays, lectures), Random House, New York, 338 pp.

1948   *A Bibliography of Modern Prosody,* Johns Hopkins Press, Baltimore, 36 pp.

EDITED

1960   *American Poetry,* Crowell, New York, 265 pp.

1962   *Prose Keys to Modern Poetry,* Row, Peterson, Evanston, Ill., 260 pp.

W. D. SNODGRASS (b. 1926)

Mr. Snodgrass was educated at Geneva College and the University of Iowa. He has taught at Cornell University, the University of Rochester, and Wayne State University, where he is at present. He has held the Hudson Review Fellowship (1958), and has received a National Institute of Arts and Letters Grant (1960), a Poetry Society of America Citation (1960), a special award from the American Academy of Arts and Letters, and the Pulitzer Prize (1960).

POETRY

1959   *Heart's Needle,* A. A. Knopf, New York, 62 pp.

STEPHEN SPENDER (b. 1909)

Mr. Spender was born in England and educated at Oxford. He was in Spain during the Spanish Civil War, and during World War II he served with the National Fire Service in England. He was an editor of the old *Horizon*, and since 1953 has been co-editor of *Encounter* magazine in London. Mr. Spender has travelled and lectured extensively in the United States and throughout Europe. He has been much honored in the United States, as in England, for his poetry and other literary work. He remains a British subject.

POETRY

1928	*Nine Experiments*, Hampstead, 21 pp.
1930	*Twenty Poems*, B. Blackwell, Oxford, 23 pp.
1933	*Poems*, Faber & Faber, London, 57 pp.
1934	*Poems*, Random House, New York, 68 pp.
1934	*Poems*, Faber & Faber, London, 69 pp.
1935	*Vienna*, Random House, New York, 37 pp.
1938	*Trial of Judge: A Tragedy in Five Acts*, Random House, New York, 96 pp.
1939	*The Still Centre*, Faber & Faber, London, 107 pp.
1940	*Selected Poems*, Faber & Faber, London, 76 pp.
1942	*Ruins and Visions*, Random House, New York, 138 pp.
1947	" " " , Faber & Faber, London, 84 pp.
1947	*Poems* (1934) (reprinted), Faber & Faber, London.
1947	*Returning to Vienna, 1947*, Banyan Press, New York, 19 pp.
1947	*Poems of Dedication*, Faber & Faber, London, 58 pp.
1947	*Selected Poems* (reprinted), Faber & Faber, London, 76 pp.
1949	*The Edge of Being*, Random House, New York, 57 pp.
1949	" " " " , Faber & Faber, London, 57 pp.
1952	*Poems* (1934) (reprinted), Faber & Faber, London.
1954	*Sirmione Peninsula*, Faber & Faber, London, 4 pp.
1955	*Collected Poems, 1928–53*, Random House, New York, 204 pp.
1958	*Inscriptions*, Poetry Book Society, London.

PROSE

1935	*The Destructive Element: A Study of Modern Writers and Beliefs*, J. Cape, London, 284 pp.

Notes and Bibliography

1936   *The Burning Cactus,* Random House, New York, 265 pp.

1937   *Forward from Liberalism,* Random House, New York, 281 pp.

1939   *The New Realism,* Hogarth Press, London, 24 pp.

1940   *The Backward Son,* Hogarth Press, London, 266 pp.

1941   *The Burning Cactus,* Faber & Faber, London, 265 pp.

1942   *Life and the Poet,* Secker & Warburg, London, 127 pp.

1943   *Jim Braidy; the Story of Britain's Firemen* (by Wm. Sansom, James Gordon, & Stephen Spender), L. Drummond, London.

1945   *Citizens in War, and After,* G. G. Harrap & Co., London, 112 pp.

1946   *European Witness,* Reynal & Hitchcock, New York, 246 pp.

1951   *World Within World,* H. Hamilton, London, 349 pp.

1952   *Learning Laughter,* Weidenfeld & Nicolson, London, 112 pp.

1953   *Learning Laughter,* Harcourt, Brace, New York, 201 pp.

1953   *The Creative Element,* H. Hamilton, London, 199 pp.

1955   *The Making of a Poem,* H. Hamilton, London, 192 pp.

1958   *Engaged in Writing,* H. Hamilton, London, 239 pp.

1962   "   "   "   , W. W. Norton, New York, 205 pp.

1963   *The Struggle of the Modern,* Univ. of California Press, Berkeley, 266 pp.

1963   *The Struggle of the Modern,* H. Hamilton, London, 266 pp.

EDITED

1939   *Poems for Spain* (Stephen Spender and John Lehman), Hogarth Press, New York, 108 pp.

1947   *A Choice of English Romantic Poetry,* Dial Press, New York, 384 pp.

1958   *Great Writings of Goethe,* New American Library, New York, 278 pp.

1963   *The Concise Encyclopedia of English and American Poetry* (Stephen Spender and Donald Hall), Hawthorn Books, New York, 415 pp.

TRANSLATED

1939   *Duino Elegies* (Rilke) (Stephen Spender and J. B. Leishman), W. W. Norton, New York, 130 pp.

1948   *Duino Elegies* (Rilke) (Stephen Spender and J. B. Leishman), Hogarth Press, London, 160 pp.

1939   *Poems by F. Garcia Lorca* (Stephen Spender and J. L. Gili), The Dolphin, London, 143 pp.

1939   *Danton's Death* (Georg Buchner), Faber & Faber, London, 142 pp.

1943   *Selected Poems of Frederico Garcia Lorca* (Stephen Spender and J. L. Gili), Hogarth Press, London, 56 pp.

1950   *Le Dur Désir de Durer* (Paul Eluard) (Stephen Spender and Frances Cornford), Grey Falcon Press, Philadelphia, 92 pp.
1951   *Das Marien-Leben* (Rilke), Philosophical Library, New York, 49 pp.
1959   *Maria Stuart* (Friedrich von Schiller), Faber & Faber, London.
1960   *Great German Short Stories*, Dell Publishing Co., New York, 284 pp.

WILLIAM STAFFORD (b. 1914)

Mr. Stafford was educated at the University of Kansas and the University of Iowa. He has worked for the U.S. Forest Service and the Church World Service. During World War II he served in the U.S. Army. He has taught at the University of Kentucky and Purdue University, and, since 1957, at Lewis and Clarke College. In 1959 he received the Union League Award for Poetry, and in 1963 the National Book Award and the Shelley Memorial Award.

POETRY

1948   *Down in My Heart,* Brethren Publishing House, Elgin, Ill., 94 pp.
1961   *West of Your City,* Talisman Press, Los Gatos, Calif., 59 pp.
1963   *Traveling Through the Dark,* Harper & Row, New York, 94 pp.

MAY SWENSON (b. 1919)

Miss Swenson was educated at Utah State College. Among the honors and awards she has won for her poetry are a Rockefeller Fellowship (1955), the Robert Frost Poetry Fellowship at Bread Loaf (1957), a National Institute of Arts and Letters Poetry Award (1960), a Guggenheim Fellowship (1960), and the Amy Lowell Travelling Fellowship (1960).

POETRY

1954   *Another Animal: Poems* (in *Poets of Today, I*), Scribner's Sons, New York.
1958   *A Cage of Spines,* Rinehart, New York, 96 pp.
1963   *To Mix with Time: New and Selected Poems,* Scribner's Sons, New York, 183 pp.

RICHARD WILBUR (b. 1921)

Mr. Wilbur was educated at Amherst College and at Harvard. He has taught at Harvard, Wellesley, and Wesleyan University, where he is at present. Mr. Wilbur served in the U.S. Army in Italy and France during World War II. Among the fellowships and honors he has won for his poetry are two Guggenheim Fellowships (1952 and 1963), an American Academy of Arts and Letters Poetry Award (1954), both the Pulitzer Prize and the National Book Award (1957), and a Ford Fellowship (1961).

POETRY

1947   *The Beautiful Changes,* Harcourt, Brace, New York, 55 pp.

1950   *Ceremony, and Other Poems,* Harcourt, Brace, New York, 55 pp.

1956   *Things of This World,* Harcourt, Brace, New York, 50 pp.

1957   *Poems, 1943–1956,* Faber & Faber, London, 136 pp.

1961   *Advice to a Prophet,* Harcourt, Brace, New York, 64 pp.

EDITED AND TRANSLATED

1955   *A Bestiary,* Pantheon Books, New York, 74 pp.

1955   *Le Misanthrope,* Harcourt, Brace, New York, 140 pp.

1957   *Candide; a Comic Opera* (by Richard Wilbur, Lillian Hellman, and Others), Random House, New York, 143 pp.

1959   *Poe; Complete Poems,* Dell Publishing Co., New York, 159 pp.